The Complete Book of Feature Writing

ABOUT THE EDITOR

Leonard Witt is editor of *Minnesota Monthly*, a regional magazine based in Minneapolis. Before that he was Sunday Magazine editor at the *Star Tribune* in Minneapolis, and is the founding editor of *Style, the Journal of the American Association of Sunday and Feature Editors*. He is a former award-winning feature editor at the Allentown, Pennsylvania *Morning Call*. He received an M.A. degree in nonfiction writing from the University of New Hampshire and taught writing courses there for two years. He also edited the book *Magic! The 1987 Minnesota Twins' Enchanted Season*, which sold more than 100,000 copies. His freelance articles have appeared in national magazines and newspapers, including the *Christian Science Monitor*, the *Philadelphia Inquirer*, *Newsday*, *The Boston Phoenix*, *The Seattle Times*, *Blair & Ketchum's Country Journal*, *People's Almanac 2*, *Wilderness Camping*, the *Physician and Sports Medicine* and *The Boston Globe Sunday Magazine*.

THE COMPLETE BOOK OF FEATURE WRITING

From Great American
Feature Writers, Editors
and Teachers

Edited by
Leonard Witt

95 94 93 92 91   5 4 3 2 1

Library of Congress Cataloging-in-Publication Data

The Complete book of feature writing / edited by Leonard Witt.—1st ed.
    p.   cm.
Includes bibliographical references and index.
ISBN 0-89879-470-6
    1. Feature writing—Handbooks, manuals, etc. 2. Journalism—Authorship—Handbooks, manuals, etc. 3. Interviewing in journalism—Handbooks, manuals, etc.   I. Witt, Leonard.
PN4784.F37C66   1991
808'.06607—dc20
                                                                        91-15256
                                                                        CIP

Edited by Chris Dodd
Designed by Joan Jacobus

For my mother, Stella P. Witt, and in memory of my father, Harry Witt.

T H A N K S

First, thanks to all the writers who helped make this book possible, and a special thanks to Donald Murray and Andy Merton who helped get my writing and editing career on track at the University of New Hampshire. I must also thank poet and novelist Stephen Dobyns, who first introduced me to the university's graduate writing program.

At the risk of slighting all of the other great writers in this book, I must highlight the names of Kay Miller and Bob Ehlert, who helped my career as an editor by producing some of the best magazine writing in the country at the *Star Tribune's Sunday Magazine* where we worked together. I'd also like to thank my agent Jonathon Lazear, and Kathy Erickson of his agency, who helped find this book a first-class home at Writer's Digest Books. And at Writer's Digest Books, I'd like to thank my editors William Brohaugh and Jean Fredette, and the book's copyeditor Chris Dodd.

And of course we can't forget the book's indexer, Diana Witt. She is, in fact, the world's greatest indexer, and I am not saying that just because she is my wife. Speaking of family, I must thank our two wonderful children, Stephen and Emily Witt, who have been supportive even after the realization that they can read faster and spell better than their father, the editor.

CONTENTS

Introduction *by Leonard Witt*   1

CHAPTER ONE
Welcome to the Features Department 3

What Is Feature Writing?
  Writer: Leonard Witt   3
A Day in the Life of a Feature Writer
  Writer: Christopher Scanlan   7
Memo to a New Feature Writer
  Writer: Donald M. Murray   14
End Words *by Leonard Witt*   18
  Afterthoughts: More Points to Remember   18
  Exercises   20
  Further Reading   20
How the Pros Do It: Writing Sample Number 1
  Mr. Lucky Ends Mr. Clean Career
  by Jay Hamburg, The Orlando (Florida) *Sentinel*   21

CHAPTER TWO
Assignments That Make Great Stories 25

Finding Feature Story Ideas
  Writer: Roy Peter Clark   25
Don't Forget the "Ordinary" People
  Writer: Madeleine Blais   31
End Words *by Leonard Witt*   37
  Afterthoughts: More Points to Remember   37
  Exercises   38
  Further Reading   39
How the Pros Do It: Writing Sample Number 2
  A Boy of Unusual Vision
  by Alice Steinbach, The (Baltimore) *Sun*   39

CHAPTER THREE
Getting the Story Down on Paper 51

On Being a Reporter First
  Writer: David Finkel 51
Interviewing Techniques: Get Them to Talk
  Writer: Kay Miller 61
Researching Your Feature Stories
  Writer: Mike D'Orso 75
A Feature Writer's Reference Library
  Writers: Jo Cates and Ken Kister 84
Organizing Your Material
  Writer: Jane Harrigan 89
Think Beginnings, Not Leads
  Writer: Leonard Witt 100
End Words *by Leonard Witt* 108
  Afterthoughts: More Points to Remember 108
  Exercises 112
  Further Reading 113
How the Pros Do It: Writing Sample Number 3
  Living In the Danger Zone
  by Claire Martin, The Denver Post 114

CHAPTER FOUR
Elevating Mundane Writing to the Sublime 124

Writing Profiles Means Going Beyond Talking Heads
  Writer: Jack Hart 124
Using Description Effectively
  Writer: Bob Ehlert 129
Writing in the First Person
  Writer: Mark Patinkin 133
When a Reporter Becomes Part of the Story
  Writer: Walt Harrington 140
Finding a Writing Voice That's Yours Alone
  Writer: Andy Merton 144
End Words *by Leonard Witt* 150
  Afterthoughts: More Points to Remember 150
  Exercises 153

Further Reading   154
How the Pros Do It: Writing Sample Number 4
A Class Struggle
An excerpt by Walt Harrington, The Washington Post   155

CHAPTER FIVE
Feature Section Specialties   157

The Art of Travel Writing
Writer: Jim Molnar   157
Eating My Words: What It Takes to Be a Good Food Writer
Writer: Mimi Sheraton   165
On Being a TV Critic
Writer: John Voorhees   167
Being a Music Critic
Writer: Daniel Cariaga   172
How to Become a Theater Critic
Writer: Dan Sullivan   175
Becoming a Film Critic
Writer: Stephen Hunter   178
Writing Freelance Book Reviews
Writer: Elliot Krieger   181
Fashion Writing
Writer: Ellen Kampinsky   186
Lighten Up! Get Some Humor Into Your Writing
Writer: Leonard Witt; Example by: Michael McLeod   190
Hooked on Morbidity and Mortality
Writer: Denise Grady   191
The Celebrity Interview
Writer: Maralyn Lois Polak   196
End Words *by Leonard Witt*   201
Afterthoughts: More Points to Remember   201
Exercises   202
How the Pros Do It: Writing Sample Number 5
Bye, Pal! Miami's Vice: It Was a Case of Art Imitating a Slice
of Life and Life Imitating the Art
by Steve Sonsky, The Miami Herald   203

CHAPTER SIX
Selling Freelance Stories to Feature Sections   211

How to Approach a Feature Editor
Writer: Neal Karlen   211

What a Newspaper Feature Editor Wants From Freelancers
Writer: Mary Hadar   219

What a Magazine Editor Wants From Freelancers
Writer: Leonard Witt   221

Feature Writing for Newspaper Syndicates
Writer: Dan O'Toole   224

Don't Forget the Alternative Papers
Writer: Sandra J. Shea   226

End Words *by Leonard Witt*   231
Afterthoughts: More Points to Remember   231
Exercises   233
Further Reading   234

How the Pros Do It: Writing Sample Number 6
A Query Letter That Found a Story a Home
by Steven Kaplan   235

CHAPTER SEVEN
Getting to The Top   237

How Feature Writers Become Great
Writer: Jon Franklin   237

Ten Surefire Ways to Train Yourself for the Next Millennium!
Writer: Ken Doctor   245

End Words *by Leonard Witt*   250
Afterthoughts: More Points to Remember   250
Exercises   251
Further Reading   251

How the Pros Do It: Writing Sample Number 7
The Poet and the Birthday Girl
by Madeleine Blais, the *Miami Herald's Tropic* magazine   251

APPENDIX
Finding a Staff Job   262

A Great Editor Tells Who He Would Hire
Writer: Richard Cheverton

INTRODUCTION

Years ago, when I broke into the field, I could have used a book like this. I had a feeling as I was writing that the stories were not quite right. Sure I was getting praise, but I was not breaking into the markets I wanted. On the year I took off to be a freelance writer I made only $1,200. But I never wrote just for money.

What piqued my desire for more knowledge and eventually added to my level of despair was the day I got a call from the *New York Times* travel section. They wanted to see a story I proposed on St. Lawrence Boulevard in Montreal.

It was a great street where waves of immigrants had lived. It had all the elements of a great feature story for the travel pages. But I didn't capture them. Upon receiving the story the editor of the section wrote back: The story had no redeeming values, and the photos weren't very good either.

I was devastated. I was ready to quit the business. Eventually I sold the story to *Newsday's* travel section, but the incident reinforced what I already knew: something was wrong with my writing. I finally went back to school and got an M.A. degree in nonfiction writing from the University of New Hampshire.

It was a great education, mainly because I got to write and experiment daily for two years. At the same time I received continuing criticism and advice from some great writers and teachers like Don Murray, whose "Memo to a New Feature Writer" is in the lead chapter.

Since the devastating day of the *New York Times* rejection, I have done all right. My writing has improved, and eventually I became editor of the feature section for *The Allentown Morning Call*, later Sunday magazine editor for the *Star Tribune* in Minneapolis, and then editor of *Minnesota Monthly*, a regional magazine in Minneapolis.

I still have my share of self-doubts about my work. And from time to time I love to sit down with colleagues and talk about the finer points of writing and editing. Then came the idea for the book. By contacting the best writers, editors and teachers to ask them to write for this book I could figuratively sit down with them whenever I chose and share their vast understanding of feature writing.

At the same time, the book makes it possible for everyone else interested in feature writing to pull up a chair with those people and share in their years of experience and knowledge.

Five years of editing *Style, The Journal of the American Association of Sunday and Feature Editors*, has assured me that there are many great feature writers, editors and teachers with plenty of tips for new and aspiring writers as well as for accomplished writers.

Their words will teach novices new ways to practice their craft and they will remind the experienced writer how many different ways there are to approach feature writing. For me, putting the book together was an experience much like feature writing itself. I was learning while spreading the good word to others.

CHAPTER ONE

Welcome to the Features Department

T he world of feature writing is a fertile one. Today daily newspapers, alternative papers and magazines of all genres need good feature writers. And there is a tremendous crossover of talent among the various types of publications. I started my own career at a give-away weekly, went to a paid circulation weekly, then to a daily newspaper feature section, then became editor of a Sunday magazine and now am editor of *Minnesota Monthly*, a regional magazine outside the world of newspapers. I got the job at the Sunday magazine after the editor there left for *National Geographic*, and one of the former editors at *Minnesota Monthly* is now an editor in a newspaper feature section. The freelance writers who write for *Minnesota Monthly* often have their articles published in daily newspapers, alternative weeklies and other monthly magazines. Skills they learn writing for one medium can easily be transferred to another. Indeed, many of the best magazine writers began in newspapers and some have even made the leap to books. I started at the bottom and worked my way up. So can you. Or you may be one of the fast-track wunderkinds, but either way, the trip getting into feature writing is hard work but great fun.

What Is Feature Writing?

Leonard Witt

Richard Cheverton, an editor at *The Orange County Register* in Santa Ana, California, is one of the nation's most respected authorities on feature writing, but not long ago he wrote, "Who the hell really understands what a feature is? I've worked for over a decade as a feature editor, and I'm not sure I could define the word 'feature' for a freshman journalism class. You can nail down a news, or sports, or business story—but grabbing the essence of a feature is like wrestling a squid; it'll soon depart in a cloud of ink. Good editors just know. Don't ask me how. They just do."

So, too, do good feature writers. They see and feel a feature when other writers around them might be focusing on the breaking story, on what used to be called the "hard news."

When I edited a feature section, we ran stories like "Roller Coasting: The Absolute Delight of Coming Back Alive"; "Charles Atlas: Puny Weaklings Still Clamor to be Muscle Men"; "Brooklynese? Hey! Dey Don't Tawk Funny"; "Airwave Psychology: Concern Growing Over Radio, TV Advice Shows." In addition to these were advice columns, theater reviews and shorts about television.

In the Sunday magazine we did stories about the risks doctors have of contracting AIDS, about a married woman who gave up her baby for adoption, and about the quirky requests celebrities make when they come to Minneapolis and St. Paul hotels.

At *Minnesota Monthly* I asked a freelancer to write a story entitled "Early Motherhood, Later Motherhood," about two friends in their forties, one with a 5-year-old daughter and the other with a 25-year-old daughter. Other stories at the *Monthly* include a profile of a museum director who is waking up a staid old institution, and another is an essay from an ex-farmgirl who laments the passing of a way of life.

The magazine does home design features, food features, book reviews and arts stories as well as entertainment listings.

The stories I've edited by freelancers and staff writers vary in length from a couple hundred words to several thousand words. The writers' styles are just as varied. The person who did the doctor and AIDS story would not be the best person to do the quirky celebrity hotel story. Her style is too serious; her strength is tenacity, research, building giant files, and then taking the time to write and rewrite to make it all read like a nonfiction novel.

The guy who wrote the celebrity story has a loose, funny style. He likes to get into a story immediately and then get it written quickly. If he used the techniques that were used in the AIDS story, his story would have lost its punch.

Just in those three publications alone—the newspaper feature section, the Sunday magazine and the regional monthly—there was writing work for just about anyone who could write well. All kinds of styles appeared. The home design story is going to be far different from the story about doctors and AIDS, which is, of course, going to be different from the one about quirky hotels.

And the stories in those three publications are going to be far different from the stories that appear in *Gourmet, Cosmopolitan* and the *New York Times*.

Each writer must decide on his or her interests and style and then begin to actively pursue editors who can provide the work. In the world of feature writing the topics are infinite and the outlets many. The key to success is hard work, fine writing, and the ability to learn and to grow in the craft.

For the most part, the people who succeed are the ones who do their research, do solid reporting, and care about their writing.

Is there one kind of feature writing that's better than another? The answer is no. However, after saying that, I should point out my personal prejudice. I love stories that read like nonfiction novels. Stories in which characters come alive. It is the most sophisticated form of nonfiction writing, but not necessarily the best nonfiction writing.

To understand the nonfiction novel approach, think of drawing a continuum from a quick-breaking newspaper story to a full-blown nonfiction novel such as Truman Capote's *In Cold Blood*. On this continuum, feature writing would begin somewhere in the middle and begin moving toward the nonfiction novel. And in fact, today, the best writing in newspaper feature sections and magazines such as *Vanity Fair* and *Esquire* is probably more closely akin to the nonfiction book than to the traditional breaking newspaper story.

So let's back up on that continuum and start with the breaking news story. Take, for example, a train-car collision in which a group of teenage girls is killed. (This, incidentally, is similar to a story done by a feature writer I used to work with.) The next-day story probably would start something like, "Four girls returning from buying their prom dresses were killed yesterday when their car was hit by a freight train." The story would give all the facts. It would tell where the crash occurred, the time, who was in the car, the name of the train engineer; it would have quotes from the family, from eyewitnesses, from officials.

Now on that continuum from news story to nonfiction book we

might have a writer—a good writer, a sensitive writer—do a Sunday piece on how the town is stunned or the story might in part re-create how the accident occurred.

Moving closer to the nonfiction book might be a rendition similar to Thornton Wilder's novel *The Bridge of San Luis Rey*.

The writer would re-create the entire day through meticulous research, by intense interviewing, and by chronicling all the important details. He might start with the engineer waking. Kissing his wife. He might describe the house, bring in telling details about the engineer. Perhaps the engineer has a daughter of his own.

The writer would have him starting out on his train; the size and speed of the train and its limitations would come alive. The train would be moving toward the fateful moment at the crossing. The writer would come back to the girls. The writer would probably take us into one of their houses. Have the girls wake, make conversation, reveal details of their lives. The writer would bring the girls in the car and the engineer on a literal head-on collision.

The reader could not let go of this story and would remember it for months. The writer would take us to the crash itself with the train rounding the slightly blind corner. We would see the branches that partially obscured the road, we'd hear the music playing loudly in the car.

To do all of this and do it factually usually requires experience. To pull this off the feature writer will have to know all the techniques of reporting. He will have a ton of notes, official reports and observations to sift through and then will have to turn in a beautifully written story with a beginning, a middle and an end. The writer will have central characters that we get to know and care about. This is feature writing in its most advanced form.

Room for Many Writing Styles

However, literary journalism is only one type of feature writing. Turn back to the lifestyle or feature sections, thumb through several magazines, and you will see many other forms. You will find writers who specialize in fashion, food reviewing, quick interviews or in-depth profiles. And the best of these writers are no lesser talents than the feature writer who moves closer to the nonfiction book. Indeed, writers like food critic Mimi Sheraton, movie reviewers Gene Siskel and Roger Ebert, and health writer Jane Brody, are among the superstars of newspaper writing. You'll find their work in the feature pages.

They know about writing, they know about reporting, and they know about their subjects. At the *Philadelphia Inquirer's* Sunday magazine, Maralyn Lois Polak conducts an interview each week with a famous person. On the continuum from breaking story to nonfiction novel her work in the *Inquirer* would be in the middle, but as a writing talent she is near the top because what she does she does better than just about anyone else. And since this is a book about feature writing, that is important to remember. In the world of features there is room for many kinds of writers with many kinds of styles and with many aspirations. Some will want to be full-time staff writers at a newspaper or magazine, others would like to make their living by freelancing, and others might want to do the occasional article while holding a nonwriting job. As an editor I have published them all and will continue to do so to ensure my magazine is fresh and lively.

Top-notch feature stories demand top-notch writing, and the best writing comes from getting away from your desk. It means getting out where the stories are. Indeed, reporting is half the fun — and many times the only fun — because all too often the writing itself means pain. As an editor, I have worked with some truly fine writers, and I have watched them struggle over pieces and watched the color drain out of their faces, or sometimes watched their faces turn red with anger, as I had to tell them their stories weren't quite right. The story needs another rewrite. And then I watched as they struggled to get it perfect and then finally watched in amazement as raw copy was turned into a masterpiece. No one understands this process better than feature writer Christopher Scanlan who is about to take you into the life of a feature writer and show you the glories, joys, tears and struggles that make feature writing one of the world's best professions.

A Day in the Life of a Feature Writer
Christopher Scanlan

6:30 A.M.
In the Waters of Boca Ciega Bay,
Off Indian Rocks Beach, Florida

Ah, the feature writer's life. Spinning gossamer webs of prose. Rivaling the foreign correspondent for glamour. No daily deadlines, no stultifying late nights with the Zoning Board.

Oh yeah? So what am I doing huddled on the bone-hard seat of a 16-foot boat bouncing along the trampoline that is Boca Ciega Bay at dawn on a stormy April morning?

Reporting, that's what. "You can't write writing," Melvin Mencher used to drum into our heads at Columbia Journalism School. At the time, it sounded like nonsense, but after 15 years writing newspaper and magazine features for a living, I realized it makes perfect sense. The essence of good feature writing is excellent reporting.

And so that's why I'm in crab fisherman Alan Frederiksen's crab boat, getting raw material for "A Day in the Life of Florida Business," a freelance assignment for *Florida Trend* magazine. I'm enveloped in one of Frederiksen's rain parkas. My tape recorder is wrapped in a plastic sandwich bag, my notebook is splattered with salt spray. But there's no other way to see the iridescent shimmer of a blue crab's claws as it clings to the barnacle-encrusted wires of the fisherman's trap. And a telephone interview wouldn't enable me to write a passage like this one:

> As morning commuter traffic rumbles over the Madeira Beach Causeway above, Frederiksen hits pay dirt: a fat stone crab. Deftly breaking off the crab's claws before tossing it overboard, Frederiksen says that the two claws alone will sell at his fish store for almost $8.
>
> Turning north in the shadow of waterfront condos, Frederiksen turns pessimistic on the future of commercial fishing in the state. "Crabbing is the one industry that will survive because the crab is a scavenger and he can live in different waters. But others—mullet, pompano, redfish, trout—they need a clean habitat, and people pollute."

Of course, writing features demands time at the desk, planning, drafting, revising and editing. But the most important part of the process is reporting. Without it you have no story. With it comes the inspiration, the excitement. Reporting is the sculptor's clay, the artist's palette, the doctor's vital signs. For the feature writer, the tools are significant details, the revelations of things said and left unsaid, the shape of narrative that forms the skeleton on which to hand the stuff of life. And the only way to obtain these elements is by putting in the time.

Much of my working time is spent hanging around, talking with people, listening, watching. A feature writer's workday is rarely nine to five. To report life in a crime-infested housing project, I spent the night in a tenant's apartment. To tell the story of a pediatric intensive care unit, I spent five full days there, and several evenings, including the late night when the life-support equipment was disconnected on a four-year-old boy pulled lifeless from a relative's swimming pool. To convey the life of a blind child, I went to school with him, to swim class, to summer camp, ate dinner with his family, watching and listening. While most of my stories have required sizable investments of time, I still work for a daily newspaper and often a story will not wait. "From Jon to Lani, the gift of life" told the story of two teenagers, a troubled girl and a clean-cut Boy Scout, who met on a train trestle after an Amtrak train severed the girl's leg. I got the assignment before lunch. It was finished before dinner. But no matter what the deadline, the essential qualities of reporting and writing remain the same: perseverance, curiosity, caring and above all, determination to find the truth and convey it in the most effective way in the time available. A feature written in a day is more of a snapshot of a story; the in-depth feature is the full-length portrait.

When I look back at the stories I've written over the years, what remains with me are the moments that captured time spent in the field, scenes from a day in the life of a feature writer, one that spans nearly two decades, half a dozen jobs, and hundreds of stories. Like all journalism, feature writing is the art of listening to what people say and what they do long enough to understand what they are all about.

7:30 A.M.
Barrington, Rhode Island

The Barton boys—Jed, 7, Bradford, 5, and Curtis, 3, are seated at the kitchen table, juice, bananas and toasted muffins before them. Jed is rubbing his right eye with his knuckles.

"Jed," his mother says sharply, "put your hand down and start eating."

The hand drops.

Jed never has to be told to stop sucking his thumb; eye-rubbing is the blind child's bad habit.

His breakfast waits, but he has to feel for it. He lifts his right hand off his lap. Fingers straight out, palm down. He starts at the edge of the table and makes a pass over the Formica. Slow and deliberate until it is over the muffin. The hand hovers, like a spaceship, and then descends. The fingers make a circle, pick up the bread, bring it to his mouth. He puts it down and the hand reaches out again, looking for the cup. It stops when he feels the plastic.

"Is this mine?"

"Yes," his mother says, "that's yours."

The feature writer's mission is to convey the reality of life beyond the writer's experience. What's it like to be blinded at birth? What's it like when your child is born blind? Or, in another story, what's it like to smoke all your life and then be stricken with cancer? What's it like for those left behind? Those questions, natural ones for a former smoker like myself, became a story entitled "The Death of a Smoker" that told the tale of Peter DeMilio who had a bad cough at Christmas and was dead by the following Mother's Day, killed by the lung cancer caused by 50 years of smoking.

2 P.M.
Fort Myers, Florida

"I never saw a man go downhill so fast in my life," his daughter says. The transplanted northerner who used to laugh at Floridians wrapped in jackets in cool weather now couldn't go outside on sunny days without a heavy coat. Since New Year's DeMilio had lost nearly 50 pounds. His hair fell out, his muscles withered away. He developed the wasted condition known as cachexia, common to cancer patients, and his doctor noted, concentration camp victims.

. . . After her husband died, friends advised Mrs. DeMilio to get rid of Pete's things: it would make the adjustment easier. . . . She used to open their bedroom closet and stare at his clothes, take them out, match up outfits for him to wear. After three months she finally gave them away. She kept his trench coat, his slippers. Sometimes she wears his blue and white warm-up jacket.

. . . Marie DeMilio is 58, a small, youthful woman with short-cropped reddish-blond hair. Grief has left its mark. Lined and tense when she talks about her husband's losing battles with tobacco and cancer, Mrs. DeMilio's face is transformed when she talks about Peter: His two left feet that couldn't accommodate a Lindy yet managed a beautiful fox-trot, his happiness on the water, how he loved to impress his family up North with his cowboy boots and hat.

Smiling at memories and snapshots in her albums, Marie DeMilio relaxes. Once again, it seems, she is a young woman very much in love with the boy who took her to the movies and held her hand as they walked down the street. Mornings and nights are the hardest for her now.

"It feels like one big nightmare," she says. "Maybe I will wake up, and he will be in bed with me. But I know it's not going to be so.

"Would you believe it? I take his after-shave lotion and spray it on his pillow just so I can smell him. Just the smell of it makes me feel like he's with me."

I write because words unlock doors and open windows. I write features because I get to write about people's lives and can strive to convey emotional truths which to me seem universal and eternal.

Will Durant, the philosopher, once observed:

"Civilization is a stream with banks. The stream is sometimes filled with blood from people killing, stealing, shouting, and doing the things historians usually record; while on the banks, unnoticed, people build homes, make love, raise children, sing songs, write poetry, and even whittle statues. The story of civilization is the story of what happened on the banks. Historians are pessimists because they ignore the banks for the river."

So are most journalists. I write to make people feel, to make myself feel, and most of all, to ride the river, watching life on the banks.

For me, reporting is an act of seduction, first of my subject and then of the reader. I must convince the widow of the man who smoked for 50 years and died in six months, horribly, of lung cancer, to open their life to me in one afternoon. And when she tells me about sprinkling his after-shave on her pillow, my heart leaps because I have found a way to communicate her loss.

I must persuade the mother of a girl in Utah who disappeared 12 years ago, presumably snatched and murdered by serial killer Ted Bundy, to tell me how that horror shaped her family's life. And I must show her that I am different from the reporter who posed as a cop to get in her front door. And when she shows me the front porch light switch, left on 12 years before for the teenager due home that night, and the piece of tape on it that has made sure it has stayed burning, my heart leaps.

7 P.M.
Pawtuxet Village, Rhode Island

In the labor room at Kent County Memorial Hospital, Jackie Rushton rose from the stretcher, her face pale and smeared with tears. A nurse pressed the fetal pulse detector against her abdomen, a taut mound stretched by seven months of pregnancy. The detector was blue, the size and shape of a pocket flashlight with earphones attached, and Jackie Rushton's eyes fixed on the nurse who strained to hear the bird-like beating of her baby's heart.

"Here's the heartbeat," the nurse said after several moments of silence. "It's 126 and it's fine."

If there's a heartbeat, why isn't she giving me the earphones so I can listen? Jackie thought. That's what the doctor always does when I have my checkups. First he listens, and then he says, "Here's the heartbeat. Listen." She didn't say, "Here's the heartbeat. Listen."

"I've lost the baby. The baby's gone."

Clearly, the writer doesn't always have to be present at the moment the story occurs. By its nature, narrative writing is an act of reconstruction, as in the opening of this piece that re-created the traumatic, but ultimately successful, birth of a baby.

Hannah Rushton had already been born by the time I heard the story of her emergency birth, but her parents' memories were still fresh the night a week later I sat in their living room. My friend Barbara Carton, a talented writer for *The Boston Globe*, uses the metaphor of portrait painting to describe her interviewing technique: You have to get people to sit still long enough to get every wrinkle. That's what I tried to do, and I pumped them for specifics. What happened then? What did it look like? What did you see? What did you say? How did you feel? What were you thinking at that moment?

Even so, I knew I couldn't reconstruct the night solely on the basis of their recollections, so I arranged to visit the maternity ward of the hospital. In the labor room, I saw the fetal detector and noticed that it looked like a pocket flashlight. I soaked in other details: the color of the room, the pictures on the wall, the overhead lamps in the operating room that looked like ice cream scoops. The use of such telling details represent what Joel Rawson, then deputy executive editor of the Providence *Journal-Bulletin*, called "pasting wafers" on a story, a reference to the last line of Chapter 9 in Stephen Crane's *The Red Badge of Courage*: "The red sun was pasted in the sky like a fierce wafer." Wafers are the images that make the reader see with the writer's eyes. They are the gold that the feature writer must pan for in every interview.

Donald Murray, writing coach for *The Boston Globe*, advises that stories start as near the end as possible. For the story of Hannah

Rushton's birth, I looked for the moment where the outcome was in doubt. It had to be the point when Jackie thought her baby had died and the nurse was lying about the heartbeat. And that, I knew, had to be my lead since I figured readers would want, need, to know what was going to happen, and I could make them read until the end to find out. If there's a trick to feature writing, it's deceptively simple: Grab the throat and never let go.

And remember: Much of what you write will be discarded. Only a phrase on some draft pages will remain in the published version. In the beginning, lower your critical standards and accept whatever pap flows from your keyboard. The writing you think is wonderful will later prove to be dreck. The stuff you know is dreck will point you in the direction of better writing.

The only way to improve a piece of writing is to rewrite and rewrite and rewrite and . . .

4 A.M.
Silver Spring, Maryland

To me, writing has always seemed like a roller coaster ride, dizzying heights of excitement and dips into valleys of despair.

Let's pick a point, arbitrarily, right after I've published a feature. Let's say it appeared on page one and people have said they liked it. I'm elated. That lasts a few seconds, replaced immediately by despair. "The story was a fluke," a little voice whispers. "Just a lucky break. You'll never be able to match it again. In fact, you'll probably never get another story idea again, and your bosses will realize you were just a flash in the pan."

But then another story idea appears; either my editor comes up with one or an idea occurs to me. I'm high again and as I launch into the reporting I start on a roll. But then an interview falls through, or I can't get to somebody. I'm back in the pits again. The only solution is to keep slogging away.

Have I got a story? That's what I'm asking myself as I come back to the office. I realize I can't let my boss know this. So I start pitching the story, and myself, and slowly, start climbing upwards again, convinced maybe there is a story here after all. But then I sit down to write and I realize it was a mirage. I start to sweat, the clock is ticking. Suddenly, at the very point of disaster, when I have hit what mountain climbers and runners call "the wall," I seem to get a second wind and push ahead and finish the piece.

I am at once elated, and terrified. What if I got everything wrong? Are my notes accurate? Have I checked everything? At 4:00 that morning, I wake up. "Oh Christ," the little voice says. "His middle initial isn't C." I race to my briefcase, fish out my notes. Yes, it is C. I go back to bed, and spend the rest of the night picking apart each paragraph.

The paper appears in the driveway at 6 A.M. This time, I vow, I won't get it. Or if I do, I won't look at my story. At 6:01 I'm outside, tearing it out of the plastic wrapper that never keeps it dry when it rains. But no, I won't look.

I look.

It looks okay.

I go to work. I hope no one notices me. I hope they crowd around my desk. I hope they forget I'm there. I hope they lift me on their shoulders. "Good story," a friend says.

"Sure," the voice says. "They're just being nice."

Someone else says it. I begin to wonder. Maybe it was okay after all. Maybe my wife was right after all. I reassess. "Hey, it's a damn fine story. One of my best. Hey, maybe it will win a prize? . . .

"Oh God, what am I going to do tomorrow?"

Christopher Scanlan is a national correspondent for Knight-Ridder newspapers based in Washington, D.C. He has written award-winning feature stories as a staff writer for the Providence *Journal-Bulletin* and the *St. Petersburg Times* and has contributed freelance articles to the *Philadelphia Inquirer*, the *Miami Herald*, and more than a dozen other newspapers, magazines and textbooks. He is the editor of the book, *How I Wrote the Story*, a collection of accounts exploring the newswriting process.

A h, if every newspaper feature editor or assigning editor at every magazine would dash off a memo like the one below, what a great profession it would be for developing writers. Unfortunately, most editors are too busy or just aren't the teacher types. All too often, you as a writer will be on your own. You'll have to read books, take courses, and experiment to develop your writing skills. However, if you do find an editor who will act as a mentor, seize the opportunity. If you are a freelancer, go to him or her as often as you can, even if the pay is better somewhere else. Learn what you can while someone is there to teach.

Memo to a New Feature Writer

Donald M. Murray

From: Donald M. Murray
Re: Writing skills

You have been given this new assignment because you have established your ability to write copy that is lively, makes the reader feel as well as think, and is not always based on a hard news peg. You have earned a reputation as a good reporter *and* a good writer. Congratulations—but don't forget the relationship between the two: you are now a feature reporter *and* writer.

We'll have some assignments for you, but we expect you to come up with your own ideas most of the time. We won't buy all of them, but whether we give you the go-ahead or not, we want you to remember—and to remind us—how much we need your ideas. Editors sit; reporters walk. Your ability to write well is based on your ability to see well, and we want you on the street, discovering what is extraordinary in what has become ordinary for the rest of us. We want to know what you catch out of the corner of your eye, what you overhear being said and not said, what you discover when you observe our world from your own point of view. We hope you'll continue to be surprised at what you find and that you'll surprise us and our readers.

Don't underestimate the importance of what you are doing. When I broke into the business, features were considered frills. They were usually assigned to women—or men who were considered slightly womanly: sensitive and rather literary. Our real job was to deliver hard news to the reader. Period. But when I look back in my mental scrapbook I find many of the features I wrote have worn far longer and better than the accounts of fires and shootings and elections and press conferences that were reported with traditional professionalism.

Hard news is still our first priority, but it is delivered today by radio and television as well as newspapers. People read today to learn what and when and who and where, but they also read to discover why and how and what it will mean in the future.

Features give us depth and implication; they put people in the story; they make the reader think and care. Features are read and clipped and passed around and photocopied and are often the real reason that readers buy our product.

Don't forget all you learned about reporting. The feature writer is a reporter first of all, and the more you work to make your writing perceptive, insightful, stimulating, and moving—the more you learn to write so that you can capture the world and hold it up for our examination—the better reporter you will become, because the writer sees better—and more—than the nonwriter.

Features Predict the News

Features used to follow the news; now they often tell the reader—and the editor—what will be news in the days, weeks, months and years ahead. To discover this news that isn't already news, you have to develop a writer's eyes that can look at the world without hard news stereotypes, catch the trend before it is a trend, spot changes in society before there is a press conference to announce the change, find stories that are not based on an event.

Perceptive, probing features give depth and texture to our coverage of the news. Features put people on our pages who walk and talk and become real—and significant—as our readers meet them.

To do this you have to get off the phone and out of the office. One technique you'll find helpful is to work off deadline. Get to the press conference ahead of time and talk to the person who puts makeup on the presidential candidate, interview the nurse who helped "harvest" a heart for a transplant, find out how a loan officer decides who should get money—and who shouldn't. Stay on the scene of the accident after the ambulance is gone, visit the victim's family a week later.

James Baldwin tells us that "the importance of a writer . . . is that he is here to describe things which other people are too busy to describe." Go into family rooms and kitchens, the high school teachers' lounge and the student hangout, visit classes and assembly lines and the American Legion bar. Find out how people buy cars and fix up their homes. Listen and find out what they fear and want and need. Sit at lunch counters, stand in the unemployment line, listen to the talk of men at the Laundromat, spend a weekend night at a hospital emergency room. Hold up the world in which our readers live so they can see, appreciate, understand, and, perhaps, change it.

Experiment With Your Writing

Many of these stories will not fit the disciplines of traditional news stories. You know that discipline. Use it, but stretch it, extend it, turn it inside out. Tell me how you think these stories should be written. It's your story, and the form of the story should grow out of what you have to say. Newspapers, like magazines, need to experiment with the normal forms of writing, use new forms, combine new and old forms to help our readers see and understand their world. Experiment not to call attention to yourself as a writer but to call attention to what you have to report. Help us find appropriate ways you can get out of the way and raise the curtain on the world.

Writing features, you'll have to pay attention to endings as well as leads, for the ending gives the reader a sense of completion. The ending is also remembered best after the story is over. Practice writing endings that give the reader a sense of completion, and you will find that knowing the ending before you draft the story may also give you a sense of direction during the writing.

Most features are people stories. We want names from you and more. The people in your stories have to walk right off the page. We need to see them physically, to hear them talk in quotes that sound like them, not you. We need to know the environment in which they live and work. We need to see them living and working. It is your job to reveal the person to the reader so that the reader sees people in action. As Mark Twain said, "Don't say the old lady screamed — bring her on and let her scream."

Let's keep talking about our craft. Share stories you like with me. Read about writing — you may want to start with the five volumes of *Paris Review* interviews published under the title of *Writers at Work* by Penguin. Visit the art museum and see what we can learn from the artist's vision of the world. Let's share what we learn from movies. Read nonfiction, fiction, poetry. Teach me whom I should read. You'll find me suggesting John McPhee, Toni Morrison, Charles Simic, Raymond Carver, Joan Didion, William Least Heat Moon, Wallace Stevens, George Simenon, William Maxwell, Susan Sheehan, William Kennedy, Eudora Welty, Graham Greene, Hilma Wolitzer, and all the other writers that keep me excited about writing.

Your stories also keep me interested in our craft. I can tell your stories even without looking at the byline. You write in your own voice. That's a rare quality, and we want you to work consciously at developing your voice so that it fits a broad spectrum of stories. Voice gives the reader the illusion of a private conversation. An effective voice carries authority, underlines the writer's caring, cements all the elements in the story so they hold together, provides momentum that carries the reader along. Be aware of your writing voice, listen to how you are saying what you are saying, read aloud as you write and learn to use that gift of voice so easily, so naturally, so invisibly that the reader is not aware of a writer laboring away at the prose but feels that the story is not being read but experienced.

Let me know how I can help you look at the world with your eye and share what you learn in your own voice. Welcome aboard.

> Donald M. Murray, who won the Pulitzer Prize for Editorial Writing, is a retired Professor of English at the University of New Hampshire. He has been writing coach at the Providence *Journal-Bulletin*, *The News Observer* and *The Raleigh Times* as well as other newspapers. His books include *Writing for Readers*, Globe Pequot Press, which is based on pieces he wrote for the staff while writing coach at *The Boston Globe*.

End Words
Afterthoughts: More Points to Remember

1. The types of feature stories are endless. The common factors for the best of them are exhaustive research, tenacious reporting and excellent writing.

2. Be sure to consider who your editors will be when looking for a feature writing job or a long-term freelance relationship. A lot of good writing at a newspaper or magazine is an indication that the editors are enlightened — i.e., they are producing an environment hospitable to good writers. Be careful about a paper or magazine with bad writing. Its management may well be so preoccupied with meeting deadlines and filling pages that they have forgotten about good writing.

3. The writer most in demand in newspaper feature sections is the generalist who can turn the quick story and do it with style. This is the entry position in any feature section. However, in the long run, it will not hurt to develop a specialty.

4. Today the most sophisticated writing in feature sections and

magazines is probably closer akin to the nonfiction novel than to the traditional breaking newspaper story. The feature writer will have to know all the techniques of reporting and will develop central characters that the readers get to know and care about.

5. Pick your own style and field of interest. Just as in baseball, a freelancer or staff writer doesn't have to be able to play all of the positions. Some people are pitchers, some are infielders, others are outfielders. Occasionally there will be a Bo Jackson, who can switch ball games, but it is not necessary. In writing, some people will shine at writing small tidbits for gossip columns, others will prosper by writing features as complex as nonfiction novels. Novice writers should take chances in order to find out which styles are best for them.

6. Even the best feature writers despair about the quality of their work, even when it is outstanding. Writing is a psychologically difficult profession, but at its best it is also mentally and spiritually uplifting for the writer and the readers.

7. Feature writing is no longer just the domain of newspaper feature sections and magazines. These days features appear on front pages of the newspapers and in news broadcasts. There's a reason for this. Readers (and viewers) want stories about people; they want to vicariously inhabit other worlds and other people's lives. Feature writing does this best.

8. Many of the best feature writers learned to be reporters first, but they always had a love for the written word and outgrew the straight news story. They intuitively know: "A newspaper should be a document of the times with all the human drama and emotion of those times." Those who follow that dictum as set forth years ago by reporter Sue Hutchinson are rewarded with the best assignments, with more time to do their stories, with more job satisfaction, and sometimes with contest awards.

9. The best writers will agree they are only as good as their editors. The best editors are not only good at helping fix stories but also recognize talent and allow writers to do their best work. That may sound obvious, but with so many deadlines and so many pages to fill, raw talent can get overlooked.

Exercises

1. Study your local newspaper's feature section. Note the different types of writing. Detail its strengths and weaknesses. Are the ideas creative? Are the stories breaking new ground or just serving up old clichés? Do you learn something new each time you read it? How is the writing? How do they localize national issues? On the continuum from a breaking news story to a nonfiction novel, where do most of the stories fall?

2. Read one or more of these newspapers' feature sections: *The Seattle Times*, the *Wall St. Journal*, the *New York Times*, *The Orange County Register*, the *Miami Herald*, *The Dallas Morning News*, the *Los Angeles Times*, the *Washington Post*, the *St. Petersburg Times*, and *The Boston Globe*. These are just a few of the country's top papers. In them you will find some great writing, but you also will find some mediocre writing. Don't let the worst stories guide you. There is plenty of bad writing everywhere. Emulate only the best. The field is overrun with average writers, but the best are always in demand.

3. Read some alternative papers. Often they are more alive and prove a better training ground than staid traditional papers. Find papers like *The Village Voice*, *The Boston Phoenix*, *Phoenix* (Arizona) *New Times*, and your local alternative papers. They usually take a lot of freelance material.

4. If you are a novice and want to build clips, look for the tiny neighborhood, suburban or school papers. Analyze one. Make a list of stories that you might write for the publication. If you are serious about this, go see the editor and ask about writing for the paper. Work for free if necessary. Use it to experiment and test your writing styles while building a clip file that will eventually get you a job or freelance assignments.

Further Reading

1. *Writing for Your Readers: Notes on the Writer's Craft from The Boston Globe* by Donald M. Murray (Globe Pequot Press, 1983). Essays on writing by Murray while a writing coach at *The Boston Globe*.

2. *How I Wrote the Story* edited by Christopher Scanlan (Providence Journal Company, 1986). Providence *Journal* stories with reporters telling how they wrote the story. Also discusses the writing process.

How the Pros Do It

Writing Sample Number 1

"Mr. Lucky," by Jay Hamburg of *The Orlando Sentinel*, is the kind of feature story most novices should learn to write. It's a slice of life that newspapers love. These stories are written in a day or so. They have humanity in them and let us see how other people live and work.

As nice as they are, they probably will not win many prizes, but they, in combination with other, perhaps harder, news stories, will give a feature or news section a good story mix. A slice-of-life story will be hard for a freelancer to place at a large newspaper because staff members can do them relatively quickly. However, freelancers learning the business can, and should, do these articles, to sharpen their talents at campus, neighborhood or small weekly newspapers, which don't have big staffs. A story like this in your clip file won't hurt in trying to land a job at a newspaper or magazine. Of course, it should be part of a greater mix.

Notice how leanly written this story is. What is left out is as important as what is used. Quotes are lean and to the point. Description is used only on those things central to the story and it helps move the story along. Notice how much the story depends on the reporter watching as well as listening to Mr. Lucky. Also notice how the writer is in control and even breaks a convention to keep story flow alive by never mentioning the man's real name until the reader is deep in the story.

Mr. Lucky Ends Mr. Clean Career
Marion Edwards Spent 37 Years Scrubbing Restaurant's Pots, Pans

By Jay Hamburg
The Orlando Sentinel, Florida

Mr. Lucky leaned over the large metal pot that sat on the restaurant kitchen's floor. The 20-gallon pot was as high as Mr. Lucky's knees, and on its curved steel sides were the remnants of red sauce, and on the bottom was a thick

Lead and description of a pot set up the rest of the story.

coating of baked-on food.

After 37 years of scrubbing pots, washing pans and stacking metal bowls, this was Mr. Lucky's last pot. He is 64, and despite a painful ailment that makes his movements unsteady, he has held on for almost four decades to a job known for its turnover. He held on for his family.

"When you've got a family, you come on in and work your heart out and ask the Lord to help you."

There was a retirement party for him Friday at work, but Mr. Lucky completed his last shift at the Villa Nova restaurant Thursday night.

He started there Dec. 19, 1950, when he was 27. He worked at night after finishing his day job at Rollins College, where he was in charge of food supplies for the company that ran the cafeteria.

At the college, he was responsible for keeping inventories, and he also stacked big slabs of beef. In 1963, though, he noticed a numbing in his arms and feet and a weakening of those muscles. He couldn't lift the heavy produce. The doctors told him it was multiple sclerosis.

The doctors said he was eligible for disability payments from the government, but Mr. Lucky had three sons and a daughter, and one of the sons suffered from profound handicaps. Although his wife worked as a housekeeper at Rollins, he needed more money than a Social Security check would provide. So that year, Mr. Lucky, unable to continue hoisting meat and produce, became a full-time pot washer at the Villa Nova, the Winter Park restaurant known for its elegant atmosphere and Italian cuisine.

It was there that Marion Edwards got the name by which all his co-workers knew him. Because the wife of a former owner couldn't remember his name, she decided to call him Lucky. And as Edwards aged and the restaurant changed hands, the younger workers and managers came to address him more formally as Mr. Lucky.

With jerky movements, Mr. Lucky spun the big pot around late Thursday, lifted it, walked awkwardly to the large metal sink and dropped it in. He sprayed hot water over it and steam rose.

Mr. Lucky's hands are scarred because he sometimes picks up hot skillets that chefs slide to him across an inside window ledge. His fingers are numb, so he doesn't always know what has happened until he sees the blister the next day.

"Sometimes I didn't like what I was doing, but I couldn't do anything else," Edwards said, as he took a scraper to the bottom of the pot. "But I learned to like it. It's just like any other job. You do it so long, you know what has to be done and go and do it. It's not a get-rich job, but it's an honest job."

Mr. Lucky cannot lift his feet very well when he walks, and back in November, he tripped and smacked his head on the floor. He needed five stitches.

"Lucky, you're a hazard to your health," Tom Lutz, the new owner, told him. Lutz, who acquired the Villa Nova in 1981, worried, too, that Mr. Lucky's next fall might injure others in the kitchen, where many people work around flames and knives. So Lutz persuaded him to retire.

None of Villa Nova's owners through the years provided pension plans, but Lutz said he will give him a retirement bonus.

"He said he'll take care of me," said Mr. Lucky, who doesn't have any plans for retirement. Maybe he'll see some baseball games with his wife. He never had the time or energy before.

Mr. Lucky took a metal scrubber to the outside of the pot. There have been a lot of changes since he graduated from the old Hungerford High School in Eatonville in 1941. His disabled son died. Another son is a musician. The third works in construction. His daughter is a nurse's aide. His grandson, the first in his family to go to college, is studying computers in North Carolina. "I feel good about that," he said.

He scraped hard with a metal spatula again. It is the same one he has used for 37 years, and he had worn it down to a jagged edge while bending over the deep sink. "As long as I'm in a crooked position, I'm okay. When I straighten up, it hurts. . . . A lot of people that have this are in wheelchairs. And some of them are dead. So I think I'm pretty lucky."

Mr. Lucky said he thinks his illness is affecting his mind, though. He can't remember things as well. "I could have a dream at night and remember it. I can't remember dreams anymore. I used to dream about this place — I'd still be out here washing pots."

He sprayed the pot another time with hot water. "This is the last one. There've been a lot of times I wished that."

Watch how the metal spatula returns later in the story.

Three-sentence quote tells us reams about Mr. Lucky.

Throughout the night, waiters and waitresses came by and offered their farewells. "I can't imagine how he's done it," said assistant chef Jeffrey Boley, 27. "I'd have gone crazy after one year. But he comes to work early. He's always grinding away."

Mr. Lucky washed off the pot and carried it off. Then he wiped up around the sink. "Last time," he said. He kissed his fingers and then slapped them on the metal ledge over which so many hot skillets had come.

"Danny," he said.

"Goodbye, Mr. Lucky," said Diennel Gaudron, a 37-year-old dishwasher who left Haiti four years ago.

"We'll see you, old pal," Mr. Lucky said. "You tell the boys to be good, and I'll holler at you sometime."

Mr. Lucky paused by the sink. He pulled open a drawer and placed some belongings in a white plastic bag.

"I feel like I don't have a place to go now—to be with people. I'll find something to do. If not, I'll get out and walk. Go down by the highway and watch the cars go by. Go into town and talk with some of my friends. I'll find something. I've just got to work into it."

Mr. Lucky rode the bus to work every day from his home near the Villa Nova, and at night one of the waiters or waitresses would drive him home. "Last ride home," he said, walking to the door. "Last ride home."

Image at the end that will stay with the reader.

He checked his watch. It was just past 11 P.M. as he headed outside with the white plastic bag by his side. In it, he carried his worn metal spatula.

CHAPTER TWO

Assignments That Make Great Stories

W riting coach and teacher Roy Peter Clark is about to tell you how to find great feature story ideas. However, if you are a freelance writer, finding ideas is only the beginning. Next, you have to be sure the ideas match your market. Even staff writers have to do this. An article about a football player might not fly in a feature section, but an article about how his family copes with the on-field violence will. On the national level, you might think *Sports Illustrated* for the player himself, but *Redbook* for his family. But that's the obvious stuff. On a more subtle level, page through the women's magazines at a big newsstand. I did it recently and found 36 different women's magazines. *LEAR'S* won't buy what *Good Housekeeping* does, nor will *Elle* buy what *Parenting* does. That's why many freelancers specialize in certain markets. When an idea comes along that's right for their market, they instinctively know it will appeal to their audience, and, equally important, to their editor. For in the end, an idea is only a good one when an editor wants it and guides it into print.

Finding Feature Story Ideas
Roy Peter Clark

The great journalists — reporters or editors — see the world as a storehouse of story ideas. They have a form of X-ray vision that allows them to see human action behind the thick walls of faceless institutions. They are curious about everything, are fascinated with how things work, and live to uncover secrets.

Where do good story ideas come from? The answer is everywhere. They come from reporters and assigning editors, of course, but also from publishers and their spouses, copyeditors, copy clerks, readers and sources. Any idea can and should be tested. No idea is inherently bad. In fact, a story concept that seems to lead through dense jungles and impenetrable thickets may be the only path to lost cities and buried treasures.

The most important source of story ideas is your newspaper and its competitors. Newpapers are filled with undeveloped stories, announcements of meetings and events, of tiny clues that could lead to interesting narratives. One day I read in the paper an announcement concerning a young minister planning to spend the weekend preaching from a little house built atop a telephone pole. He called it his "polepit," and all were invited to hear him preach the gospel from on high.

The story reminded me of those ancient hermits who would preach from mountaintops or high trees or poles. So I rushed down to interview the minister. As soon as I arrived at his church, I understood what this event was all about. His church was on a street with about a dozen other churches. What I had was a story about this town's competition for souls, and the preacher's publicity stunt could be judged in that light. The seed for the story was the little announcement in the paper.

There are secret stories even in the press release describing the new phone book. When I received that assignment, I challenged myself to take this lemon of a story and make lemonade. I first thought that I would turn the story into a book review, imagining the phone book as having more characters than a Russian novel. Someone suggested that I call the first name listed in the book, but it turned out to be AAAA Roofing, followed by all the businesses with AAA initials. There was a business story there, perhaps. But I found my way while looking up the last name in the book: "Z. Zyzor." What a strange name, I thought, and what must it be like to be on the bottom of every alphabetical listing ever conceived?

I called the number and got the cafeteria of the local post office. I dialed again, and got the same number. No one knew of any Z. Zyzor. I used the city directory and discovered that, indeed, the address next to the name was that of the post office. I called the personnel department of the post office, but got nowhere.

When I had almost given up hope of solving this little mystery, I got a call from the postmaster. "I hear you've been asking about Z. Zyzor."

My palms were sweating. Finally he told me the story.

Back in 1948, the letter carriers decided to pitch in money to get a telephone installed at the post office for their personal use. "We invented the name Z. Zyzor. We told our families: 'If you need me in an emergency, just look up the last number in the book.' "

That is how a story about the new phone book made the front page of the local section on a pretty busy news day.

But what about reporters who are not so ingenious? What if they have learned, perhaps from bad editors, to see news, and the world, in the most conventional ways? What kind of coaching will help them open their eyes and ears? Try these approaches:

Find the Person Behind the Story, and the Story Behind the Person

A follow-up to a story about a postal rate increase became a tale about the unpopularity of postal clerks. The story began with this lead:

"When Marion W. McDonald went to work for the postal service back in 1945, you could mail a letter for three cents and a postcard for a penny."

After a description of the rate increases, there is this quote:

" 'Shakespeare could explain why the post office gets such bad press,' said McDonald to a reporter. 'Do you remember Mark Antony's words over the body of Julius Caesar?'

"The reporter looked down at his notes like a nervous schoolboy.

"McDonald peered hard into the reporter's eyes. His forum was framed by scales, meters and postal charts. He spoke his lines accurately and with conviction:

" 'The evil that men do lives after them, the good is oft interred with their bones.' "

I was fascinated and delighted by the postal worker who quoted Shakespeare. I wanted my readers to share that same experience.

Go One Step Beyond What Is Expected of You

I remember reviewing the movie *Midnight Express*, a powerful film about a young American trapped in a brutal Turkish prison. Some other reviewers wondered whether the film had been unfair to the Turkish people, depicting them as torturers and sadists.

I felt the need to go one step beyond the review, which led me to a column idea. I called the project manager, who defended the film, and was surprised how easy it was to get the deputy Turkish ambassador to the United Nations on the phone. It took two simple phone calls. "For years we've been stereotyped as being brutal, terrible, the mustachioed, scimitar-bearing people," said Altemur Kilic.

"Unfortunately, this film uses all the tricks in the book to come out against the Turkish people. As an American, when you come out of the movie house you come out with hatred against the Turks — not with hatred against the Turkish prison system. If I were paranoiac, I would say there was Greek or Armenian money behind it."

The young reporter should know: 1) That he or she can reach almost anyone in the world on the telephone at almost any time; 2) That making just one more call may give you just what you need to construct a great story.

Don't Be Afraid to Use Your Life as a Mirror of Some Larger Reality

In the days before Madonna and MTV, I tried my best to protect my daughters from Barbie. "I hate Barbie," I wrote, "I hate her grown-up polyethylene breasts, her glamorously expensive outfits, her superstar image, her camera, her microphone, her motor home, her sports car, her bedroom set, and especially her blond boyfriend Ken with his rose-tinted sunglasses, his mink coat, and his suede jumpsuit."

I checked the clips and found the name of another man who hated Barbie. He lived in a town called Oakland, Oregon, and I got his phone number from directory assistance. The man, Bill Barton, disapproved of the way Mattel was marketing Barbie. He was concerned that she was too sexy and flashy for little girls, and that she was being marketed in a way that conditioned little kids to be aggressive consumers. What makes Barton's criticism of Barbie relevant? He invented her.

Journalists live in the world, too, and their experiences may lead to legitimate story ideas. Perhaps there are suddenly a number of houses on your block for sale. Or garbage trucks are tearing up your street. Or it seems that traffic problems make getting to work more difficult. Or you can't find places to park downtown. While it is a conflict of interest to write a story that offers you personal advantage, it is right to assume that your problems and concerns may be shared by many other citizens.

To the Tuned-in Journalist, Even Nothing Can Be Something

When the local bluenoses failed to raise a protest about the arrival of the stage play "Oh! Calcutta!," it inspired this story:

"Like the floozy she is, 'Oh! Calcutta!' will strut her stuff into town this week, spend the night and move on.

"The controversial nudie musical makes its first St. Petersburg appearance in a one-night stand at 8 P.M. Wednesday at the Bayfront Center.

"Although the play faces protest from some church and community leaders in other Florida cities, such as Melbourne and Lakeland, 'Oh! Calcutta!' comes to St. Petersburg without a whimper of opposition."

When I learned that the play was facing protests in other Florida communities, I assumed that protesters would be out in force in St. Petersburg. I braced myself for their emergence, and prepared to write a story about it. At first I was disappointed when there was no outcry, but then realized that the lack of protest was a break from the trend, providing me with an even better story. Nothing became something.

Great Feature Writers and Their Editors Cultivate an Eye for the Offbeat

John McPhee of *The New Yorker* wrote a piece on Atlantic City by visiting the locations mentioned on the Monopoly board, including Jail.

Jeff Klinkenberg learned the value of an offbeat perspective at the now defunct *Miami News*, an afternoon paper which always looked for a fresh angle on a story.

Jeff, who went on to become an outdoors writer for the *St. Petersburg Times*, once found a young man who set up a NERF-ball fantasy basketball league in his own garage: "By day he is the mild-mannered vice president of a small family business which stuffs plastic bags with nuts and bolts. At night, on the basketball court, things are different. Terry Lewis, 20, is a superstar . . . It's only a one-man basketball league. The applause rings only in his imagination. But Terry Lewis has scored 25,000 points in 780 games in his garage-turned-gym. He's a holy terror."

An old army medal in a drawer inspires a reminiscence; a piece of sheet music becomes a story on its composer; a high school year-book becomes a window onto 20 years of educational change.

A waitress takes an order, not on a pad, but on a hand-held computer. A small public school is established at a large GE plant. Little kids are collecting baseball cards not for fun, but for invest-ment. Suddenly a grain of narrative appears before the writer's eyes.

But good writers also go against the grain, avoiding what Don Murray calls "clichés of vision." Handicapped people are not always heroic. Women and old people are not always victims. Capitalists can be altruistic. Some writers even develop strong counter-intuitive sensibilities about the news in their own paper. They wait and watch, weigh the evidence, and find another way.

These are just some of the "idea skills" that can be passed from editor to reporter, and back again.

Many of these attitudes come from a rich life of reading. Sadly, too many writers fail to read their own newspaper. The smart ones scour the paper for new ideas and angles. They might spend an after-noon poring through current periodicals in the library. They wisely read books which carry them beyond the boundaries of their special interests. Through their reading they can see the world through many lenses.

The productive feature writers get so many ideas they need places to store them. Those places may be in a computer file, or in a compost heap of papers, or in a folder, notebook or journal. Ideas are tricky creatures; if you don't capture them in words, they can fly off into space, where you may have to pray for their return.

Roy Peter Clark is a writer and teacher of writing. He is dean of the faculty at the Poynter Institute for Media Studies, a journalism teaching institution supported by the stock of the *St. Petersburg Times*. He has established a national newspaper center at the institute to hold seminars and workshops for editors, reporters and teachers. He is editor of *Best Newspaper Writing, 1979-85*, and is working on a book entitled *Coaching Writers: The Human Side of Editing*.

T he rich and famous have access to the press, and writers seek them out. Their good, and often not so good, deeds dominate the news. But we as writers can't forget the ordinary people. The beekeeper, the nun who has devoted her life to hospice work, the woman who fights for better safety standards after her husband dies on the job, the outstanding teacher, perhaps even your own mother. They all have potential stories. Most often their stories are told in small features in newspapers or in the front or back sections of magazines. Often these small features will provide writers entrée to do full-length stories. Indeed, many magazines will first try out new freelancers with small assignments about ordinary people, and if they work, the assignments will grow in numbers and often in story length. Sometimes that will mean writing about more important people, but it might just mean developing a full-length feature about an obscure person with an extraordinary story to tell or simply a story so rich in emotion and detail that it merits a magazine-length story. No one is better at writing about everyday people than Madeleine Blais. Her stories have earned her a Pulitzer Prize in feature writing and respect among her peers. Here she shares how she finds the people who help make award-winning stories, and how she makes those people come alive on the pages.

Don't Forget the "Ordinary" People
Madeleine Blais

All journalists live by certain private treasured precepts about what they are willing to do or not to do in order to get a story, and of all the lofty principles I hold dear, none is more lofty than my refusal to interview mayors.

By "mayors" I mean that whole raft of humankind, actually usually mankind, who occupy some great official seat in worldly matters and whose primary goal in communication is obfuscation, preening self-advancement or windy filibuster. What this means for me as a journalist is that most of the people I interview are obscure, and I am interviewing them because something in their unsung lives has struck me as important and worth documenting. The advantage to interviewing the kind of people I interview is that I almost always start out liking them, or if not liking them, at least appreciating something about their circumstances that makes them in my mind worth the intense attention of a full-length feature story.

How Does One Find These People?

One source for these stories, obviously, is in the regular news pages, when someone formerly obscure has been thrust into sudden prominence because of what is usually a cataclysmic, sometimes tragic, event. I am a great reader of newspapers and have been all my reading life; by the third grade I possessed that journalist's addiction to current events; when my classmates discussed the comics, I recited headlines. Even then I used to wonder what happened to the people in the news after they stopped being in the news. This curiosity about the human condition (or plain nosiness) never really left me, and so I often pick as subjects people whose situation continues to haunt me after the glare of publicity has dimmed.

Another source is word of mouth.

People are always suggesting that someone they know would make an interesting interview. This is not always encouraging: They could mean their Aunt Myrtle, who makes macrame thingies for her annual church fair, or their new neighbor, an expert on mung bean seedlings. My suggestion is to do your best to find out what they find so compelling, keeping in mind that as a feature writer you want not just a story, but also a plot. The best definition of the difference between a story and a plot comes from E.M. Forster. "The king died and the queen died is a story. The king died and the queen died of grief is a plot."

Here's an example of a word-of-mouth suggestion that worked. It came from a friend who arrived in the office, filled with enthusiasm from a dinner party she had attended the night before.

"There were some people there that would make a story," she said.

Who?

"This woman named Hannah Kahn. She's in her early seventies."

So are a lot of people.

"For 40 years she has sold furniture at the same store in Miami."

Am I being gently mocked?

"But really she's a poet."

A lot of people think they're poets.

"Who's been anthologized in more than 30 languages."

That's impressive. But still, she's not famous; we're talking a minor writer.

"She lives with her daughter who has Down's Syndrome."

A lot of people live with people in their families who are damaged. Situations like that are hard to describe well because they have so much built-in sentimentality. One has to fight hard to strike more than one note. Everything's too smooth, like scaling a sheer cliff. Where's the foothold?

"This daughter, Vivian, goes to a class in genetics at the University of Miami Medical School every year so the students can see the kind of progress a Down's Syndrome person can make in their life with the proper care. Vivian also writes poems."

That's more than heartwarming: that's news.

"For years Hannah told her daughter she was 16, in the belief that that would make her more acceptable to the small children who were her same age socially. But now Hannah is ill, she has cancer. Vivian's fortieth birthday is coming up, and she wants to tell her the truth. . . ."

There's a foothold, an edge, a point of pure tension. In the end, I spent weeks with Hannah and Vivian, on and off, discovering that in some fierce maternal way, Hannah's greatest poem was her daughter.

Everyday Sources of Feature Stories

Very young journalists are often led to believe that they should not be involved in their communities; they are encouraged in a kind of carpetbagging mentality that makes them think of themselves as not quite accountable: The person you treat unfairly in print one day will never materialize in your life again. The older you get, the more likely you are to attach yourself to the fabric of a community, especially if you invest in a house or have children. Sometimes, the everydayness of your very life becomes a source of stories. I like first-person stories, and if I were an editor I would routinely ask my best news writers to write about themselves, if only because the compassion and goodwill they are likely to bring to a personal story might serve them well in their coverage of strangers. But also, when we write about ourselves, we see grayness, nuance, something other than that sharp division that characterizes most news in which people have either won the lottery or they lost it bad.

Once in a while one will meet an anonymous someone in the course of one's daily life who seems somehow worthy of coverage. I once did a piece called "Monica's Barrel," about a Jamaican immigrant who sent huge cardboard cylinders back to her homeland every few months or so. She worked, long hours and hard ones, as a live-in domestic five days a week, but on her free days she devoted herself to trolling for goodies at the flea markets, the sidewalk bazaars, in her own cupboards. The impulse to send these barrels seemed to me almost religious: to give thanks for her life here and to appease the gods of envy. After the piece appeared, someone asked how it was I had discovered Monica, and I explained that her friend Velma sometimes babysat for my children, and whenever the children had outgrown toys or clothes, Velma would take them to give to Monica for her barrels.

Often, a writer will get a letter or a phone call from a member of the vast unknown public pitching a story, usually concerning something personal in their own lives, almost always of a saddening nature. One develops a certain antenna for the contents of these letters, and the ones in which every word is underlined or put in caps or in contrasting ink usually come from someone so, shall we say, fevered, that they are too disordered to convey the news in their life on their own. Even so, I made it my policy to investigate every request. In the case of Trish, the story of a schizophrenic bag lady, the letter came from her sister Meg, an advertising executive. Meg's letter was so measured and sympathetic and urgent that I remember calling her back within seconds of opening it, literally seconds. I had no doubts about the worthiness of the story: Here was a large family, eight children in all, in which everybody was willing to talk for the record, names and all, about an important social ill.

Making People Come Alive on Paper

The disadvantage to interviewing the Trishes and Hannahs and Monicas of this world is mostly one of a literary nature.

In one regard, the jobs of a feature writer and a fiction writer are not dissimilar. If novelists are faced with the artistic challenge of getting people who are not alive to seem alive, the journalist faces essentially the same problem: how do you make people who are alive in reality come alive on paper?

This is when I sometimes wish I could break my own rule: generally, mayors and governors and presidents are already quite familiar to readers and there is no extra pressure to prove their existence, to round it out by describing how they talk, or walk, or to find the identifying gesture that stands as a symbol for their whole personality.

I wish I had a surefire formula to pass along to ensure the easy discharge of this task, but I don't. My main suggestion will seem frightfully paltry, but since it has worked for me I pass it along in the hope that maybe it will work for you.

There are, we all know, two parts to the interviewing process. One is the formal part, where the journalist is officially on duty, notebook out, pen poised, face fixed in an expression of pure attention. Generally we are intent on getting down what the person says, and may be less attuned to how they are saying it or to what they look like at that moment.

And then there is also the down time, those casual, informal interludes when perhaps we are walking alongside our subject or helping him or her prepare the coffee that has been offered or clear the clutter off the couch.

It is during those times, those unofficial moments, that the subject is engaging in the gestures that often constitute the most telling physical description. My basic advice is to get time on your side. Try to become the world's champion at hanging out. I always advise young reporters to take it as a rule of thumb that they should generally be willing to work twice as hard as anyone twice their age.

One way to make time your ally is to work on several stories at once. Since they will usually be in various states of completion, each will be demanding a different aspect of your creative energies. The image that comes to mind is of a cook overseeing a complicated menu in which some things are baking slowly, others simmering in pots, while something else must be quickly deep-fried at the same time fresh ingredients are being assembled for yet a new item.

For example, I began the story about Hannah and Vivian the day I heard about them, with a phone call to Hannah. We met in person soon after, but she professed reluctance. "I don't know, the spotlight, who needs it?" I said I was still interested if she changed her mind and she could call me anytime.

That was that, for several months. I did my other stories. And then by chance we ran into each other at one of those outdoor arts festivals, a Miami winter tradition. In our quick conversation, I could sense her ambivalence. When I called the next day, she said yes.

Then the hard part began. I had to make this ordinary person come alive on paper. To do this I began stalking the colorful descriptive phrase. One afternoon I found myself with Vivian in the apartment she shared with her mother. We were waiting for the older woman to return home from work and we were both looking out the picture window in the living room that faced the parking lot. In the distance I could see Hannah, her silver hair at the steering wheel, and I watched as she nearly hopped out of the car and headed home at a fast clip, an unmistakable no-nonsense brisk pace. At the time my first child was barely two years old, and I was touched by Hannah's movement, recognizing it as the always hurried pace of mothers with young children, and that is how I described it in the piece.

The basic point is that as a reporter you need to marshal all your senses, not just your ears, to come up with a rounded portrait.

I guess one of my pet peeves about reporting is that too often quotes seemed to be the only route reporters take to establish the character of the person they are talking about.

There's nothing wrong with quotes.

In fact, the way people speak often reveals a wealth of detail: their age, ethnic background, their fancifulness toward life, their level of education, their gender. Speech is a dense, rich code.

But too often, feature pieces seem to be an onslaught of uninterrupted quotes, the purpose of which has less to do with advancing the narrative than billboarding the reporter's pride at actually having compiled so many quotes.

The ability as readers to really hear what a person has to say is enhanced by some kind of word picture about what he or she looks like. But just as important as the color of someone's hair or eyes, and sometimes much more telling, are the gestures, all those mannerisms and habits, the pacing and the knuckle-cracking, the sighs and the strokes of the chin, all those outward signatures that stand for something inward.

In other words, listen hard, but also keep an eye on the little gestures and nuances that make your ordinary people special and make them come alive.

Madeleine Blais is an associate professor in the Department of Journalism at the University of Massachusetts at Amherst and writes a twice-monthly column for *Newsday*. She was a Nieman Fellow at Harvard University in 1985-86 and won the Pulitzer Prize for feature writing in 1980 while at the *Miami Herald*'s *Tropic* magazine.

End Words

Afterthoughts: More Points to Remember

1. Sometimes ideas alone are worth money. Magazines like *People* and *Money* pay local stringers to keep them supplied with a steady stream of ideas from around the country. Of course, the main sources of the stringers' ideas are their local newspapers. The passing news story is often the seed for a more in-depth story for the feature section or for a magazine.

2. When constructing a story, don't assume well-known or important people are too important to talk to you. Try. Most will take or return your calls. And if they don't, you have lost nothing.

3. Don't forget to tap into your own experiences to develop story ideas. Lifestyles include every facet of life and that includes every facet of your life. When you plan to travel, think travel stories. When you try a new food, think of the food sections. When your own life is touched by tragedy, probe to see how you can relate the experience to others. The more life experiences you have, the richer the source of story ideas you will become. In other words, read and write, but don't forget to live.

4. Take national issues and think how you can localize them. The best way to localize any story is to tell that issue through a living human being. In the words of Don Murray, don't write about a war or battle—write about the soldier in the battle. Another writer put it this way: Don't write about mankind, write about a man. Localizing a story is the perfect venue for doing this. In fact, the major issues, from AIDS to exercise, demand that they be told through experiences of local people.

5. When you get an idea, write it down before you forget it. Inspired ideas are fleeting; besides, there is nothing better during a dry spell than to turn on the computer, call up your idea file, and see a storehouse of excellent ideas that you had all but forgotten.

6. Don't forget the ordinary people. Listen to all story suggestions. Ask questions to find out why those who suggest them think the story is compelling enough for you to spend hours, days or weeks on. Most ideas will not pan out, but some will become the great stories of your writing career.

7. Look for stories with an edge, tension or a plot. Often asking yourself if they have a beginning, middle and end will help in making the decision on whether or not to pursue a story.

8. Never underestimate your region for potential story ideas. For years, reporters and editors at the *Star Tribune* in Minneapolis carped that all the Pulitzer Prize-winning stories were done in the more dynamic cities like New York, Miami, Dallas, or Los Angeles. Not in the quiet Midwest. Then the *Star Tribune's* competitor, the *St. Paul Pioneer Press Dispatch*, won two Pulitzer Prizes. People at the *Star Tribune* were rudely reminded that great story ideas are everywhere. Soon afterwards the *Star Tribune* won its own Pulitzer Prize.

9. Be flexible with your ideas. Often you will go into a story with one plan, but as the research and reporting develops, the original premise might change. Usually, it is best to go with what will make the better story. However, let your editor know if a story is taking a different tack than agreed upon. Established freelancers or staff writers often instinctively know when changes will be well received. But if you are a new freelancer it would be foolish to put your sale in jeopardy simply because you didn't make a call to the editor buying the story. Editors love to be kept informed, and they, too, want the best story.

Exercises

1. Start a clip and idea file. Use your computer, notebook or even a drawer or envelope. For a two-week period, see how many ideas you can develop from all your life experiences — from hobbies, emotions, family, TV, reading — everything. When an idea comes to you, write it down. Sometimes you will be just writing a few words, other times an avalanche of details will come to you. At the end of the two weeks, go back over your ideas, cull the best of them, and turn them into feature stories or into well-thought-out assignment ideas you can present to your editors. Of course, don't stop after two weeks. Keep the file active.

2. Again for a two-week period, read your hometown newspaper or newspapers every day, concentrating on the local news. Which stories are underdeveloped and have the potential for a richer story?

Does the little item about a pizza chain opening in town mean the beginning of the end for the local family-owned pizza parlors? Is the teen auto accident death the beginning of a feature on teens and alcohol? At the end of the two weeks, see which stories could be turned into features. Continue the habit of studying your local papers for potential feature stories.

3. For another two weeks, read national magazines and papers like the *New York Times* for national trends. Write a brief note on how you would localize the stories. List some people who would know what is happening locally. Don't just list experts; what about the everyday people who might become the focal point of your story? And don't do everything from your desk and telephone; do legwork by visiting places that might give you insights into your story. To use the pizza chain example again: You read that national pizza chains are growing by leaps and bounds. A visit to a few family-run places might show that erratic quality and poor service might be what is doing them in. Only by an on-site visit would you and your readers get a feel for what is really happening.

Further Reading

1. *Free-Lancer and Staff Writer* by William L. Rivers and Alison R. Work (Wadsworth Publishing Company, 1986). A textbook for college students who have mastered basic writing and are interested in newspaper and magazine feature writing. It has plenty of sample articles, as well as advice on how to write and sell them.

2. *Best Newspaper Writing* edited by Don Fry (Poynter Institute for Media Studies, Annual since 1985). Contains stories and commentary by each year's winners of the American Society of Newspaper Editors competition. Although these books deal with all kinds of newspaper writing, they still benefit feature writers. The writing itself is interesting, as are the commentaries by writers describing how they go about their work.

How the Pros Do It

Writing Sample Number 2

The feature story that follows won a Pulitzer Prize, the highest award in journalism. There is no fancy wordplay, no great metaphors, just writing that sounds as if the writer is talking to a friend. The writer is in control. She breaks conventions by occasionally reading her descriptions to the blind boy who remarks on them. This is not the detached writer. This is a writer who is in the thick of it, who is making things happen.

It is a story about a blind boy with courage, and his family's perseverance to ensure he has a good life. It is not a story about what it is like to be blind or how blindness strikes youth. The writer defined her territory and stuck to it.

It is a deceptively simple story, but at the same time it is an uplifting story.

In his book *Writing for Story*, Jon Franklin, who has won two Pulitzer Prizes, says, "To the eternal chagrin of angry adolescents who yearn to pen indictments against a world they do not yet understand, successful stories generally have happy endings." I'm not sure Franklin is entirely right, but these kinds of stories certainly make the reader feel better. And what Franklin calls "constructive resolutions" do help us better understand the human condition, as does this piece by Alice Steinbach.

A Boy of Unusual Vision

By Alice Steinbach
The (Baltimore) *Sun*

Opens with description that focuses only on his eyes, which is what the story is about.

First, the eyes: They are large and blue, a light, opaque blue, the color of a robin's egg. And if, on a sunny spring day, you look straight into these eyes—eyes that cannot look back at you—the sharp, April light turns them pale, like the thin blue of a high, cloudless sky.

Notice the writer uses the story to interact with the subject. The experiment works in this case. Good writers take risks when appropriate.

Ten-year-old Calvin Stanley, the owner of these eyes and a boy who has been blind since birth, likes this description and asks to hear it twice. He listens as only he can listen, then: "Orange used to be my favorite color but now it's blue," he announces. Pause. The eyes flutter between the short, thick lashes. "I know there's light blue and there's dark blue, but what does sky blue look like?" he wants to know. And if you watch his face as he listens to your description, you get a sense of a picture being clicked firmly into place behind the pale eyes.

He is a boy who has a lot of pictures stored in his head, retrievable images which have been fashioned for him by the people who love him—by family and friends and teachers who have painstakingly and patiently gone about creating a special world for Calvin's inner eye to inhabit.

Picture of a rainbow: "It's a lot of beautiful colors, one next to the other. Shaped like a bow. In the sky. Right across."

Picture of lightning, which frightens Calvin: "My mother says lightning looks like a Christmas tree—the way it blinks on and off across the sky," he says, offering a comforting description that would make a poet proud.

"Child," his mother once told him, "one day I won't be here and I won't be around to pick you up when you fall—nobody will be around all the time to pick you up—so you have to try to be something on your own. You have to learn how to deal with this. And to do that, you have to learn how to think."

Quote almost works like a summary paragraph, in that it telegraphs what the story is about.

There was never a moment when Ethel Stanley said to herself, "My son is blind and this is how I'm going to handle it."

Calvin's mother:

"When Calvin was little, he was so inquisitive. He wanted to see everything, he wanted to touch everything. I had to show him every little thing there is. A spoon, a fork, I let him play with them, just hold them. The pots, the pans. *Everything.* I showed him the sharp edges of the table. 'You cannot touch this; it will hurt you.' And I showed him what would hurt. He still bumped into it anyway, but he knew what he wasn't supposed to do and what he could do. And he knew that nothing in his room—*nothing*—could hurt him.

"And when he started walking and we went out together—I guess he was about 2—I never said anything to him about what to do. When we got to the curbs, Calvin knew that when I stopped, he should step down and when I stopped again, he should step up. I never said anything, that's just the way we did it. And it became a pattern."

Calvin remembers when he began to realize that something about him was "different": "I just figured it out myself. I think I was about 4. I would pick things up and I couldn't see them. Other people would say they could see things, and I couldn't."

And his mother remembers the day her son asked her why he was blind and other people weren't.

All writing above
is done in formal
interviews.
Parts could even
have been done
on the phone.

"He must have been about 4 or 5. I explained to him what happened, that he was born that way and that it was nobody's fault and he didn't have to blame himself. He asked, 'Why me?' And I said, 'I don't know why, Calvin. Maybe there's a special plan for you in your life and there's a reason for this. But this is the way you're going to be and you can deal with it.''

Then she sat her son down and told him this: "You're *seeing*, Calvin. You're just using your hands instead of your eyes. But you're seeing. And, remember, there is *nothing* you can't do.''

Notice transition
from formal inter-
viewing to show-
ing that there is
nothing Calvin
can't do. Para-
graphs above
were telling,
paragraphs be-
low are showing.
Showing is usu-
ally better than
telling.

It's spring vacation and Calvin is out in the alley behind his house riding his bike, a serious-looking, black-and-silver two-wheeler. "Stay behind me,'' he shouts to his friend Kellie Bass, who's furiously pedaling her bike down the one-block stretch of alley where Calvin is allowed to bicycle.

Now: Try to imagine riding a bike without being able to see where you're going. Without even knowing what an "alley" looks like. Try to imagine how you navigate a space that has no visual boundaries, that exists only in your head. And then try to imagine what Calvin is feeling as he pedals his bike in that space, whooping for joy as the air rushes past him on either side.

Writer has taken
you outside with
Calvin. Notice
the details. First
details only the
sighted can see.

And although Calvin can't see the signs of spring sprouting all around him in the neighboring backyards — the porch furniture and barbecue equipment being brought out of storage, the grass growing emerald green from the April rains, the forsythia exploding yellow over the fences — still, there are signs of another sort which guide him along his route:

Then details Cal-
vin can't see, but
uses.

Past the German shepherd who always barks at him, telling Calvin that he's three houses away from his home; then past the purple hyacinths, five gardens away, throwing out their fragrance (later it will be the scent of the lilacs which guide him); past the large diagonal crack which lifts the front wheel of his bike up and then down, telling him he's reached his boundary and should turn back — past all these familiar signs Calvin rides his bike on a warm spring day.

Ethel Stanley: "At 6 one of his cousins got a new bike and Calvin said, 'I want to learn how to ride a two-wheeler bike.' So we got him one. His father let him help put it together. You know, whatever Calvin gets he's going to go all over it with those hands and he knows every part of that bike and what it's called. He learned to ride it the first day, but I couldn't watch. His father stayed outside with him."

Calvin: "I just got mad. I got tired of riding a little bike. At first I used to zigzag, go all over. My cousin would hold onto the bike and then let me go. I fell a lot in the beginning. But a lot of people fall when they first start."

There's a baseball game about to start in Calvin's back-   More showing.
yard and Mrs. Stanley is pitching to her son. Nine-year-old Kellie, on first base, has taken off her fake fur coat so she can get a little more steam into her game and the other team member, Monet Clark, 6, is catching. It is also Monet's job to alert Calvin, who's at bat, when to swing. "Hit it, Calvin," she yells. "Swing!"

He does and the sound of the ball making solid contact with the bat sends Calvin running off to first base, his hands groping in front of his body. His mother walks over to stand next to him at first base and unconsciously her hands go to his head, stroking his hair in a soft, protective movement.

"Remember," the mother had said to her son six years   Action sequence
earlier. "There's *nothing* you can't do."   ends as it began.

Calvin's father, 37-year-old Calvin Stanley, Jr., a Balti-   Now back to for-
more city policeman, has taught his son how to ride a bike   mal interviewing.
and how to shift gears in the family's Volkswagen and how to put toys together. They go to the movies together and they tell each other they're handsome.

The father: "You know, there's nothing much I've missed with him. Because he does everything. Except see. He goes swimming out in the pool in the backyard. Some of the other kids are afraid of the water, but he jumps right in, puts his head under. If it were me I wouldn't be as brave as he is. I probably wouldn't go anywhere. If it were me I'd probably stay in this house most of the time. But he's always ready to go, always on the telephone, ready to do something.

"But he gets sad, too. You can just look at him sometimes and tell he's real sad."

The son: "You know what makes me sad? *Charlotte's*

Organization: This whole section has a theme; it is about sadness, and each ensuing paragraph plays off the one before it.

Web. It's my favorite story. I listen to the record at night. I like Charlotte, the spider. The way she talks. And, you know, she really loved Wilbur, the pig. He was her best friend." Calvin's voice is full of warmth and wonder as he talks about E.B. White's tale of the spider who befriended a pig and later sacrificed herself for him.

"It's a story about friendship. It's telling us how good friends are supposed to be. Like Charlotte and Wilbur," he says, turning away from you suddenly to wipe his eyes. "And when Charlotte dies, it makes me real sad. I always feel like I've lost a friend. That's why I try not to listen to that part. I just move the needle forward."

Something else makes Calvin sad: "I'd like to see what my mother looks like," he says, looking up quickly and swallowing hard. "What does she look like? People tell me she's pretty."

The mother: "One day Calvin wanted me to tell him how I looked. He was about 6. They were doing something in school for Mother's Day and the kids were drawing pictures of their mothers. He wanted to know what I looked like and that upset me because I didn't know how to tell him. I thought, 'How am I going to explain this to him so he will really know what I look like?' So I tried to explain to him about facial features; noses and I just used touch. I took his hand and I tried to explain about skin, let him touch his, and then mine.

This section is resolved. And the resolution makes it easy for the reader to move on to the next section. But it is so emotional the reader needs a pause before moving on.

"And I think that was the moment when Calvin really *knew* he was blind, because he said, 'I won't ever be able to see your face . . . or Daddy's face,' she says softly, covering her eyes with her hands, but not in time to stop the tears. "That's the only time I've ever let it bother me that much."

But Mrs. Stanley knew what to tell her only child: "I said, 'Calvin, you *can* see my face. You can see it with your hands and by listening to my voice and you can tell more about me that way than somebody who can use his eyes.' "

Think of these breaks between sections as seams in cloth, but in this case well-tailored seams.

Providence Hospital, November 15, 1973: That's where Calvin Stanley III was born, and his father remembers it this way: "I saw him in the hospital before my wife did, and I knew immediately something was wrong with his eyes. But I didn't know what."

The mother remembers it this way:

"When I woke up after the cesarean, I had a temperature and couldn't see Calvin except through the window of the nursery. The next day a doctor came around to see me and said that he had cataracts and asked me if I had a pediatrician. From what I knew, cataracts could be removed so I thought, 'Well, he'll be fine.' I wasn't too worried. Then when his pediatrician came and examined him, he told me he thought it was congenital glaucoma."

This is another self-contained section; this one gives us historical perspective.

Only once did Mrs. Stanley give in to despair. "When they knew for certain it was glaucoma and told me that the cure rate was very poor because they so seldom have infants born with glaucoma, I felt awful. I blamed myself. I knew I must have done something wrong when I was pregnant. Then I blamed my husband," she says, looking up from her hands which are folded in her lap, "but I never told him that." Pause. "And he probably blamed me."

A good interviewer builds trust and people tell secrets they often won't tell, even to those closest to them.

"No," says her husband, "I never really blamed her. I blamed myself. I felt it was a payback. That if you do something wrong to somebody else, in some way you get paid back for it. I figured maybe I did something wrong, but I couldn't figure out what I did that was that bad and why Calvin had to pay for it."

Mrs. Stanley remembers that the doctors explained to them that the glaucoma was not because of anything either of them had done before or during the pregnancy and "that 'congenital' simply means 'at birth.' "

They took Calvin to a New York surgeon who specialized in congenital glaucoma. There were seven operations and the doctors held out some hope for some vision, but by age 3 there was no improvement and the Stanleys were told that everything that could be done for Calvin had been done.

"You know, in the back of my mind, I think I always knew he would never see," Mrs. Stanley says, "and that I had to reach out to him in different ways. The toys I bought him were always toys that made a noise, had sound, something that Calvin could enjoy. But it didn't dawn on me until after he was in school that I had been doing that— buying him toys that would stimulate him."

Thirty-three-year-old Ethel Stanley, a handsome, strong-looking woman with a radiant smile, is the oldest

Last paragraph helps make transition to this section which is mostly about Calvin's mother.

of seven children and grew up looking after her younger brothers and sisters while her mother worked. "She was a wonderful mother," Mrs. Stanley recalls. "Yes, she had to work, but when she was there, she was with you every minute and those minutes were worth a whole day. She always had time to listen to you."

Somewhere—perhaps from her own childhood experiences—Mrs. Stanley, who has not worked since Calvin was born, acquired the ability to nurture and teach and poured her mothering love into Calvin. And it shows. He moves in the sighted world with trust and faith and the unshakable confidence of a child whose mother has always been there for him. "If you don't understand something, ask," she tells Calvin again and again, in her open, forthright way. "Just ask."

When it was time to explain to Calvin the sexual differences between boys and girls, this is what Mrs. Stanley said: "When he was about 7 I told him that when you're conceived you have both sexes. It's not decided right away whether you're going to be a boy or a girl. And he couldn't believe it. He said, "Golly, suppose somebody gets stuck?" I thought, 'Please, just let me get this out of the way first.'

"And I tried to explain to him what a woman's sexual organs look like. I tried to trace it on the table with his fingers. I said, well you know what yours look like, don't you? And I told him what they're called, the medical names. 'Don't use names if you don't know what they mean. Ask. Ask.' "

Back to Calvin.

"When he was little he wanted to be Stevie Wonder," says Calvin's father, laughing. "He started playing the piano and he got pretty good at it. Now he wants to be a computer programmer and design programs for the blind."

Again notice use of details.

Calvin's neatly ordered bedroom is outfitted with all the comforts you would find in the room of many 10-year-old, middle-class boys: a television set (black and white, he tells you), an Atari game with a box of cartridges, a braille Monopoly set, records, tapes and programmed talking robots. "I watch wrestling on TV every Saturday," he says. "I wrestle with my friends. It's fun."

Quote reminds us that Calvin's world is different from ours.

He moves around his room confidently and easily. "I know this house like a book." Still, some things are hard for him to remember since, in his case, much of what he remembers has to be imagined visually first. Like the size and color of his room. "I think it's kind of big," he says of the small room. "And it's green," he says of the deep rose-colored walls.

And while Calvin doesn't need to turn the light on in his room he does like to have some kind of sound going constantly. *Loud* sound.

"It's 3 o'clock," he says, as the theme music from a TV show blares out into this room.

"Turn that TV down," says his mother, evenly. "You're not *deaf*, you know."

From the beginning, Ethel and Calvin Stanley were determined their blind son would go to public school. "We were living in Baltimore county when it was time for Calvin to start school and they told me I would have to pay a tuition for him to go to public school, and that really upset me," Mrs. Stanley says. "I had words with some of the big honchos out there. I knew they had programs in schools for children with vision problems and I thought public education should be free.

"We decided we would move to Baltimore city if we had to, and I got hold of a woman in the mayor's office. And that woman was the one who opened all the doors for us. She was getting ready to retire but she said she wasn't going to retire until she got this straight for Calvin. I don't know how she did it. But she did."

Now in the fourth grade, Calvin has been attending the Cross Country Elementary School since kindergarten. He is one of six blind students in Baltimore city who are fully mainstreamed which, in this context, means they attend public school with sighted students in a regular classroom. Four of these students are at Cross Country Elementary School. If Calvin stays in public school through the 12th grade, he will be the first blind student to be completely educated within the regular public school system.

Two P.M., Vivan Jackson's class, Room 207.

What Calvin can't see: He can't see the small, pretty girl sitting opposite him, the one who is wearing little rows of red, yellow and blue barrettes shaped like airplanes in her braided hair. He can't see the line of small, green plants growing in yellow pots all along the sunny windowsill. And he can't see Mrs. Jackson in her rose-pink suit and pink enameled earrings shaped like little swans.

Showing rather than just telling us he likes loud sounds around him.

First tells us about getting him into schools, now shows him in school.

Sense the
warmth between
the writer and
her subject.

("Were they really shaped like little swans?" he will ask later.)

But Calvin can feel the warm spring breeze—invisible to *everyone*'s eyes, not just his—blowing in through the window and he can hear the tapping of a young oak tree's branches against the window. He can hear Mrs. Jackson's pleasant, musical voice, and later, if you ask him what she looks like, he will say, "She's nice."

But best of all, Calvin can read and spell and do fractions and follow the classroom work in his specially prepared braille books. He is smart and he can do everything the rest of his class can do. Except see.

"What's the next word, Calvin?" Mrs. Jackson asks.

"Eleven," he says, reading from his braille textbook.

"Now tell us how to spell it—without looking back at the book!" she says quickly, causing Calvin's fingers to fly away from the forbidden word.

"E-l-e-v-e-n," he spells out easily.

It all seems so simple, the ease with which Calvin follows along, the manner in which his blindness has been accommodated. But it's deceptively simple. The amount of work that has gone into getting Calvin to this point—the number of teachers, vision specialists and mobility instructors, the array of special equipment—is staggering.

Patience and empathy from his teachers have played a large role, too.

For instance, there's Dorothy Lloyd, the specialist who is teaching Calvin the slow and very difficult method of using an Optacon, a device which allows a blind person to read a printed page by touch by converting printed letters into tactile representation.

And there's Charleye Dyer, who's teaching Calvin things like "mobility" and "independent travel skills," which includes such tasks as using a cane and getting on and off buses. Of course, what Miss Dyer is really teaching Calvin is freedom; the ability to move about independently and without fear in the larger world.

There's also Lois Sivits who, among other things, teaches Calvin braille and is his favorite teacher. And, to add to a list which is endless, there's the music teacher who comes in 30 minutes early each Tuesday to give him a piano lesson, and his homeroom teacher, Mrs. Jackson, who is as finely tuned to Calvin's cues as a player in a musical duet would be to her partner.

An important part of Calvin's school experience has been his contact with sighted children.

"When he first started school," his mother recalls, "some of the kids would tease him about his eyes. 'Oh, they're so big and you can't see.' But I just told him, 'Not any time in your life will everybody around you like you — whether you can see or not. They're just children and they don't know they're being cruel. And I'm sure it's not the last time someone will be cruel to you. But it's all up to you because you have to go to school and you'll have to deal with it.' "

Calvin's teachers say he's well liked, and watching him on the playground and in class you get the impression that the only thing that singles him out from the other kids is that someone in his class is always there to take his hand if he needs help.

"I'd say he's really well accepted," says his mobility teacher, Miss Dyer, "and that he's got a couple of very special friends."

Eight-year-old Brian Butler is one of these special friends. "My *best* friend," says Calvin proudly, introducing you to a studious-looking boy whose eyes are alert and serious behind his glasses. The two boys are not in the same class, but they ride home together on the bus every day.

Notice the writer goes beyond just talking to Calvin and his parents.

Here's Brian explaining why he likes Calvin so much: "He's funny and he makes me feel better when I don't feel good." And, he says, his friendship with Calvin is no different from any other good friendship. Except for one thing: "If Calvin's going to bump into a wall or something, I tell him, 'Look out,' " says Brian, sounding as though it were the most natural thing in the world to do when walking with a friend.

"Charlotte would have done it for Wilbur," is the way Calvin sizes up Brian's help, evoking once more that story about "how friendship ought to be."

Nice to come back to earlier emotional points in the story.

A certain moment:

Calvin is working one-on-one with Lois Sivits, a teacher who is responsible for the braille skills which the four blind children at Cross Country must have in order to do all the work necessary in their regular classes. He is very relaxed

Works in what it could have been like for Calvin in another time. Shows just how much progress has been made.

with Miss Sivits, who is gentle, patient, smart and, like Calvin, blind. Unlike Calvin, she was not able to go to public school but was sent away at age 6, after many operations on her eyes, to a residential school—the Western Pennsylvania School for the Blind.

And although it was 48 years ago that Lois Sivits was sent away from her family to attend the school for the blind, she remembers—as though it were 48 minutes ago—how that blind, 6-year-old girl felt about the experience: "Oh, I was so *very* homesick. I had a very hard time being separated from my family. It took me three years before I began getting used to it. But I knew I had to stay there. I would have given anything to be able to stay at home and go to a public school like Calvin," says the small, kind-looking woman with very still hands.

Feature writers have to follow their subjects around to capture these kinds of scenes.

Now, the moment: Calvin is standing in front of the window, the light pouring in from behind him. He is listening to a talking clock which tells him, "It's 11:52 A.M." Miss Sivits stands about 3 feet away from him, also in front of the window, holding a huge braille dictionary in her hands, fingers flying across the page as she silently reads from it. And for a few moments, there they are, as if frozen in a tableau, the two of them standing in darkness against the light, each lost for a moment in a private world that is composed only of sound and touch.

There was another moment, years ago, when Calvin's mother and father knew that the operations had not helped, that their son was probably never going to see.

"Well," said the father, trying to comfort the mother, "we'll do what we have to do and Calvin will be fine."

He is. And so are they.

CHAPTER THREE

Getting the Story Down on Paper

P eople come into feature writing because they're confident they can write. So, in the beginning at least, most believe they are writers first. If they were just reporters, they would probably work on the news side. But the lesson all these would-be feature writers must learn, and a lesson that is preached over and over again, is that feature writing is nothing without reporting. And what is reporting? It is everything that precedes writing. I have asked the contributors to this section to break the process down in terms of research, interviewing and then organization. Beyond that there is the art of simply hanging around, of being there for the right moment. David Finkel, a writer at the *The Washington Post Magazine*, puts it all together for us, and we see how the best nonfiction writing can't happen without solid reporting.

On Being a Reporter First

David Finkel

One day, long ago, an editor took aside his new feature writer and tried to make a point.

"I just want to tell you, you're some kind of writer," the editor said. "In fact, it's an interesting thing. Whenever there's a hole in one of your stories, you write around it so smoothly that most readers probably aren't even aware a hole is there."

"Thank you," I said, missing the point.

And with that, I was put on the police beat.

"It's time you learned to be a reporter," the editor said. "Some-day, you'll thank me."

Well. I don't know about that, but in the dozen or so years since that day, I have learned two general truths about journalism.

One is that writing, for the most part, isn't a lot of fun. Some people may think otherwise, and that's fine. I have met all kinds of people over the years, including those who think it's fun to mock the injured and razz the dead. In such a world, surely there's a place for those who think writing is a good time. Not me. Writing and I have had our moments, but for the most part I'd rather be reporting.

Truth number two: reporting, for the most part, is fun. Tracking down the arcane, interviewing the reluctant, observing the hidden — all of that can be a joy. And a good thing, too, because in the line of work we've chosen, reporting — hard, solid reporting — is at the center of what we do.

Think about the best journalism you have read, and you'll real-ize this is true. The best stories may seem to turn on wonderful writing, but if you look closely enough you'll discover the true strength of these stories is that every sentence reports some specific piece of information. Maybe it's a fact that gives context. Maybe it's a quote that establishes tone. Maybe it's a description that defines the background.

Whatever it is, it provides some kind of essential detail, and when all the details are added together, the result is a story that takes a reader to a particular time and makes it so real it's as if the reader is his own witness.

The best stories, in other words, are more than a retelling, they're an experience of the senses. A reader doesn't only learn some-thing from a good feature story, he feels it. He sees it, smells it, hears it. He comes to know it down to its most affecting details. He is there.

That's the reader's end.

The writer's end is to regard feature writing as anything but a soft, comfortable undertaking. Put simply, the best stories require a lot of work. There is no formula for producing these stories, but there is a general process to follow that can be broken down into three broad areas: research, interviewing and observation.

In this process, writing is the translation. Reporting is the key.

Research

A colleague of mine, Jack Reed, knows about research.

One time, tracking down a trail of receipts involving a local sheriff, Reed ended up in a small building in North Carolina. "It was a metal shed, like something you'd put your lawnmower in," he says. "It had a metal door and one window that didn't open. It was hot and filled with boxes of gas-purchase receipts for airplanes. It was right off the end of an airport runway, and when jets took off the noise was deafening."

Reed spent a day and a half in that shed sifting through thousands of receipts and never found what he was looking for. A year and a half later, the miseries of those hours were assuaged when he received a Pulitzer Prize for the things he did find. But to this day, the time in the shed remains fresh in his mind. "I'll never forget it," he says. "It was like hell."

The point is, Reed did it because of the potential to make a good story better, and that, at its most basic, is what research is. It's an essential source that can provide you with all kinds of information, from what you don't know to what you haven't thought of. It's a necessity no matter if you are doing an investigative piece like Reed or a simple feature story.

The wonderful part of research is that the paths it can take you down are almost limitless. There are the obvious sources, such as newspaper and magazine clippings, but I've also gotten information from probate files, divorce files, voters' registration records, the Census Bureau, the Weather Service, old high school yearbooks, even the documentary stamps attached to someone's recorded land deeds.

At the least, research provides names, addresses and other starting points for interviews. At best, it provides the kind of authoritative detail that can set a story apart.

Such was the case when I set out to write about a man named Charles Griffith, who was about to go on trial for first-degree murder. This was the lead I wrote:

> MIAMI—He was a distraught man that day, a man who sang lullabies and wept. With one hand, he held a gun. With the other, he stroked the smooth face of his daughter, a 3-year-old existing in limbo between life and death.
>
> An hour before, he had given her what he thought was a fatal dose

of Valium. But here she was, still breathing, her tiny chest rising and falling rhythmically, if ever so slightly.

She was in a crib at Miami Children's Hospital, lying on her back. She had been there for eight months, since the day she nearly suffocated. He leaned over the crib railing and looked at her eyes. They were open.

They stared ahead, mirrored no emotions, saw nothing. It was the same for her other senses. The damage to her brain was total and irreversible, and because of it, she couldn't hear his weeping, and she couldn't feel his last touch goodbye before he aimed the gun at her heart.

He shot her twice. He dropped the gun. He prayed that her suffering was over. He fell into a nurse's arms, cried and said he wanted to die. He said, "Maybe I should get the electric chair to make things even. I killed my daughter. I shot her twice. But I'm glad she has gone to heaven."

What makes that lead worth bringing up is that it was built entirely from documents. Griffith, in jail at the time, would only consent to a brief interview. It was the same for the police and attorneys, and none of the witnesses scheduled to testify would talk at all.

Fortunately, there was a fat court file. At first I went through it for basic information, such as names of nurses and other witnesses to call. Then, when it became apparent that none of them wanted to talk to a reporter, I went through the file again, this time concentrating on sworn statements the witnesses had given attorneys in pretrial proceedings. Those statements, balanced against each other and bolstered by police and hospital reports, provided every detail in my lead as well as the emotional heart of the rest of the story. Documents, nothing more, allowed me to write of the little girl's life:

She would sleep with her eyes open. She couldn't swallow. She was fed through a tube into her stomach. For the first few months, a bolt was inserted into her head to monitor any swelling in her brain. She was kept from further deterioration only through incredible medical wizardry: Nystatin in her mouth to fight off infection. Lacri-Lube in her eyes when they got too dry. Tylenol as a suppository to control her temperature.

And an entire medicine cabinet fed into her through the gastronomy tube: Pedialyte for nourishment, Colace for constipation, Phenobarbital to control seizures, Bactrim to control infection, Valium to relax her muscles, and more.

Also:

He would dab lemon juice on her lips. He would run a cloth under cool water, lay it on her leg and say, "Joy, this is cold." He would put filters over a flashlight, aim it toward her eyes, and say, "Joy, this is red."

He would say, "This is Daddy. If you can hear me, move your toes.

"If you love me, blink your eyes."

Admittedly, it's a rare case when documents are so complete. In almost any story, though, a few hours of research will at least provide a solid beginning. It will give you background. It will help you focus an idea. If you start the reporting process by building a foundation of information, it will be easier to move on to the next step, which is going out there to meet your story head on.

Interviewing

COCOA—Behold the fat man. Go ahead. Everybody does. He doesn't mind, honestly. That's how he makes his living. Walk right up to him. Stand there and look.

Stand there and stare. Gape at the layers of fat, the astonishing girth, the incredible bulk. Imagine him in a bathtub. Or better yet, on one of those flimsy antique chairs. Boom! If you're lucky, maybe he'll lift his shirt. If you're real lucky, maybe he'll rub his belly.

Don't be shy. Ask him a question.

"What's your name?"

"T.J. Jackson. Better known as Fat Albert."

"How old are you?"

"Forty-three."

"How much do you weigh?"

"Eight hundred and ninety-one pounds."

"Gawd! How many meals you eat a day?"

"Three."

"What—three cows?"

Now there was an easy interview. For three hours, I stood next to Fat Albert and watched his night on the midway unfold. I was prepared to ask him all kinds of questions, but I didn't have to. The people who came by asked every question I had thought of, and more. They asked him how much he weighed, how much he ate, whether he had a girlfriend, whether he had sex, exactly how he was able to have sex, and on and on. They asked, and I became a stenographer.

If only it was always that easy. It isn't, though, which is why so many writers worry endlessly over interviews. They worry about the order of their questions. They worry about impressing the person they're interviewing. They worry about whether to come across as tough or sympathetic. They worry about what to wear and whether to use a tape recorder.

I know they worry about these things because I worry about them, too.

In truth, though, I know that interviewing isn't a complicated process. Here's what you do: You think of some questions. You start with the easy ones. And then you let things drift where they might until the interview becomes a conversation. Sometimes it happens right away. More often, it takes several attempts. But it does happen.

I interview the main subjects of a piece two, three, four times, usually over a period of days, until I feel I've gotten a true sense of who they are.

I remind myself that I'm not conducting the interview to impress the person I'm writing about, that my obligation is to readers. In this equation, no question is too trivial or inane if it leads to a clearer, stronger piece.

Finally, I remind myself that lots of things are going to go wrong. Maybe everything.

That's what happened when I interviewed a man named Jack Bowman, whose daughter had been murdered by serial killer Theodore Bundy. For 10 years, Bowman never said anything publicly about the case. Then, two hours after Bundy was executed, Bowman consented to an interview.

This was the lead I wrote for a sidebar to my newspaper's main execution piece:

> Jack Bowman was up most of the night. At 6 A.M., when it was clear he couldn't fall back asleep, he got out of bed and walked down the hall toward the kitchen. His wife Runelle already had the coffee on. He said good morning to her. He turned on the radio. He turned on the TV, too, keeping the sound low.
>
> At 7 A.M., the news came on, and Bowman watched intently. The pictures were of the scene at Florida State Prison. The prison itself, a long flat shadow, was in the background. In the foreground was a steady stream of cars, and in the cars were people holding signs. One

of the signs read, "Burn Bundy Burn." Another read, "Roast in peace." Another read, "Chi-O, Chi-O, it's off to hell I go."

At 7:18, the phone rang. It was the Florida Attorney General's Office in Tallahassee. "Mr. Bowman, this is Paul Freeman," the caller said. "This is to let you know that the sentence has been carried out. The execution occurred at 7:07, and he was pronounced dead at 7:16."

In St. Petersburg, Jack Bowman hung up. A sensation of relief spread through him. It was a vague feeling—"flat" is a word he would use to describe it later—but relief nonetheless. Theodore Bundy was dead. At last.

What's instructive about the lead is that it came from an interview that went as badly as one can go. Bowman didn't want to talk at his house so he came to the newspaper where I work. The small room I had reserved for the interview couldn't be used after all, so we ended up in the middle of an auditorium. I decided the best way to begin the interview was to ask Bowman about his daughter; as soon as I did, he began to weep. Things disintegrated from there. My questions were awkward. My pacing was awful.

The saving grace is that Bowman, even in grief, was a decent man who allowed me to ask questions endlessly. And I did. I knew I wanted the story to begin with Bundy's death, and when Bowman wouldn't let me be with him during the time of the execution, I knew I would have to ask the kind of trivial-sounding questions that would allow me to put the reader there anyway.

So for a couple of hours, I asked Bowman what time he got up, what time his wife got up, who made the coffee, who turned on the TV, how many steps it was from the bedroom to the living room. I asked everything I could think of until I had enough material to describe a private, pivotal scene as if I had been in attendance.

The interview never did achieve the level of conversation, and yet it was ultimately successful because it did the most important thing of all. It got the details, and the details are what make a story vivid.

In a good story, in other words, the TV isn't just on, its volume is at a certain level.

In a good story, a paranoid schizophrenic doesn't just hear imaginary voices, he hears them say, "Go kill a policeman," and "You can't tell Aretha Franklin how to sing a song."

In a good story, an 11-year-old girl isn't just trapped in the rubble of the Soviet Armenian earthquake ... "she was afraid to open her eyes out of fear of what she might see. She heard a noise and grew more afraid until she realized it was the sound of her own breathing. Only then did she conclude she was alive. She opened her eyes, saw nothing, held her breath and listened, heard nothing, tried to move, couldn't."

Observing

The girl in the rubble was named Ani Gabrielian. I met her a few months after the earthquake when she and her father Simon came to the United States for medical help. Shortly after they returned to Armenia, I traveled there to find them. The result was a series of stories that, for me, reinforced the importance of observation in the reporting process.

To anyone who has written a story, the value of observation is obvious. The most compelling stories are often a succession of pivotal moments, and seeing those moments unfold, rather than trying to re-create them, leads to a stronger, richer narrative.

It's obvious — and yet when I go out on stories, I often get so wrapped up in interviews that I forget to step back and become a passive observer. Lately, to overcome that, I've started doing two things.

When I arrive in a strange town, I don't go immediately to my first interview. Instead, I drive around for a while to get a feel for the landscape, the neighborhood, even the street the person I'm interviewing lives on. Doing this helps me settle down after a plane flight, and it also allows me to have a sense of place in mind when I begin asking questions.

I also try to look at any site that will be the focus of a narrative passage as if I were a photographer. I not only stand near something, I move away for a long view, I crouch down, I move left and right. I try to view it from every angle possible to see what might be revealed.

As you might imagine, I do see different things, all of which end up in my notebook. I fill up lots of notebooks on stories because I tend to write down everything I see, even if it's something like, "2 rocks off to left — sedimentary?? — resemble poodle."

My hope is that as the reporting process continues, the significance of my notations will emerge. Usually, that doesn't happen; out of a 50-page notebook, I'll have 5 pages of possibly usable quotes, 10 pages of other possibly usable notes, and 35 pages of hieroglyphics.

Sometimes, though, as with Ani and Simon Gabrielian, it does happen.

If ever a story called for observation, it was Armenia after the earthquake of December 7, 1988. More than 25,000 people were killed in the earthquake, including Ani's mother and four of her seven brothers and sisters. Ani's primary injury was physical: She had a leg amputated. Her father Simon's injury was psychological: He was destroyed when he lost most of his family, and then he was destroyed again when, after seeing how well people in America live, he returned to Armenia where he had no place to live but an old railroad boxcar.

He and Ani spent four months in America. While they were here, I visited them frequently, interviewing them about what their lives had been like and what happened to them when the earthquake began. I also read everything I could find about Armenia, and I conducted dozens of interviews with academicians, geologists, architects, search-and-rescue experts, Soviet officials and Armenian-Americans.

Then, Ani and Simon left for Armenia, and I followed a few weeks later. The interviews and research I'd done helped tremendously, providing context for what I observed. But in the end, I used almost none of it because it was the observations themselves that made Ani and Simon's story at all affecting.

One section in particular demonstrates what I mean. It was the ending to the third day of a four-day series, and it described a private moment in Simon's life that came upon his return to a relative's apartment after he visited the graves of his wife and children:

> The day is cool. The window is open. Simon sits in the living room, just sits, until his sister-in-law brings him an album of photographs of his children.
>
> He opens the album and looks at the pictures slowly. After a while, his niece, Irina, comes in and begins playing the piano. She plays a piece by Beethoven, a sonata. Simon stops looking at the photographs, closes his eyes and listens.
>
> In any city, in any place, there are the sounds of a day going by. On this day, in this place, the sounds are of some people whose lives are slowly coming to order.
>
> There are footsteps crunching in the gravel.
>
> There is a hushed conversation, too quiet to really hear.
>
> There is a baby crying, and a car door closing.

There is a sonata being played on a piano.

There is a man beginning to cry.

And, soft as a whisper, there is the sound of someone bringing some photographs to his lips, photographs of some children who have died, the quiet sound of a kiss.

I remember the day that story was published. I was awake before dawn. I waited in bed, listening for the sound of the paper being delivered, and when it arrived, I remember reading those nine paragraphs and thinking that, after 12 years of writing newspaper stories, I finally wrote something I liked.

Six months later, those are some of the only paragraphs I've written that I can reread and feel a sense of accomplishment over, and the reasons are twofold.

First, being with Simon that day was one of those privileged moments that make feature stories worth doing. As I sat with Simon, I learned not only about him, but about people in general and about myself. When measured against the devastation of much of a country, the act of Simon kissing some pictures was a little thing to be sure, but it revealed a universal kind of emotion that helped readers see how deep and prolonged someone's grief can be.

Second, I was able to witness that scene because of preparation. I had done enough research about Armenia to have a basic understanding of its history. I had done enough interviews to understand the severity of the earthquake. And I had spent enough time with Ani and Simon for a rapport to develop. I have had people cry before in interviews, and often, as their tears flow, they look at me to see if I have noticed. It wasn't that way at all with Simon. At that point, he trusted me enough to act as if I wasn't there. I was transparent that day, and he was a grieving man alone. It was the purest form of reporting of all.

A Sense of Control

What all of this means is that a good story isn't just a bunch of pretty words. It's a flow of information in which every sentence has something to say. And—as my editor suggested so long ago—it's reporting that allows that to happen.

It's getting to know your subject. It's interviewing for the tiny details. It's watching events unfold.

If you do these things, you'll finish the reporting process in good shape. You'll be able to focus your story. You'll be able to organize your notes. You'll feel like you're in control. You might even feel giddy with success. And then, just when you thought you were having fun, you'll sit down and begin to write.

David Finkel is a staff writer on *The Washington Post Magazine*. Before that he was a national reporter for the *St. Petersburg Times* in Florida. He also contributes magazine articles to publications ranging from *Esquire* to *Urology Times*. Among the citations he has received for his work are a Distinguished Writing Award from the American Society of Newspaper Editors in 1986.

Interviewing is an unnatural act. You must sit with notebook and pen in hand, while scribbling notes, perhaps as a tape recorder runs nearby. In the back of your mind you know that accuracy is primary. That means you might have to frame a question several ways until you understand what is being said. At times you will feel a question is embarrassing or dumb, but you must ask it because it is much dumber and more embarrassing to write a story that is incomplete. Fortunately, most people want to talk about themselves. Often they will tell you things they have never said to anyone else. Sometimes an editor will ask you to do a simple interview, let's say with an author passing through town who will give you just an hour on his busy schedule. Then you will want to focus your interview around one theme. It might be as simple as how he came to write his new book. Some magazines have a vitae-like section where you might just have to ask the questions to fit the format. At other times you will be asked to do a full-blown profile, in which case you want to spend as much time with your subject as possible. One interview will probably be less than ideal because you want to dig beneath the veneer to find out what the subject is really made of. No one is better at this digging than Kay Miller of the *Star Tribune* in Minneapolis, who can get people to reveal things they normally would reserve only for close friends.

Interviewing Techniques: Get Them to Talk

Kay Miller

I love interviewing. I love preparing to talk to someone I don't yet know. I love sparring with people who don't expect me to know as much as I do and emerging with a story they never intended to tell me. I love piecing together bits of information from one person to ask the salient question of another. I love spotting quirks of character.

I even love the odd situations interviews put me in: Crawling through the cold muck of an underground cave. Talking with Jewish dissidents in the Soviet Union. Listening to river people dicker with a traveling pearl buyer. Watching a child be born in the filth of Calcutta. Following a homeless family in their search for a clean, well-lighted place to live.

I love packing my beat-up black purse with notebooks, a handful of pens, and my tape recorder. And I love leaving my office, getting in my car, and driving where no one knows how to reach me.

But most of all I love entering another person's life at the time it is most intense: Birth. Death. Discovery. Magnificent failures. Ignominious successes. In such times, philosopher Joseph Campbell would say human beings feel the rapture of what it is to be alive. We don't pick dull times to write about. So we catch people in the drama and paradox of life. At such times people have wisdom to share. And it seems to me that at such times they are more inclined to tell the truth.

During those times a great interviewer is rather like a great psychologist: In his presence people often reveal far more than intended, while the interviewer listens and watches.

Learn to Listen

Not long ago, my friend Martha Sawyer Allen was permitted onto the Rosebud Reservation in South Dakota to cover a religious purification rite. Martha didn't want to blunder into asking offensive questions. So before she left, she asked several Indians' advice on the best way to interview people for her story on native American spirituality.

"Don't take notes. Don't take pictures. And above all, don't ask questions," the Indians advised her. "Just watch. And listen."

Watch. And listen. People will *tell* you what's important, often in ways other than words. Once a psychologist told me that only a small part of communication is words. That means that the majority of what we learn about other people comes through their facial expressions, the tone of their voices, the set of their bodies. Sometimes people say more in the silences between words than through all that they utter. Sometimes they speak most loudly in their choice of words or the themes to which they repeatedly return.

Of course, over the telephone you will get none of this. From face-to-face interviews, you observe how they have arranged the artifacts of their lives. You watch how they interact — or don't — with their kids, wives, neighbors and friends. Over the hours, you have them reconstruct their life histories, recalling the sights, sounds and color of seminal events.

There are stories that can be done on the fly. But my bias is that to do a thorough job of writing requires multiple interviews in as many settings as makes sense.

I have never encountered a person who told me in the first interview everything about his or her life that was crucial to an understanding of the person. There is a paradox in interviewing people: They crave being known and understood. Yet people hide out emotionally from reporters: Perhaps you will spot in them the very thing that they dislike in themselves.

In first interviews, people select their words carefully. They censor stories they wouldn't want to see in print. Their self-description too often sounds like advertising copy. Perhaps unconsciously, people want to know if you will be repulsed or will exploit them if they reveal their true selves.

I think of a 33-year-old woman who two years before had gotten out of prostitution. She was extremely bright: an honors student in English before she dropped out of college.

At first she talked about prostitution in a detached, clinical way, as if she were a sociologist describing someone else's life. But the more we talked, the harder it was for her to distance herself from her experiences. In an emotionally wrenching third interview, she talked about how loathsome she found sex with strangers. For her to survive, it became imperative that she focus on anything but the intrusion on her body. During sex, she silently recited poetry from her college days. She laughed when she told me that the only poem she could recite in its entirety was "Old Ironsides."

Yet, she said her revulsion was so great that after a time, the poetry was insufficient to block her feelings. So she devised a grisly visualization in which she would mutilate a part of herself. With each sexual encounter, she advanced the image, like installments in a serial:

"I would take a knife. And I would slice around my heart. I would slice off pieces of my heart, and I would watch the blood flow. That sounds kind of psychotic. It worked very well. . . .

"Every time I took another layer off, I would say to myself, 'See? This doesn't hurt. See, this doesn't hurt.' And I did that for a long time. Until the image—my HEART—kept getting smaller and smaller. At some point I didn't have to do it anymore. And I was glad. I was real glad because then I knew I didn't feel anything."

Of course, the more time you spend with people the harder it is to write a one-dimensional story. You begin to see your subjects as human beings, with many traits. I usually approach stories with an underlying hope that the people I've chosen to write about will prove to be admirable characters. They aren't always. And their stories aren't always pretty. Human beings are complex, and the more time you spend with them, the harder it is to write stories that are black and white.

Getting the Interview

Unless you're an investigative reporter with a hidden agenda, it's important to be candid about the focus of your story and what your interviewees can contribute. Let them know how much time the interviews will take and whether they can be done over the phone or should be done in person. On sensitive stories, face-to-face interviews are not only reassuring to the person you're talking with, but they are almost always more productive. And many times an interview isn't simply asking a series of questions and getting a series of answers. Many times it's more, even, than a great conversation. It's putting yourself in the sweep of a person's life, so that you understand the context for all those conversations.

On the other hand, if I'm talking with a relatively minor character—someone who's out of town or somebody who will provide a small slice of background for the story, some historical perspective, another portion about a profilee's background—I use the phone. Generally I do not tape-record these conversations. I'm a very fast typist and take computer notes as they talk. When they're going too fast, I say, "Just a second, could you reiterate that last point?"

When I am contacting someone for an in-depth profile, I let them know that most likely this will take multiple interviews. For a profile of a Minnesota politician I interviewed him six times, with many more calls in between. Each interview lasted at least two hours; some took as long as four. After that long, my mind turns to mush and paralysis sets into my writing hand.

At the close of an interview, I often tell my subject what has been particularly helpful for my story. Then I schedule our next interview.

Invariably during the interview new questions crop up in my mind. If I don't want to interrupt the flow of conversation, I jot them on the inside cover of my reporter's notebook. Other questions occur as I'm reviewing notes or listening to tapes. These I write down in the front of a notebook, ready for our next interview.

For profiles, I might ask to follow the person through a normal day — or sometimes through a unique day that gives me insights into their work — as I did when I followed pearl buyer Nadine Nelson from her tiny shop in Stockholm, Wisconsin, to watch her negotiate for rare pearls found in Mississippi River clams.

Unpredictably, the greatest insights I had about Nelson came during our three-hour drive home in the dark, where conversation was more relaxed than it had been before. I stopped taking notes and simply listened to stories from her life. She told me about growing up rich in Morocco and later living a hand-to-mouth existence with her artist husband. She told me about dirty tricks played on her by some competitors. Good quotes from that drive were lost. But everything else I knew about Nadine Nelson made more sense.

Stay Away From Restaurants

By far the worst places to conduct interviews are restaurants. They are noisy and distracting. If you've ordered something delicious, you're too preoccupied to eat it. Invariably your subject tells you something compelling just as you've picked up a sloppy sandwich and you look like a fool scrambling for a pen.

There are, of course, exceptions that prove the rule. My colleague Bob Ehlert did a stunning profile of playwright August Wilson drawn from interviews conducted in a restaurant where Wilson did much of his writing. The point is to select locations for interviews that will tell you more about the person you're interviewing: If you're profiling a prosecutor, get him in court. If it's a pearl buyer on the river, get her with river people. If it's a clothes buyer, follow her to showrooms.

If you're doing a series of interviews, it makes sense to let your subject chose where he or she will be most comfortable for the first interview—and you do the moving.

If your story also relies on photographs, think about whether the sites you select will provide action shots or boring, static pictures. My original interviews with a doctor who had been exposed to the AIDS virus were in a hospital office and later in his home—neither of which would have produced compelling photographs. Photographer David Brewster joined me in the emergency room with the doctor and got some very dramatic photos.

Preparation

The kind of interview you plan to do will shape your preparation. If you're planning a profile, you'll want to read everything possible about the person. Usually I mentally store away interesting anecdotes, crisis points, controversies, points of heroism or shame that I'd like expanded upon.

If the interview is going to be tense, or time is strictly limited, I prepare a set of questions that follow a logical progression from least threatening to most difficult. My hope is that by the time we reach the tough questions, both the person I'm interviewing and I will be relaxed enough so that I can ask almost anything—and have it be answered. The point is to know—going in—what kind of material you want coming out of the interview. If the interviewee raises a relevant subject, it can be the perfect foil for raising the tough questions.

Once I've grown conversant with a topic, I rarely need prepared questions. I know what gaps I need that person to fill in for me.

Just a word about dress: Whenever possible, I dress according to the expectations of the people I'm interviewing. In 1982, I went to a conference of American Catholic Bishops in Washington, D.C. The first day, my interviews went very smoothly. My notebook was loaded with good material. But the second day, the bishops seemed more standoffish. I sensed a reluctance that hadn't been there the day before. Though I was puzzled, I didn't give it much more thought.

I left the conference directly for the airport. On the plane trip home, I fell into a conversation with a businessman who owned a small but thriving computer company. Tending to the details was the secret of his success, the man said, and that included such items as requiring all his female salespeople to wear business suits with skirts, not pants.

Bristling at the notion of women working under what constituted a dress code, I pointed to the maroon silk pantsuit I'd been wearing on the final day of the bishops' conference. It made no difference to my interviews whether I wore these slacks or the dress I had on the previous day, I said.

"That may be," the man said skeptically. "But if you came to interview me dressed like that, I would make you work twice as hard for the interview."

Timing

Deciding who to interview and when can be crucial to the success of an interview and your entire story. After a national discussion on banning assault weapons, my editor and I decided I should follow the life of a single gun. I wanted a case that was about two years old, one that already had been adjudicated so I'd have a court record to rely on. I settled on the case of one Browning 9mm Hi-Power semiautomatic. I chose it after a prosecutor recalled that one of the central characters referred to the murder weapon as "my favorite toy."

On this story, I began by interviewing more peripheral characters—police, prosecutors, weapons manufacturers, officers at the Federal Bureau of Alcohol, Tobacco and Firearms. This I did for tactical reasons: First, I knew that they had no stake in the case and therefore it would cost them nothing to help me. Others might have dozens of reasons not to be interviewed. Second, I am characteristically tongue-tied on unfamiliar topics; I stumble looking for the right terminology. By starting at the outer ring of characters, I learned the language of weapons, as I gathered useful data and gained a foothold on the story. Then I was ready to interview people in the center of the drama.

From police records I got the name of Stephen Petersen, the accountant and sometime-firearms dealer from whom the guns had been stolen. Originally I had no idea how important Petersen would be in the story, so our first interview was over the telephone. As it turned out, Petersen had become obsessed with the theft, spending all his spare time for two years seeking prosecution of the men involved in the theft and sale of his guns. However, when the Browning Hi-Power turned up in the hands of a murderer, the police decided not to tell him:

> Not until Petersen was contacted by a reporter did he know that his 9mm Browning had found its way into the hands of an armed robber. Worst of all was the news that the weapon he bought to protect his family was used to murder a man.
>
> "My gun killed a man?" All the bravado in Petersen's voice seeps away. At first Petersen sounds as if he does not want to believe this. Then there is no sound from him at all.
>
> Quietly he tries to make conversation again: "My worst fear's come true.
>
> "Now, I'm not responsible for that man's death. I feel a moral responsibility. But the bottom line is that it could just as well have been another weapon. From that standpoint, if it wasn't mine, it would have been someone else's."
>
> In a flash Petersen switches from morose tones to angry ones in which he talks about the need for longer prison sentences and capital punishment. Then he shifts back to the morose tone again.
>
> "You see what happened? My efforts failed. We *knew* who burglarized the house and failed to put them away. A killing took place 10 months later. *We* failed. I failed because I didn't get the job done. I wanted those guns swept off the street."

Earlier, I talked about starting at the outer ring of characters on a complex story. Waiting to interview principal characters can, however, be risky.

Doing a story on an internecine family feud over an elderly mother's care, I made the tactical error of contacting the family's minister before letting all her adult children know I was doing the story. Within a day, the woman's favorite grandson called me, sputtering with rage, saying that the minister had told him some reporter was snooping around. Not only was this well before I was prepared to talk with the grandson, but he was so angry he refused to participate in the story. And he poisoned the well for me with his mother, aunts and uncles also.

Moral of the story: It's important not to wait too long to contact a principal person in a story, lest the person think you've got sinister intent and resolve not to work with you.

An Ideal Example

For me the structure of my first and subsequent interviews with Mark Dayton, a politician and member of the Dayton-Hudson department store family, comprised a textbook case on how I conduct interviews.

Our first of six interviews was at Dayton's home. He met me at the door, his posture ramrod straight. He was extremely cordial. Yet, even when Dayton smiled, he looked sad. His face seemed drawn down hard around the prominent bones of an aristocratic face. He led me into his living room and left to get coffee and mineral water. I picked a chair at right angles to a sofa. That way I could comfortably look him in the eye, without having to turn my body. There was a coffee table on which to set my tape recorder.

When Dayton returned, we made small talk briefly. Then we agreed to ground rules for the interview.

"Where's a good place for us to begin?" I asked.

Dayton began a detailed, fairly dry monologue that followed a strict chronology from the time he was last in the public eye to present day. From experience, I knew this first interview would lay the foundation for our subsequent meetings. I simply let it take its own course, seldom interrupting. I told Dayton that it is my style to try to put the reader in important scenes and that it would help me if he would describe settings, people, feelings, with as much detail as possible. Those are the elements of story telling. Some people are storytellers and some are not. Dayton was not.

From his word choices, the looks on his face, the falters, I would have to figure out which were the salient scenes to describe and return to for details later. Despite Dayton's clear willingness to please, the entire interview felt oddly stiff and contrived.

Every time I stepped into a tender area, asked a highly personal question, Dayton sidestepped it or declared it off limits:

Were there times in alcoholism treatment that stick out in your mind as particularly powerful?

"It was all powerful. . . ."

What factors contributed to the breakup of your marriage?

"I don't feel it's appropriate to get into. . . ."

Do you remember times in your childhood when growing up that were especially painful?

"I'm not going to get into that here. . . ."

Tell me about the new relationship you had that stopped last spring?

"I'm not going to say anything about that, except for the power of the experience. . . ."

Walls kept going up. I was frustrated.

Impressions

After returning to the office from an important interview, I try to record impressions, as I did for this story: "Has a need to be socially correct . . . So prissy he starts off one slightly off-color story saying, 'This is off the record' . . . Walls go up . . . Clearly knows what he will talk about, what he won't. You'll be getting someplace, then the walls go up . . . Everything about Dayton is controlled, everything planned."

Later my impressions of Dayton changed dramatically as I began to see the depth of his character, warmth and humor. But these notes gave me a reference point.

Dayton had set our first interview in the living room of his home. While comfortable, it is also formal, with implied boundaries. So when he offered to get me coffee during our second interview, I traipsed out to the kitchen behind him, settling myself on a high stool around an island counter, talking while he poured.

That began a modest ritual: Before each interview, we'd talk for half an hour or so about our lives, kids, articles we'd read, other politicians, sports, whatever came to mind. Sometimes Dayton would catch himself saying something unguarded: "Are we off the record?" he'd ask. To which I'd reply, "We are now, but I may want to ask you about it later."

These informal conversations gave Dayton a chance to know me better. It's a scary thing to open yourself up to a reporter. And I believe these talks gave Dayton reason to believe that I wouldn't abuse his trust. Perhaps in stepping over the initial boundary, I unconsciously had broken down some of the psychic distance that Dayton had set up.

Soon he would talk about his family and about how his divorce devastated him. As Dayton described those feelings, both he and I cried. Particularly wrenching was telling his older son that Daddy was moving to another house:

"Just the look of horror on his face. . . ." Dayton's eyes are closed again, and he looks slightly ill. "Even when I think about it now, it's just very moving. I mean he was so small and so innocent and vulnerable. And his world was about to be changed drastically."

Several days later the boy was to spend the night at Dayton's townhouse for the first time. Sensing that it might be rough, Dayton tried to smooth the transition by letting him pick out his own bed, desk and dresser.

That night Dayton read his child a book and put him to bed. Like always.

"I think I'd rather sleep in your bed," his son said. So they trucked down the hall to Dayton's room.

"I tucked him in my bed, and I lay down beside him. After just a couple minutes he said he thought he'd rather go back and sleep in his bed at his house. As I drove him back to our house I didn't blame him. I would've rather been back there too.

"I remember coming back here after that point, just breaking down into tears—the awfulness of the reality of that just driving itself in."

Using a Tape Recorder

I always tape-record important interviews. Invariably there is rich material in my tape recorder that never made it into my notebook. In the five years since I left news side to write for the *Minneapolis Star Tribune*'s Sunday magazine, one of the most satisfying feelings is the sense that I am not leaving great material out of stories.

Moreover, people speak in voices that are distinctive to them—their idiom—and the ear is not always quick enough to pick these up. Tapes capture the power and subtlety of human exchange in a way I have found impossible with handwritten notes. In my 14 years of reporting I have yet to meet a reporter whose hearing is so keen and whose hand so quick that he or she can catch every word accurately in sentences to be quoted later. That includes me. Sometimes I'm appalled at the lapses in my own notes.

I use a small tape recorder that fits into my purse with a reporter's notebook. On the slow setting, one tape will record two hours' worth of conversation. I generally keep an extra box of microcassettes and a handful of batteries at the bottom of a large, embarrassingly cluttered purse.

Before I turn the recorder on, I make sure that's all right with the person I'm interviewing. "It's a way to keep me honest," I might quip. "That way I'm not going to quote you saying something you never did."

Not only does that give them some assurance, but when people know you are taping, they are less inclined to later accuse you of inaccuracy or taking things out of context. That may well be, because you're less likely to commit those journalistic sins.

A small tape recorder rapidly becomes unobtrusive in a way that note-taking never is. Taping also frees me to jot down descriptions—of the person, his surroundings, his demeanor—without missing chunks of the discussion. Sometimes I get so excited when people expound on an important idea or are at last telling me the true grit of their emotion, that my hand freezes up. I miss things I know I'll need.

Moreover, as I listen to tapes, I feel as if I'm back in Mark Dayton's living room, sensing his human frailties and strengths. Carrying that feeling into writing brings some unquantifiable, intangible bonus.

All those are taping's rewards. But it carries a steep price: the time involved in transcribing tapes. To limit that amount of time I spend transcribing, I circle material in my notes that I want to retrieve from the tape. Next to quotes that were great, but I couldn't write fast enough to capture entirely, I typically write "get." Or I circle or star seminal ideas. Nevertheless, there's a tremendous temptation to listen to whole tapes and transcribe far more than can ever be incorporated into a piece.

The other downside of taping—and this is far worse—is that machines and tapes and batteries can fail. So can the operator: I've unwittingly taped an interview with explorer Will Steeger right over a key talk with St. Paul school's superintendent William Bennett. I've left the pause button on in an interview with a Canadian woman who helped Vietnam draft dodgers settle in Toronto. I've had a tape-recorder refuse to run during a conversation with AIDS physician Dr. Frank Rhame. It is daunting to think you've got a terrific interview socked away, only to discover that the tape is blank.

Your only salvation is taking good notes so that you don't come up empty.

It's Just Conversation

In many respects interviewing is just conversation with someone you want to know. Think about how you are with a stranger you find intriguing and want to know more about. You face the person, eyes trying to make contact. You tell him or her a little about yourself searching for common ground. With your expression and the power of your entire being you say, "There is nothing at this moment more important than what you are saying to me."

In a society where people are so prone to interrupt each other and to discount others with the disdain of disinterest, there is nothing so satisfying as someone who listens, really listens to you.

Another way to make an interview more of a conversation is to make it two-way. Often I find myself talking about my children and the things I have learned from them — or the trying times. This is done without guile or premeditation. It's simply the way I am in conversation. Yet I understand that it makes me less threatening. If interview subjects are sometimes appalled at the things they have told me, there are times that I am incredulous at those intimate details I have shared with them about my life.

You also have to be tough enough in interviews to ask questions that will cause discomfort. My style in asking such questions varies. Most often I ask tough questions straight on, without flinching.

Yet I was sufficiently intimidated by the process of asking one prominent interviewee if she really spit on her best friend in a rage, that I backed into the question:

"I've been dreading asking you about this, but a number of people have mentioned it. . . ." I started. My tone was so timid and apologetic that *she* burst out laughing.

"Oh the spitting incident. . . ." She claimed that among her group of friends, spitting on one another had become a silly, idiosyncratic joke.

Sidestepped Questions

Many times I ask questions that people really don't want to answer, no matter how gingerly they're asked. When I don't get an answer that's satisfying or smacks of truth, I return to it.

Sometimes I laugh to hear on my tapes how many different ways I've asked the same thing and how many times I have persistently returned to an unanswered question someone has sidestepped, as Dayton did when I asked him how much he was drinking in the depths of his alcoholism. The first time he ducked the question, answering one I'd never asked. So I asked again. He paused for a long time. "I drank enough that it was a problem," was the closest he came to answering.

If a question is particularly important and the person continues to avoid answering it, I sometimes say pointedly, "I know I've asked this before, but I don't feel that I have a satisfying answer yet. . . ." Alternatively, I might comment that this area seems to be one that he or she is avoiding and ask if there's a reason.

Which takes us to another point: Pay attention to your instincts. If you sense a certain reaction to a particular question, chances are it is an area you should delve into. If someone laughs at an odd time or if his or her eyes mist over unexpectedly, there's more there.

When It's Over

Generally I assume that everything people say is on the record and open for me to quote, unless they specify otherwise in advance.

If they ask to see the article before it's published, I explain that I never do that, but that I routinely review my stories and will likely get back to them to double-check details. If they feel there's a point that I've missed, we should go over that now, I'll say. And they may call me back to make sure I really understood points they made.

I consider double-checking an important part of interviewing, and I tell people to expect me to call back as I get close to completion of the story. Before I call them, I go through each line of the story and jot numbered questions on every item that I am not absolutely sure of.

On the story about Dayton, there were 50 items—some large, some small—to check. Even in thorough interviews, I have left some gaping holes or made egregious assumptions. Double-checking is the only way to get it right.

Toward the end of every interview I ask a variation of the same question: "Is there anything else I should be asking about?"

People are often startled and generally gratified for this question to be asked. To them it signals that I understand my own limitations and biases, that I am open to new lines of thinking. I also ask if there are other people who would be worth talking to.

Even material that never gets into the stories can be important. During one of my kitchen chats with Mark Dayton, I mentioned that I always sing to my daughters at night. I asked whether he and his boys sang together. No, he answered. Of course, his sons sang songs from school. He loved listening to them, but he never joined in. He'd never sung as a child.

Later, Dayton and I were sitting in the darkened balcony of Westminster Presbyterian Church, where Dayton went during his darkest times to pray and sort things out. Our talk was random and about nothing very important. He mentioned a song from the seventies that I couldn't place.

"How does that go?" I asked.

At that, Dayton sang in a voice deep and melodic. Gone was any self-consciousness. For the first time in six interviews, I felt that the walls had come down. I felt I had glimpsed the real Mark Dayton. And I liked him a great deal.

I kept looking for a way to work the singing in, but it didn't fit. As it happened, I ended the Dayton story with a scene of him in the balcony. But that was the story of his epiphany, not of his song:

> During the times that Dayton felt most humbled, during the darkest night, he spent a good deal of time in the sanctuary of Westminster Church. Three, sometimes four times a week, he'd climb to the balcony to find God, if there was God.
>
> There, he could be quiet and look for light coming through the darkness. Once silence was his enemy, a reminder of his isolation and profound alienation from himself. As Dayton came to be at peace with himself, he sought the silence and called it solitude. . . .

Kay Miller is a Sunday magazine staff writer at the *Star Tribune* in Minneapolis and has worked at the newspaper since 1978. She has concentrated on human interest stories, which have taken her to such places as India and the Soviet Union and have won her numerous writing awards, including first place in general excellence in the American Association of Sunday and Feature Editors' "Excellence in Feature Writing Competition" in 1989. She has a master's in print journalism from American University in Washington, D.C.

R esearch is essential for every feature writer. A freelancer who doesn't begin with research is generally doomed to failure. Even the initial idea has to be tested via research to ensure it hasn't already been done by the publication you are writing for. Selling the idea to an editor has to be more than just an idea off the top of your head. It has to be grounded in facts and details that come from research. This can mean reviewing previous magazine and newspaper stories, looking up data, digging out names of sources. It is a lot of work. However, this is a golden age for freelancers working at home who need to do research. A

writer with a computer and a modem can tap into all the research databases currently available, plus all the traditional sources such as the *Reader's Guide to Periodical Literature* and the *New York Times Index* at the
library. Indeed, you'll see the traditional print sources worked fine for Mike
D'Orso in this next piece.

Researching Your Feature Stories

Mike D'Orso

A few years ago, the writer John McPhee said to the editor of an
anthology titled *The Literary Journalists*:

"... you've got to understand a lot to write even a little bit. One
thing leads to another. You've got to get into it in order to fit the
pieces together."

Getting into it, for McPhee, means spending months, even
years, immersing himself in his subject, whether it is the orange
industry in Florida or volcanoes in Iceland. Few journalists have the
luxuries of time and space to study and shape the sorts of stories
McPhee writes. The pieces he fits together become books, while the
rest of us rarely end up with more than a couple of pages in the
Sunday paper.

But that's enough to have a goal as high as McPhee's: to want
our writing to touch the reader, to draw him in, to keep him there
until we're finished, and to leave him with something he did not
feel, know or fully understand before. We want our readers to trust
and believe us, to hear the voice of authority in our words. We are
storytellers, but our stories are grounded in fact. And so, like Mc-
Phee, we must begin in the same place:

With research.

Know Where to Dig

As writers in the realm of reality, we are only as good as our material.
But rarely is that material lying right before our eyes. More often
than not, we have to mine it. To do that, to know where to dig and
how, takes preparation. And that is what research is — simple, solid
preparation.

What do I need to know? Who do I need to ask? With research, these questions begin to be answered, the story starts to take shape, the targets become focused, and we can approach them armed with the ammunition of at least a little knowledge.

Without research, we are shooting in the dark.

Not long ago I got the idea to write a piece about hearses. More specifically, it was about people who own and drive *used* hearses. I had noticed a few around town and decided to track down the drivers, to find out who in the world would turn a funeral coach into the family car.

First I walked upstairs to our newspaper library back-story file, fearing the off chance that this story might have been written before. It wasn't. There are times, of course, when I go to our library *hoping* to find something. Sometimes I'm not even sure what it will be, as in the case of the 25th anniversary of John F. Kennedy's assassination.

Here was a story that had been approached in every imaginable way over the quarter century. My task was to imagine a new one. When I began scanning the microfilm of our newspapers from the weeks before and after November 22, 1963, I had no idea exactly what I was after—until I found it, on an obituary page printed a few days after Kennedy's death.

A seven-year-old boy named David White had died Friday, November 22, at 2 P.M., the same day and time as Kennedy. I pulled the phone book and checked his parents' name at the address given in the obituary. They still lived there, after all these years. No one had ever talked to them about the timing of their son's death. When I called, they were stunned. But they were also ready to talk—to me and to each other—about feelings they had never fully faced.

No reporter had ever talked to June and Gerald Winters either. But after I called several local hospitals and had them each search their birth records for November 22, 1963, I discovered June Winters had given birth to a boy the same afternoon Kennedy was shot—a boy she named John.

Finally, I followed up on a headline I had noticed in the November 23 sports section. There had been one local high school football game that was not canceled the night of Kennedy's death. A fullback had scored six touchdowns in that game, setting a state record that still stands. He was not listed in the phone book, but when I called the athletic department at his old high school, they led me to Frankie

Culpepper. He was living with his mother, who still pulls out scrapbooks of his fullback days.

I had my story.

> It was Friday afternoon, the day Alice White normally headed home from the hospital after her husband Earl replaced her at her little boy's bedside.
>
> But this Friday was different. The couple's 7-year-old son David, who had been battling a kidney disease for a year, had suddenly taken a turn for the worse. He was lying in an intensive care ward, surrounded by doctors scrambling to save his life. Earl was on the highway, rushing from his Virginia Beach job to the hospital in Richmond. As Alice sat in a waiting room wondering if her son would survive, a cluster of nurses stood around her in tears.
>
> "They were all crying," recalls Alice White.
>
> "Crying," she says, "for Kennedy."

That is how the first of the three profiles began, portraits of people whose private tragedy and triumph had become linked to and shadowed by the public pain of a president's death. I would never have found their stories if not for some old microfilm, some accurate hospital files, and a reporter's best friend, the telephone.

Try the Library

The telephone eventually helped me with the hearses, but before making some calls I went to another library — the one at the local university. The *Reader's Guide to Periodical Literature* and the *Newspaper Index* are there. They contain listings of major magazine and newspaper stories, respectively, indexed by subject. The *Newspaper Index* goes back only a few years. The *Reader's Guide* goes back beyond the turn of the century, and I have occasionally gone back that far with it, nibbling at anything I could find on subjects ranging from bowling to hoboes.

You've got to have a tenacity bordering on obsession to stay with a search like this, but sometimes the payoffs are delicious. To prepare for an interview with Mary Travers of Peter, Paul, & Mary, I found dozens of magazine stories written since the sixties. Skimming those helped give me a frame of reference, but it was Travers' appearance as a teen food editor in a 1953 issue of *Seventeen* magazine that gave me an offbeat icebreaker I used in our interview. When I mentioned her recipe for pineapple-braised pork chops, Travers nearly choked. She loved being thrown for a loop like that. Celebrities can be tough nuts to crack, but we can usually find a way if we do our homework.

Sometimes that homework uncovers something that totally transforms the story we thought we were doing. I recently found a former sumo wrestler who had arrived in town to train at a local gymnasium. The Japanese wrestler didn't speak a word of English, but his American coach told me all about the plans to turn him into an Oriental Hulk Hogan. What I wasn't told was that this sumo had been tossed from his sport back in Japan after he hit the 88-year-old chief of his sponsor's group in a fit of temper. I learned about that in a *New York Times* report I dug up as I was searching the *Newspaper Index* for anything on the sport of sumo. My story on this stranger in a strange land had now become more than merely odd—it had the tint of tragedy.

Occasionally it is worth looking beyond a library's reference room to check out what's in the general catalogs. (Yes, sometimes even reporters can take time to look at a book.) If not for a 1937 tome titled *Llamas and Llamaland*, I would never have known that the Incas used to decapitate and sacrifice these animals before feasting on their flesh. I had found that information before going to roam the grounds of the International Llama Convention a couple of summers back. It came in handy as I prodded these people about their peculiar pets. The mention of barbecued llama got me enough quotes to fill a couple of notebooks. I even found room for the Inca anecdote in my story.

If I hadn't looked at a few books about Dick Gregory before meeting his daughter at a local college, the story on her arrival in town would have gone nowhere:

> It was not until she was in college that the young black woman heard comedian/activist Dick Gregory speak. "I never knew he was so funny," she said. "I was in tears."
>
> She never read *Nigger*, Gregory's 1964 autobiography, until a friend gave it to her three years ago. "It was tragic. I was crying," she said. "I didn't know anything about his childhood."
>
> She was surprised when a reporter mentioned that Gregory was wounded during the 1965 rioting in Watts. "You mean shot?" she asked. "Like, with a bullet?"
>
> She was confused when a photographer told her he had photo-

graphed Gregory in Selma the same year. "What went on down there?" she asked.

"Marching and stuff?"

She admits it is odd that a black third-year college student majoring in mass media and enrolled in a course in Afro-American history knows nothing about Selma. Even stranger, she admits, is how little she knows about Dick Gregory.

He is, after all, her father.

There was a void in Pam Gregory. But the details I had gathered beforehand gave the void a context. And *that* became the story.

Make Your Own Good Luck

Unfortunately, all I found on hearses at the library were an article in a magazine called *Canadian Business* about that nation's most successful hearse manufacturer, a slim piece on horse-drawn hearses in *Americana Magazine*, and a *People* magazine feature about a California couple who rent hearses and caskets. No books. No luck.

There are ways to make your own luck. One is to keep your eyes — and your mind — open all the time. Some of the stuff you stumble across while researching one story can lead to another. I recently wrote a piece on a group called the Vietnam Veterans Motorcycle Club. While researching the biker culture, I looked at several magazines with titles like *Outlaw Biker* and *Iron Horse*. Inside those magazines I noticed a few ads for products aimed specifically at Vietnam vets. A few months after I finished the biker story, I went back to those magazines and picked up a few more, new publications with titles like *Vietnam* and *Vietnam Combat*. The trend I had sniffed in those biker ads was all over the pages of these war magazines. I began clipping ads, dozens of them, then called each of the companies that had placed them. Finally I tracked down some veterans, including Jan Scruggs, the man behind the building of the Vietnam Veterans Memorial wall. My story, titled "Milking Vietnam," began like this:

War is hell, but it sure can sell.

Just ask the Battlefield Replica Company of Magnolia, Ark., which will ship you an M1911 Automatic pistol — "the gun that blazed away in Khe Sanh, Khan Duc and Hue" — for $9.95. Order now and receive a "Vietnam Death Card Patch, the card often seen decorating helmets of Vietnam jungle fighters."

Or call the Pieces of History company in Wildomar, Calif. They've got something called the Republic of Vietnam Air Force Northern Expeditionary Medal, which, says the company, "was authorized by decree of Lt. Gen. Nguyen Van Thieu but was never awarded for unknown reasons."

For $40 (plus $2 postage and handling), the medal is yours.

If your tastes run toward collectible ceramics, Nilsson's Fine Porcelain of Solvang, Calif., has just the thing: "Dust-Off," first in a series of four "collector's plates honoring the Vietnam Veteran."

Rimmed in 24-carat gold, each saucer is decorated with a drawing of Marines clearing a helicopter landing zone in the Vietnamese jungle.

Price: $29.50 a piece.

And it ended like this:

"It makes me ill," says Murphy. "I think it's disgusting, a rip-off. All most of these companies are in this for is the money. They couldn't care less about the Vietnam vet, about the pain that was suffered, the damage that was done. They're simply using the current awareness and interest in Vietnam as a marketing tool."

Even the Vietnam vets who are making money off the war bother Murphy.

"Look," he says, "your service to your country is just that. It doesn't give you any special license to come back and sell something based on that."

But David Grieger disagrees.

"It's the American way," says Grieger. "And if you don't like this kind of thing, don't buy it. These are some of the freedoms those 60,000 or so names on the wall up there in Washington died for."

Noticing those magazine ads made that story. They were the root of my research. The rest was follow-through.

The hearse piece, however, did not fall in place so quickly. After I left the library, I went back to the office and began dialing local funeral homes. None of them sold used hearses. None of them knew any owners of used hearses. But I did learn a little bit about how they buy hearses, and I discovered that most funeral homes sell their old hearses back to the manufacturer. That led me to the largest hearse maker in the nation, the Superior Coach Company in Ohio. I called Superior's vice president for sales and got more information than I could ever want on the hearse industry. My talk with him and with several other companies gave me an idea of how many of these vehicles were entering the market each year and at what prices. Although I still had nothing on used hearses, I was circling the subject, beginning to zero in.

The *Encyclopedia of Associations*

Some of the best background information on any story having to do with an industry or a business comes straight from the companies themselves. And almost every industry, or organization, or interest of any type has at least one association representing it. Most of those associations are listed in one of the most valuable—and fascinating—reference books a feature writer can find: the *Encyclopedia of Associations*. Its two volumes, updated each year, contain more than 2,000 pages listing almost 22,000 organizations representing almost every conceivable subject. Addresses, phone numbers and brief synopses are included on groups ranging from Puzzle Buffs International (39,000 members, headquartered in Cuyahoga Falls, Ohio) to the Flying Dentists Association (500 members, based in Dunwoody, Georgia) to the Maine Sardine Council (7 members, located in Brewer, Maine).

The only hearse club listed in the encyclopedia's index was the Hearse and Car Owners Association ("address unknown since 1970"; no other information available). But the Superior Cadillac salesman mentioned a group called the Professional Car Society and gave me the home number of its president in Ohio. I talked with her a bit—her husband owns a seven-passenger Packard hearse—and she gave me the Dayton number of her club's expert on funeral wagons.

He was a gold mine. Not only did he know everything there was about the history of hearses, not only did he tell me where I could find a copy of *American Funeral Cars and Ambulances Since 1900* (the author sold the book out of his Florida home), not only has he owned a half dozen used hearses in his lifetime and was full of stories about the ins and outs of bartering for the relics, but he had in his Rolodex the name and number of the only used hearse dealer in the nation.

Now I was getting somewhere. Besides picking up information along the way, I was beginning to collect characters who would become part of my story. The used hearse dealer, in Cincinnati, described his strange range of customers across the country, from a softball team that travels to tournaments by hearse to a restaurant owner who uses his to deliver pizzas. The dealer estimated there were

2,000 used hearses on the road for purposes other than hauling dead bodies. And one of his best customers, he told me, lived one town away from our newsroom.

Bingo. The trail of research had now come full circle, landing me in my own backyard with a lead on the first of several local hearse owners who would become part of my story. It had taken two days of roaming the library and sitting on the phone, but the digging was worth it. And I knew when I had enough. It is easy for writers to be seduced by research, to become what *Wall Street Journal* editor William E. Blundell calls "scholastics":

> ... who, against all reason, try to learn everything about a subject before writing anything. Lacking a sense of scope, they report and report until their desks are hidden under stacks of papers and notes. They become prisoners of their stories.

We can't learn everything about our subjects. We can, as McPhee says, "understand a lot." It is up to a writer to decide how much that is, and to know when his material is threatening to control him rather than vice versa. Remember, too, that much of that material will never find its way into the story. A mistake young writers often make is trying to cram everything they know into the text. What they have to remember is that their readers—and their editors—don't care about all the behind-the-scenes sweat they shed scouring courthouse records, locating government reports, filing Freedom of Information requests. All that matters is the story. Most of my hearse material was left in my notes, but it all guided my voice as I began to write that story:

> Ask Phil Rubino about his hearse. Everyone else does.
>
> They lean out at traffic lights to see what he's got in the back. They snap his picture as he passes them on the interstate, his STIFF license plates disappearing in the distance. His neighbors would probably like to know how much longer he plans to park that shiny chocolate brown '76 end-loading Superior Cadillac out by the curb as if it's just any other family car—which it is for Rubino and his wife and daughter.
>
> After all, it is a Caddy. Which means it's got cruise control, power windows, power seats, double-air, and it fits eight with enough comfort to make you forget it was built to carry corpses.
>
> Some people will never get used to seeing a hearse anywhere but at graveside. Never mind that used funeral coaches have been showing up in strange hands for years.
>
> There was a wave of hearses among rock bands in the late 1960s.

Chimney sweeps have used them for decades—you can shove a lot of ladder into a 25-foot-long limo. Grateful Dead fans have been following their heroes in hearses for 20 years. And there have been recent sightings of hearses in Virginia Beach, where surfers seem to have found the perfect car for storing their boards and throwing a party— as well as raising eyebrows.

"The average person meets a hearse owner and automatically assumes he's meeting a ghoul," says Bernie DeWinter. "That's just not true."

DeWinter should know. He is the historian of the 600-member Professional Car Society, a national organization of hearse, ambulance and limousine owners headquartered in Ohio. A 38-year-old tool grinder by day, DeWinter's hobby has been hearses since he was a little boy sketching the ambulances and funeral coaches that paraded past his Dayton classroom window.

"The school was right on the route to the hospital and the cemetery," he explains.

Research. No writer should be caught dead without it.

Mike D'Orso is a feature writer for *The Virginian-Pilot* and *The Ledger-Star* newspapers in Norfolk, Virginia. His work has also appeared in several national publications, including *Sports Illustrated*. He won a 1988 National Headliner Award for general feature writing and has been included three times in *Best Sports Stories*, an annual anthology published by *The Sporting News*. His first book, *Somerset Homecoming*, written with the subject of one of his newspaper stories, was published by Doubleday in 1988. A collection of his nonfiction stories, *Fast Takes: Slices of Life Through a Journalist's Eye*, was published by Hampton Roads Publishing Company, Inc. in 1990.

Where do you begin to research a story? It can be as simple as looking at newspaper clips or as complex as using the vast array of computer databases. Jo Cates and Ken Kister give you some of the places where you can start your search.

A Feature Writer's Reference Library
Jo Cates and Ken Kister

A feature story is only as good as the research that goes into it.

Accurate, up-to-date information is not always easy to come by. Part of the problem, paradoxically, is the sheer amount of information available, much of which is duplicated, dated and either un-reliable or unsubstantiated. Since Gutenberg and the development of movable type, raw information has accrued at a dazzling pace, its output said to be doubling every ten years or so. Just the vastness of, say, the literature of medicine is enough to overwhelm all but the most intrepid researchers. One authority, for instance, estimates that it would require fifty-four centuries merely to read all of the medical literature generated last year alone. Pity the writer who tackles a luxuriant subject like sexually transmitted diseases.

But do not despair. An impressive array of reference material exists, designed to bring the knowledge glut under control and lead you through the information thicket. This material falls into two broad types of reference sources: print and electronic.

Print sources, the more familiar of the two, are traditional reference books found on library shelves, such as almanacs, dictionaries and encyclopedias.

Electronic sources, on the other hand, are comparatively new and innovative research tools that provide automated access to information via machine-readable disks and databases. Because they manipulate large quantities of data at lightning speed, electronic sources offer greater potential for effective retrieval of information than their print counterparts, but they also tend to be more expensive, and require training and skill on the part of the user.

Print Sources

First on any list of indispensable reference tools is a general desk dictionary, the writer's *vade mecum*. We emphatically recommend *Webster's New World Dictionary* (Third College edition), published in 1988 by Simon & Schuster. Adopted by the wire services and practically all major U.S. newspapers as their dictionary of first referral, *Webster's New World* is the most up-to-date, authoritative, best designed and user-friendly general English-language dictionary currently on the market.

Most writers also find a thesaurus or synonym dictionary a handy companion. Among the dozens available, we suggest *Webster's Collegiate Thesaurus* and *The Random House Thesaurus*. Likewise, there are few writers who will not find Strunk and White's little classic, *The Elements of Style*, helpful when dealing with the basics of standard English usage and composition.

A high-quality encyclopedia of basic knowledge, another essential source for any feature writer, provides both trustworthy factual information and easily understood summaries of complex subject matter. The 22-volume *World Book Encyclopedia* is, page for page, the best general encyclopedia published today.

Those who cannot afford or have no space for a multivolume encyclopedia should consider the single-volume *Concise Columbia Encyclopedia*, an inexpensive, reliable desk-sized compendium of encyclopedic knowledge.

Almanacs, yearbooks, handbooks and manuals complement encyclopedias, furnishing the researcher with a wealth of quick reference information. *The World Almanac* and the *Guinness Book of World Records* come readily to mind, and every subject field has its quick reference sources. In the case of medicine, for example, two important references are *The Merck Manual of Diagnosis and Therapy* and the *Physicians' Desk Reference*.

Writers frequently need geographic information found in atlases and gazetteers. Several excellent world atlases are on the market, but most critics agree that the current edition of *The Times Atlas of the World* (cartography by John Bartholomew & Son of Edinburgh) is the standard choice; it does cost more than $100 however. The smaller *Goode's World Atlas* represents an inexpensive alternative in paperback. For the United States, the *Rand McNally Commercial Atlas and Marketing Guide* provides excellent state maps as well as much population and business data. Another very serviceable atlas is the annually revised paperbound *Rand McNally Road Atlas*, a longtime favorite that covers the U.S. (including a map for each state), Canada and Mexico.

Feature writers constantly require biographical information about people of all types. Among the best general sources are *Webster's Biographical Dictionary*, which offers brief sketches of roughly 40,000 historically significant persons, and the *Almanac of Famous People*, a three-volume set that covers some 25,000 notables from biblical times to the present. *Current Biography*, as its title suggests, covers contemporaries in the news; since its first appearance in 1940, *Current Biography*, which is issued monthly and cumulated into annual volumes, has set the standard for carefully researched yet readable short biographical profiles. *Who's Who in America*, on the other hand, offers only thumbnail data for biographers, but it does cover nearly 80,000 living persons, most of whom are Americans.

Writers and researchers should know that many libraries subscribe to a service called *Phonefiche*, a collection of nearly 3,000 telephone books (both white and yellow pages) from around the country on microfiche.

Covering private organizations is another essential directory, the *Encyclopedia of Associations*, which describes well over 25,000 groups concerned with everything from brain research to life insurance to sex (one recent edition, for instance, cites eleven organizations in the index under "Sexually Transmitted Diseases"). Two heavily consulted business directories are *Standard & Poor's Register of Corporations, Directors and Executives*, which offers basic information on some 50,000 businesses and their executives, and *Thomas' Register of American Manufacturers*, a multivolume listing of products and services.

Books in Print, now grown to ten volumes (three for authors, three for titles, three for subjects, and one for publishers), is essential for bibliographic data about books currently available from U.S. publishers. *BIP* is supplemented by the quarterly *Forthcoming Books*, which reports on books just published or announced for publication. Reviews of books can be located through *Book Review Digest*, which includes both citations to and excerpts from published reviews, and *Book Review Index*, which gives only citations.

Finding articles published in magazines entails use of indexes like the H.W. Wilson Company's *Reader's Guide to Periodical Literature*, a popular library reference item since 1905 that provides subject indexing for close to 200 general interest magazines, and *Magazine Index*, a newer source developed in 1976 which lists approximately twice as many titles as *Reader's Guide* but is available only on microfilm.

Several major dailies have developed their own individual indexes, most notably the *New York Times* and the *Wall Street Journal*. The *New York Times Index* is especially valuable for the feature writer, in that it furnishes detailed subject access from 1851 to the present to what most observers consider to be the newspaper of record in North America.

Electronic Sources

While many of the aforementioned print sources also are available on-line via computer, there are multitudes of databases for which no print equivalent exists.

Computer searching is not an act of magic. It's not a matter of pressing a few keys and — voilà — the information you seek is served up on a silver monitor. It is true, however, that with the aid of database systems and a savvy on-line searcher, a writer can unearth useful information on just about any issue, event, person, place or thing.

Searchers can link up with more than 3,000 on-line databases ranging from *Coffeeline* (yes, a database devoted entirely to the literature of coffee) to *America: History and Life*.

By using key words and controlled vocabulary or free text searching, users can retrieve everything from full text articles to citations to unpublished documents available on microfiche.

Computer searching can save you time. In addition, you can search for buzzwords or jargon that printed sources might not currently list, and, as you might have guessed, on-line sources are almost always more current than printed sources. But it is not a perfect world; most bibliographic databases date back no further than 20 years. (Most full text newspaper databases contain articles only from the 1980s.) For many topics, you must still rely on print and microfilm sources. Too, the costs of computer searching can be prohibitive.

The *NEXIS* system, probably the most familiar to journalists, is one of the most widely used systems in news libraries. Produced by Mead Data Central, the service contains full text articles from more than 160 newspapers, magazines and newsletters, including the *New York Times*. Mead also offers *LEXIS*, a database covering legal information, court decisions, statutes, legal cases, etc.

Other full text services, such as *DataTimes* and Knight Ridder's *Vu/Text*, focus on regional newspapers. *DataTimes* contains articles in newspapers ranging from the *Arkansas Gazette* to *Newsday*.

So how do you access these sources? Contact your public, university or state library and speak with a librarian or information professional trained to perform on-line searching. A good librarian can do you much more good, in fact, than all the fancy databases, and can save you money.

Jo Cates has been Chief Librarian of The Poynter Institute for Media Studies since 1985 and is the author of *Journalism: A Guide to the Reference Literature*, published by Libraries Unlimited. She has an M.S. in library science from Simmons College and a B.S. in journalism from Boston University.

Ken Kister is a freelance writer. He has worked as a librarian at the Poynter Institute for Media Studies and at *The Tampa Tribune* in Florida. He is also author of several reference book guides, including *Best Encyclopedias* (Oryx Press, 1986).

Y ou have done your reporting and research. You might have been working on your material for only a few hours or maybe a few months. Now what do you do with it? How do you make the leap from raw notes and research to a story that flows?

You get yourself organized.

On short, "quick-hit" features, you might be able to work out the organization in your head, and then get it quickly down on paper. But as you grow in the profession and try more in-depth stories, you will probably find organization becomes more of a problem. You might have interview notes in one pile, tapes in another, legal documents in a third, newspaper clips in a fourth, and public relations handouts in a fifth.

For almost all writers this is the hardest stage of writing. And it will never be easy. But Jane Harrigan, a professor at the University of New Hampshire and former editor, can help you get all the pieces together.

Organizing Your Material

Jane Harrigan

Landing my first reporting job in 1976 taught me a few things that my journalism professors had neglected to mention. I learned how to live in New York on $8,000 a year, and I learned that writing is a process made up of distinct steps. In those days, a model of my writing process would have looked like this:

report — write — curse & eat cookies — rewrite

Today, a few zillion stories and students later, I'd map the process this way:

report — ORGANIZE — write — curse & eat cookies — rewrite

Recognizing that second step has cut down on the cursing and rewriting, if not the cookies. But I fought organizing for years, and I've seen plenty of other writers fight it, too. Organizing sounds mundane. We want to believe that writing ability is some sort of cosmic gift — otherwise, how are writers different from other people? We want to believe that if we just plant ourselves at our typewriter or the terminal, the story will spring from our fingers, perfect and clear.

Occasionally it does. Mostly it doesn't, and here's why: Writing is not the act of putting marks on paper. Writing is synthesizing, comparing, ordering—in short, writing is thinking. *That's* how writers are different from other people: Each of us wields our unique vision like a chisel, giving form to our raw observations. If you don't believe that writing is thinking, walk into any newsroom and look around. You won't see hordes of harried writers hunched over keyboards. Instead, you'll see a few people typing and a lot of people twisting their hair, bending paperclips, and counting the holes in the ceiling tiles. All of them are writing. Or, as the writer-bird explained to his nephew in Jeff MacNelly's comic strip "Shoe": "Typists pound keyboards. Writers stare out windows."

Four Vital Questions

Getting organized means giving yourself permission to stare out the window. Most people recognize the importance of thinking at one key stage in the process, the lull between reporting and writing. That's the time for asking yourself, over and over, the Universal Writer's Query: *What have I got?* But that's not the only time that organization comes into play. You also need to organize before and during reporting. Later in the process, you may need to *re*organize as a prelude to rewriting. In other words, organization involves asking yourself four questions: What's my subject? What am I trying to say about that subject? How do I want to say it? Have I said it well enough?

Let's consider those questions individually.

What's Your Subject?

A good feature writer is a sponge, soaking in sights, sounds, smells and quotes in hopes that some of them, somehow, will bring the story to life. Like sponges, however, writers have limits; after a while, new details hit your saturated brain with a thud and simply drop away, unabsorbed. How can you be sure that the good ones sink in? The trick is to be organized, and part of the trick to being organized is remembering that you're not alone. Talk about your ideas with a fellow writer, a friend, a tolerant spouse. You never know when one of you will drop the comment that makes your brain shout, "That's

IT!'' And when you're looking for someone to talk to, don't forget your editor.

Editors are not the enemy. They want the same thing you do — to publish a terrific story — and it's in their best interest to do everything possible to achieve that goal. Smart writers also recognize another goal of editors: never to be unpleasantly surprised.

The more you and your editor discuss your story in advance, the less time the editor will spend "fixing" the story to fit some image you didn't know he or she had. So it stands to reason that, even if you're freelancing, you should let your editor know what you're up to. Remember that editors are busy, and make sure not to disturb them on deadline. But remember, too, that exploring a story's possibilities with the writer is many editors' (and teachers') favorite part of their job. It certainly is mine.

Recently, one of my best feature-writing students told me that she wanted to do a story on bulimia. As I fought the urge to groan, she added, "I know everybody writes about eating disorders, so I want to do something different. Can you think of an angle?" We talked about why the subject interested her, and about the stories we'd both read. Gradually she decided that she wanted to focus on treatment, perhaps building the story around the experiences of a young woman who had acknowledged her problem and gone for help. We made a quick list of potential sources and then, 15 minutes after she'd arrived in my office, she was on her way. She had a focus. She was organized.

Once you start reporting, organization points you toward the appropriate details. When I spent a day with a roving newspaper photographer while researching a book, I knew that much of my chapter, like much of his workday, would take place inside his car. Having decided that, I could collect many more specifics than I would have otherwise: how many miles on the odometer, how many pairs of shoes in the trunk, what sounds came over each of his five radios.

Organization can also save you much grief during interviewing, allowing you, for example, to nudge a meandering subject back on track with a gentle, "That's very interesting, Mr. Smith, but I'd really like to hear about X." Unless you've clearly defined X, for your subject and for yourself, you won't be able to tell a digression from a revelation. Of course, stories change as you report them; if they didn't, writing would be a dull affair. Taking an occasional minute to reorganize, and perhaps bounce new thoughts off your favorite sounding board, can pay big dividends later.

What Are You Trying to Say?

It's three hours before deadline and you're driving back to your office with 20 pages of notes and not much idea how to pull off the "quick, easy feature" your editor wanted. Or it's three days before deadline, and you're sitting on the floor surrounded by papers, wondering why this idea for a major feature sounded so good two weeks ago. In either case, you've reached the moment of truth, when a voice from on high — in my case it sounds a lot like Woody Allen's — needles you with the unshirkable question: "So what's the story?"

You need a focus. Then you need a form for expressing that focus. Those are the two steps to organizing your writing. Here are some exercises to help you climb the first step. You can try them while sitting at your desk, but most work equally well while you're driving your car or riding the subway or standing in a checkout line.

1. Write a summary sentence. What is your story about? Say it in one sentence, and be tough: The sentence must have a specific subject and an active verb. Or try writing it as a headline; that way, you can't settle for, "This is a story about X."

For one of my first features for the Associated Press, I remember panicking as I drove away from the final interview. Knowing I'd never be able to think once I returned to that madhouse bureau, I started talking to myself, telling myself the story. "Company sells house kits," I tried, then laughed at my own lameness. "House kits gaining popularity." *Ugh.* "You can build by numbers." *Closer.* "Dummies can build houses." *Hmmmm . . .* "Even klutzes can build their own castles." *Okay!* As soon as I uttered that sentence, I saw how the story could unfold. Mentally, I flipped through my notebook, labeling the categories of information I'd collected and then inserting each like a branch into the trunk formed by the summary sentence. Although the words "klutz" and "castle" never actually appeared in the story, the sentence kept me centered throughout the writing process.

Some writers carry tape recorders in their cars so as not to lose the ideas that can surface when the mind roams free. Even if you arrive at your focus by some method other than writing a summary sentence, however, you'd be wise to try writing one before you submit your story. If you can't write the sentence, the story isn't finished yet.

2. Rehearse leads. Sometimes you write leads to figure out your focus. Sometimes you write leads because you have a focus but aren't sure where to take it. Either way, you're probably going to write a lot of leads for a feature — six, ten, maybe dozens. How to write those leads is the subject of another section of this book. At this point, though, it's important to realize the role the lead plays in organizing your story. A good lead pushes you forward with the energy created by your own words. You know you're onto something when you hit the end of the lead and just keep writing, sure of your direction. While a few writers can write the story first and the lead later, most of us find organizing without a lead as difficult as hiking on an unmarked trail.

Lead-writing, too, can be done at places other than your desk. Just create a blank screen in your mind; I picture the one on the silly black fortune-telling ball I had as a kid. Then see what floats to the surface. Often what you'll see is a contrast, especially a contrast between expectations and reality. The expectations might be your own (what you expected Miss America to be like, versus the tough-talking feminist you encountered), but more likely they'll be your subject's (the whiz-kid entrepreneur whose dreams went bust). Or the trigger might be a moment — like the moment when Paul Newman took off his jacket at a Walter Mondale campaign event in 1984, and every teenage girl in the room started to scream. Driving home hours later, I saw that moment over and over and knew it was the lead for my story on celebrity campaigning. The trigger might be a sound — like the voice that journalist Oriana Fallaci used to dismiss the admiring questions of young writers at a seminar. I drafted dozens of leads for that story, but her voice kept drowning them out. Eventually I realized that her attitude was not only the lead but the backbone of the story.

Whatever leads form on your mental screen, make sure they either fit the focus you've chosen or point you toward a new one you can carry throughout the story. The Paul Newman lead worked because the story showed that celebrities simply build excitement for political campaigns. It wouldn't have worked on a story alleging that celebrities actually sway votes. As you organize your story, you're going to throw away a lot of good information and even more good leads. A wonderful lead becomes a terrible lead at the moment that you realize it leads nowhere.

3. Write an ending. Organization means knowing where you're going before you start. Carrying this dictum to a logical extreme, try writing the ending first. The ending can serve as a tow rope, pulling you up the long hill that looms between you and a finished story. This technique only rarely works for me, but I know many writers who swear by it. One caution: Don't save all of your best stuff for the end. Readers might never get there.

4. Write without notes. Obviously, no responsible nonfiction writer works entirely without notes. But sketching out a draft "freehand" can go a long way toward showing you what you want to say. Notes are like Velcro. As you try to skim them, they ensnare you, and pretty soon you can't see the story for the details. In my work as a writing consultant for newspapers, I'm often asked to help intelligent, interesting people who write dull stories. Almost invariably, it turns out that these people are trying to transform their notes into the story—sometimes physically, by typing their notes into a computer and then rearranging them into sentences. They do this because they don't trust their own instincts. In the great tradition of writers everywhere, they lack confidence.

Until you develop confidence as a writer, fake it. Fake it by repeating these words over and over, like a mantra: "The story is not in my notes; the story is in my head." Then believe it. No matter how many wonderful details you've jotted down, the details are not the story. A video camera can collect details and play them back; a writer must do more. The story is what you make of those details—the connections and patterns you see, the way you arrange them to support your focus. Hiding your notebook as you start to write can release you from the tyranny of details, freeing you to see the big picture.

How Will I Say It?

Now that you have a focus, you need a structure, a container to keep your ideas from oozing onto the page in a shapeless mass. Although the classic inverted-pyramid structure isn't an option for a feature, some other established structures might be worth considering. First, however, you'll want to organize your notes and make an outline. Much as you may pine for divine inspiration, the fact is that good writers plan each story. If the plan refuses to take shape in your head, or fades as quickly as it forms, it's time to organize on paper.

Organizing your notes needn't take long. Read through them once, quickly, and then make a list—not of the facts, but of the broad categories of information. For example, when one of my students finished researching the decline in Peace Corps volunteers at our university, she skimmed her notes and listed these categories: Statistics, History, One Volunteer's Story, The Recruiter's Perspective, Student Expectations, Peace Corps Expectations, Outlook for Future. She chose an abbreviation for each category, then labeled each section of her notes with the appropriate abbreviation. Because the material seemed manageable, she didn't cut her notes apart by category and put each category into a separate folder. That's something to consider, however, when you're tackling a long, complex story. For a fascinating account of the system used by a master organizer and writer, read the introduction to *The John McPhee Reader* (Farrar, Straus and Giroux, 1976). You'll never look at darts in the same way again.

After labeling, you're ready to synthesize. It's a lot easier to figure out the relationships among seven categories of facts than it is to impose an order on hundreds of separate pieces of information. Look at your categories, choose the one you think is most important or interesting, and outline possible ways of tying the remaining categories to the central one and to one other. Don't panic at the word "outline." We're not talking about the Roman numeral exercises that tormented you in grammar school—the ones that Pulitzer-winning feature writer Jon Franklin calls "English Teacher's Revenge." (Franklin describes his own elaborate outlining system in his book *Writing for Story*, Atheneum, 1976.) An outline can be as simple as a few words scrawled on a scrap of paper, or as elaborate as a detailed "recipe" you keep on one side of your computer's split screen. Either way, the point is to apply your intellect to your material. Outlining is to the writer what visualizing is to the athlete. Just as high jumpers visualize their jump mentally before performing it physically, writers outline their course before embarking on it.

The writer of the Peace Corps story, for example, considered using the volunteer's experiences as a frame for the other information she'd collected. But the story "refused to be outlined" in that form, she told me, so she tried another idea. She decided to write the story as a series of contrasts—between past and present, inside and outside, the average student's apathy, and the volunteer's enthusiasm. When an outline based on that idea came together in two minutes, she raced out to start writing.

Five Writing Sructures

Organizing and outlining take much less time than you'd think. Valuable as they are, they can become a convenient way to procrastinate, to avoid facing the blank page or screen. When you find yourself wondering whether you're ready to start writing, you probably are. That's when you'll encounter, head on, what's simultaneously most exciting and most intimidating about feature writing: There are no rules. You can put the information together in any way you please. As long as you stick to the facts, you have every conceivable writing technique at your disposal. Before long, you'll be inventing structures that no one's ever used before. When you're new to the game, however, it can be reassuring to try some of the many structures that have worked for other writers before you. Here are five:

1. The hourglass. This term, christened a few years ago to describe certain news stories, can apply to features as well. An hourglass story starts out like an inverted pyramid, arranging information in descending order of importance. Then, at the "waist" of the hourglass, the story shifts gears, relating the remaining information in chronological order. You'll often find the hourglass structure in crime stories, where a few paragraphs answering the 5 W's are followed by a sentence such as, "Police gave this account of the robbery." Feature writers can apply a variation of the hourglass to stories that follow a natural time sequence, such as day-in-the-life stories (a day in the life of a substitute teacher, or a judge, or a radio d.j.). Just be sure that your introduction establishes your focus and tone and promises enough surprises so that readers don't feel they're reading a transcript.

2. The spatial story. Most stories are organized logically, but some are organized spatially, using physical space to determine the order. This structure can work especially well when geography defines the focus. For example, in a story chronicling the economy's effects on one neighborhood, you might want the story to move from house to house, leading the reader on a tour of the street. A spatial structure defines a world, as National Public Radio did when Tip O'Neill retired from Congress. A reporter followed O'Neill from room to room in the Capitol as he said his goodbyes and described the memories that flooded him. Another variation of the spatial story mimics an actual shape, as in a story on bureaucratic waffling that is deliberately written in circles, or an environmental story that doubles back on itself to show how species are interrelated.

3. The story in scenes. Ever since Tom Wolfe's 1972 essay defining the New Journalism (indispensable reading for any nonfiction story-teller), writers have recognized the importance of scene-by-scene construction. Most stories stitch the scenes together into a seamless narrative. Occasionally, however, a story can best be told in short bursts, through discrete scenes separated by bullets or some other typographical device. You'll sometimes see this structure in profiles, where the writer shows the subject in different situations to reveal different personality traits. A story on a large event, such as a protest march, can also lend itself to this technique, allowing readers to see the action through many different people's eyes. I remember especially fondly a story I once read on Valentine's Day, in which an accumulation of short scenes showed both how ridiculous people thought the holiday was, and how seriously they were taking it.

4. Parallel narratives. Reading is an integral part of writing, and you can't give yourself a better gift than the chance to reread Truman Capote's *In Cold Blood.* There you'll find all the nascent techniques of literary journalism, plus a structure you might be able to borrow — parallel narratives. Throughout the first part of the book, killers and victims follow their separate courses, moving toward the inevitable collision. Parallel narratives can also work with less dramatic subjects: the young man and woman in their frantic separate preparations for the prom, the daily routines at two schools of the same size but different budgets. I once edited a story that interspersed scenes of a potter working at her wheel with scenes from her everyday life as a secretary. It worked; each narrative illuminated the other, and by the end the reader felt the same longing as the secretary who couldn't afford to devote herself to art.

5. Distance as structure. As a writer, you view your subject through an adjustable lens, choosing for some purposes a distant, wide-angle view, for others an up-close, telephoto study. In some stories you can use these varying distances to establish the structure. To show how old-timers and newcomers are clashing as New Hampshire grows, for example, *The Boston Globe* reporter Bob Hohler took readers to the town of Bath. His story starts with a description of the town as if seen from a distant hilltop. It moves in closer and closer until, by the end, the reader is inside the apartment of the couple whom many old-timers blame for the town's changes. Readers might not notice the device, but they do notice their growing understanding of the controversy. This structure can also be used in reverse, starting close to an issue and then backing up to place it in a wider context.

Whatever structure you choose, you'll quickly realize that an organized story does not need transitions, at least not the words like "however" and "therefore" that you were taught to use back in the days of English Teacher's Revenge. Instead, think of each idea in your story as an island. Your task is to write bridges between the islands to keep your readers from drowning. The only strong building material for these bridges is logic. From each paragraph pull out one thread, one aspect of the paragraph's central idea, and bring it forward to the next paragraph, knotting it securely by repeating a word or showing a similarity or difference. If this logical connection doesn't exist, or isn't spelled out clearly enough for readers to recognize, no number of transitional words will be strong enough to ferry readers to the next island.

Have I Said It Well Enough?

In the ideal world, you would write a feature, walk away from it for at least a day, then go back and polish it. In the real world, you'll sometimes be lucky to walk away from it for an hour. Even a few minutes of "downtime" will suffice if you can discipline yourself to return to the story with a fresh eye. (If you can't, have a blunt friend read your draft and ask you questions.) Editing yourself requires a complex shift in outlook that takes time to develop. You can speed the process by learning to handle two common situations: a story that needs reorganizing, and a story that needs reconceiving.

Let's return to the Peace Corps story. Although the writer started out feeling organized, she later came to my office with her first draft and announced, "This is a mess." On one hand, she was wrong: The information was strong. On the other, she was right: It seemed to come in no particular order. Together we resurrected the list of abbreviations she'd used to label her notes, and we applied those categories to the story. In the margin next to each paragraph, she labeled the type of information it contained. Then, reading down the margins, she was able to see places where the categories followed in a logical sequence, and others where the sequence either wasn't logical or wasn't explained well enough for readers to see its logic.

By this time she was so tired of the story that she grabbed some scissors, cut the text into paragraphs, and reassembled them on her bedroom floor. A little mechanistic, perhaps, but it worked. It can work for you, too—at least the labeling of paragraphs can—when you can't figure out why a story doesn't flow. Try it the other way, too. When you read a story you admire, cut the paragraphs apart, mix them up, and, as you try to put them back in order, see if you can figure out the structural devices the writer used.

The writer of the bulimia story had a different problem. Her first draft was thoroughly reported, wonderfully organized, and very dull. She knew it, but she didn't know what to do about it, and neither did I. That's where talking with your editor can come into play again. The writer and I sat and talked about the bulimia story, neither of us knowing where the conversation would lead. Gradually, as she explained her interest in the subject, we both began to realize that the story was much more personal than her writing had acknowledged. Her friend Wendy had nearly died of bulimia before getting treatment, and the writer herself had veered perilously close to the disorder from time to time. She decided to rewrite, using Wendy's story to frame the other information and adding occasional first-person sections for her own view.

This time, she wrote the ending first. It describes a moment after Wendy had returned from the hospital, feeling wonderful and no longer obsessed with food. "She told me she was going to throw her scale away," the writer wrote. "I told her to give it to me instead."

The process of feature writing presents you with a choice: You can fight organization as an annoying waste of time, or you can accept it as a challenge that will sharpen both your thinking and your writing. Once you really begin to concentrate on organizing, you may amaze yourself by starting to enjoy it—even the outlining. Suddenly an idea will fall into place with an almost audible click, and you'll remember why you wanted to be a writer.

Organization and structure can't happen without focus. So I'll leave you with the example of my friend Sue Hertz, a magazine writer whose skills I've always admired. One afternoon as I was climbing the stairs to her apartment, she yelled down a warning: "Watch out! I'm in the middle of a piece, and the place is a mess." Inside, her writing room looked just like mine, piles of papers covering every horizontal surface. Then something on the windowsill caught my eye. It was an index card with a single sentence written on it.

"What's that?" I asked.

"That's the point," Sue replied. "I put it there so I always know where to find it."

Jane Harrigan directs the journalism program at the University of New Hampshire. She has been an Associated Press reporter and managing editor of the *Concord* (N.H.) *Monitor*. She is the author of *Read All About It!*, a book tracing one day's activities at *The Boston Globe*, and of a forthcoming book on editing to be published by St. Martin's Press.

If writing were a religion, what you are about to read would be considered blasphemy. Nonetheless, here it is: *Striving for throat-grabbing, punchy leads is mostly a waste of time.* Say that aloud—especially in a newsroom—and hordes of old-time copy and news editors would puff up into great balls of indignation and fall upon the infidel with very sharp little pencils. But, alas, we are talking feature stories, and here rules are made to be broken, especially when they have little relevance to the real world of writing. So clear your mind, forget what your teachers and mentors may have been preaching all these years about snappy leads, and listen to the good word about beginnings.

Think Beginnings, Not Leads

Leonard Witt

After spending a lot of time trying to find wonderful leads, I came to the conclusion that leads are not as important as they have been made out to be. At first I wanted to do as William Ruehlmann did in his book *Stalking the Feature Story*, where he gave examples of leads like this one written by Mike Winerip for the Louisville *Courier-Journal*:

Louisville is home for Ralph W. Ray, leading dustpan magnate of the free world.

In less than three seconds, his dustpan factory, J.V. Reed & Co., produces a dustpan. (Thump-a-blimp.) More than 20 a minute. (Thump-a-blimp, thump-a-blimp.) More than 1,300 an hour. (Thump-a-blimp, thump-a-blimp, thump-a-blimp.) More than six million every year. (THUMP-A-BLIMP!) Twenty percent of the dustpans for the non-Communist world.

It is a clever lead. At one time or another all feature writers have written a lead like this. And that is fine. The writer was striving to make the words work. To have fun. To break traditional rules. There's rhythm in the writing; it plays off the subject. But, alas, it is a gimmick that you might use once in a few hundred stories.

I know because I read several hundred leads in search of clever ones and I found almost none. However, as I searched for great leads I found that I was getting pulled into many stories even though the leads were not special. They were simply honest to the story's subject matter. I read on if the story was compelling and if the opening words moved the story along. The leads did not grab me by the throat as great leads of yesterday were supposed to do. In fact, many times those throat grabbers draw so much attention to the writer that you think more of the writer than of the flow of the story. Sometimes that works, but, in the long run, leads don't make great writers — well-written, compelling stories do.

Now my discovery was not really a revelation. I have been fortunate to have worked with many great feature writers over the years, and their best stories rarely have throat-grabbing leads. Most often they ease you into the story instead.

This does not mean beginnings of stories are unimportant. They are extremely important. They set the tone for the whole story. However, the problem with the concept of a *lead* is that it is most often approached as a separate entity. Over the years, the lead has been viewed in terms of a hook or almost a gimmick. The "thump-a-blimp" leads were praised, especially in newspapers, because all too often the beginnings of newspaper stories were so convoluted and boring they simply went "thump."

No one wants a story, and especially its beginning, to go thump. So instead of spending a lot of time thinking of the clever lead, think of the whole story. Most well-written features, like most well-told stories, have a beginning, a middle and an end. The writer will know about reporting, voice, tone, rhythm, character development, dialogue and scene setting — and will bring these rich writing traditions to the opening of the story and keep them flowing throughout. Punchy and clever might work for some stories, but the writer who aims for that combination in every story is aiming far too low.

Prevent Lead Anxiety

Once you think of the story as a whole, the beginning comes almost naturally. However, it won't necessarily come easily. I remember reading somewhere about how Jimmy Breslin hunched over his typewriter and stuffed a piece of paper in it; he'd type a few lines, then rip the paper out of the typewriter, crumble it into a ball, and toss it to the floor. This exercise would go on for a while with sheet after sheet of paper ripped from the typewriter, wadded up, and cast to the floor. Eventually, however, a sheet would go into the typewriter and the keys would begin slapping against the paper and would not stop. One sentence, then another, then another, and Breslin was on his way to writing his story.

Today, in the age of the computer, there are fewer wadded up pieces of paper, but no less anguish in trying to start a story. The anguish comes not just from the fear of having a thumpy lead, but also because in the beginning there is nothing in front of you. No words on the paper with which you can start an inner dialogue. But once the words begin to flow, one word plays off another, then one sentence off of another, then one paragraph after another, and finally a story is written.

As an editor I try to help writers identify possible beginnings in the prewriting stage. As they collect information while reporting, I ask plenty of questions, and I listen to their answers for potential leads.

When James Thornton, an excellent St. Paul-based freelance writer, was working on a story about moms getting called to war, he told me of one military family where both mother and father were called to the Persian Gulf and their 18-month-old child had to stay with relatives in Minnesota. A pediatrician told the family the child would quickly forget what his parents looked like. To help him remember, the temporary guardians would unfold a life-size photo of the parents once a day. The child would stop whatever he was doing, move toward the photo, and smile. As soon as I heard that, I knew we had a story and a lead. As it turned out, Thornton opted for another lead, but this one would have been there if needed.

As I write this, another freelancer, Jon Tevlin, is working on a story on open enrollment in Minnesota schools. Parents in the state can send their kids across district lines to whatever school they deem best for the kids' education. Each morning one family in exurbia puts their kids in a cab and sends them off to another school district. The cab fare is some $80 a week or $4,000 a year. In my mind I can see the story beginning with the cab stopping at the house, mom kissing the kids good-bye, and the kids leaving in the cab, which weaves around a lake or two and eventually arrives at the school. The kids quite conspicuously get out of the cab and begin their day at school.

Again in the prewriting stage, I can see a possible lead. And seeing it early helps take the pressure off both the writer and the editor. Tevlin might find a better lead or decide this anecdote works better somewhere else in the story. But no matter, there is a potential lead and he has identified it early, and it will take pressure off him when he eventually sits down to write.

Forget the Rules

As with all writing, there really are no fixed rules. Stories can begin with quotes, description, dialogue, questions, anecdotes or an action sequence. It all depends on the tone that you as a writer want to present. Some people advocate writing many leads to get a story started and that is not a bad idea. On the other hand, if those first sentences are not coming to you as quickly as you might like, my recommendation is to stop fretting and start writing. If the lead doesn't work after you look at the finished story, then rewrite it. Or search in the finished story to see if the real lead floated down further into the story. Editors often talk of the throat-clearing syndrome where writers seem to have a couple of false starts before really letting the story begin.

Here is an example of a story I recently received where I believed the writer was just one paragraph away from the true beginning. He started his story like this:

> Ann Smith, a native Bostonian, graduated from Carleton College in Northfield, Minnesota, 20 years ago. That same day she hitched a ride to the North Woods, where she still resides, living her dream in a cabin three miles northwest of Ely, Minnesota, in the Superior National Forest, on the edge of civilization.

Just after that opening he wrote:

> One night last July Smith was awakened at 12:30 in the morning by
> the sound of an intruder in her kitchen. She did what any modern
> frontierswoman would do, she dialed 911. But a half hour passed and
> the sheriff's deputy hadn't arrived. The intruder was making a suspi-
> cious amount of noise, so Smith poked her nose downstairs. There
> she found, seated at the kitchen table, a yearling bear—butt on chair,
> elbows on table, face buried in a pan of brownies her son had baked
> that evening.

The woman whom he describes in his original first paragraph
really plays no part in the rest of the story, so there was little reason
to develop her. With a little rewriting that second paragraph should
have been the lead. It is more compelling and honest to the rest of
the story, which is about black bears and their relations to humans.

Honesty Is the Best Policy

Honesty to the rest of the story is important. Readers do not want to
be deceived. You shouldn't promise them one thing and then deliver
another. However, you can make your beginning interesting even if
the root of your subject matter might be dull. A medical column by
Neil Ravin in *The Washingtonian* magazine began like this:

> He was 12 years old, and every day he pedaled furiously on his station-
> ary bicycle for as many hours as they would allow him. He was so
> absorbed in his effort that it was all they could do to get him to stop
> for meals.
>
> In fact, before he was hospitalized at a psychiatric institution he
> had been unwilling to stop for meals, for schoolwork, for the simple
> exchanges of ordinary life. At age 12, he had lost almost 30 pounds.
> He looked, in the language of the ward, cachectic, or in the language
> of his friends, as if he had been an inmate in a concentration camp.

This lead forces you into the story. It provides mystery, an element that William Blundell touts in his book, *The Art and Craft of
Feature Writing*. Blundell says not revealing everything will force the
reader to get into the story, and once a reader has made a commitment, he will read on as I did with the story about the "bicycle boy."
I read on even though the story turned out to be a rather complicated
one about Lyme disease—a story I would not have read if the lead
had not captured me, and one I might have stopped reading if the

mystery had been revealed too quickly. This "bicycle boy" lead, which really went on for eight paragraphs, did one other thing. It humanized a story that otherwise would have been a fairly dull medical story. Getting people into beginnings will often make the story more readable, and feature stories provide the most opportunities of any stories to get people into them.

However, just having people in a lead is not enough. If the medical writer had started his story with a woman having arthritic knees, it might have been too weak a way to start out a story on Lyme disease. If our kids going to another school district had just boarded a school bus rather than a taxi, that too might not have been enough. They would not have been special anecdotes. Think of your own life. Most of what happens to you is mundane. But occasionally a wonderful or unusual thing happens and you tell that story often. In mining for lead material in your reporting, don't settle for the mundane; look for the compelling, humorous, sad, offbeat or intriguing.

Sometimes, however, the simple, straightforward lead is just fine. Not long ago Cheryl Lavin, a feature writer, was a finalist in the "Best Newspaper Writing Contest" sponsored annually by the American Society of Newspaper Editors. Among her entries was this very straightforward lead:

> A lot of people who think they love Lily Tomlin really love Jane Wagner. Jane puts the words in Lily's mouth. She writes her material, she creates her characters, she makes her sound smart, she makes her sound funny. She works with her, she lives in a Spanish-style house in the Hollywood Hills with her, she protects her, she mothers her, she fusses over her, she finishes her sentences, she even reads her mind.

Forget about the idea of mystery here. Lavin has told everything right up front. She summarized the entire story in the first paragraph, and if you care about Lily Tomlin you will read on. As an editor, my own inclination would have been to push the writer to start out setting a scene, where we could see them interacting rather than just have Lavin tell us. But Lavin took a different approach, and it worked. She started out *telling* us about Wagner and Tomlin and then went on to *show* us in the second and succeeding paragraphs as follows:

> The two are huddled over breakfast at the Mayfair Regent Hotel.

They're talking about the cult following inspired by Wagner's play, "The Search for Signs of Intelligent Life in the Universe." Tomlin starred in the one-woman show for a sold-out year on Broadway and recently moved it to L.A. She called it "the Saturday Night Fever of the theater" because the diehards come back to see it over and over again.

Says Lily, "People have come to see it five, six times, even mo . . ."

". . . one woman told us she had seen it 17 times!" says Jane.

"Well, she was a little over the edge," says Lily. "She also had 'Jane' tattooed on her arm. Uh . . ." She catches herself and stops.

"What were you going to say?" a reporter asks.

She shakes her head. "Nothing."

"She's afraid this all sounds so self-serving," says Jane.

And on Lavin goes, establishing throughout the story what she set up in the beginning. Hers is not a delicate or funny lead, but simply a workhorse that got us into the story and mapped out a direction for it. More often in fine writing that direction setting is more subtle than the Tomlin/Wagner beginning, but to be effective it has to direct us into the story and give us a realistic idea where the story is going. It also has to move us forward.

Using Description

In the hands of novices, stories that start with description often slow us down rather than move us forward. Lead descriptions shouldn't be just description for description's sake.

Too often it is written as if someone is sitting on a bench looking at a flower garden—a very passive business. However, when I go to a park I hardly ever see anyone just sitting. Most people are on the move. Walking, jogging, skating, biking. In a like manner, your story beginnings should have the metaphorical feel of leading someone down a path to a destination. Walk them slowly and let them sniff the roses or get them moving at breakneck speed. The pace is up to you.

Paul Theroux's travel story "Sunrise with Seamonsters," in a collection of his work by the same name, is a wonderful example of a quiet, descriptive lead that moves the reader right into the story. It begins:

The boat slid down the bank and without a splash into the creek, which was gray this summer morning. The air was woolly with mist.

The tide had turned, but just a moment ago, so there was still no motion on the water—no current, not a ripple. The marsh grass was a deeper green for there being no sun. It was as if—this early and this dark—the day had not yet begun to breathe.

I straightened the boat and took my first stroke: the gurgle of the spoon blades and the sigh of the twisting oarlock were the only sounds. I set off, moving like a water bug through the marsh and down the bendy creek to the sea.

You are the writer, and should be in control. It is your story. Make things happen. Keep movement in the story, but the movement doesn't have to be breathless, quick-paced writing. Theroux, for example, gives the reader plenty of time to smell the morning, but never gets bogged down in the marsh.

Quotes and Questions

As for starting with quotes and questions I would follow the advice of Andre Fontaine and William A. Glavin, Jr. in their book *The Art of Writing Nonfiction*. They wrote, "Two types of leads used by inexperienced writers usually fail: quotations and questions. The quotation lead is generally ineffective because most quotations need explanation to be understood, and explanatory material can slow down the lead. Besides, any writer who can't write better than most people speak, is in the wrong field. Having said all that, we should point out that . . . in writing all rules are made to be broken. As for questions, a good rule to follow is that a writer's job is to answer them, not ask them."

Now underline the part above about breaking the rules because here comes Gay Talese with his classic magazine piece on boxer Joe Louis:

> "Hi, sweetheart!" Joe Louis called to his wife, spotting her waiting for him at the Los Angeles airport.
>
> She smiled, walked toward him, and was about to stretch out up on her toes and kiss him—but suddenly stopped.
>
> "Joe," she said, "where's your tie?"
>
> "Aw, Sweetie," he said, shrugging. "I stayed out all night in New York and didn't have time—"
>
> "All night!" she cut in. "When you're out here all you do is sleep, sleep, sleep."
>
> "Sweetie," Joe Louis said, with a tired grin. "I'm an ole man."

In the next couple of weeks spend some time reading leads. Analyze them. You'll find they come in all shapes and sizes just as do the writers themselves. Borrow the techniques from the best writers. But don't look for a formula. Let each story dictate its own beginning, and (I might add) its own ending also.

Endings are, in fact, as important as beginnings because when written well they allow the reader to walk away with a lasting reminder of what the story was about. Some people talk of summary endings, where the story is quickly summed up at the end. Others talk of a circle where the end plays off something that happened in the beginning of the story and tends to wrap it all together. Another category is the snapper where there is a shock or revelation.

However, as with leads, the endings should not be gimmicks, but logical conclusions. Once the words start coming out onto the page, they should lead the writer as much as he leads them. Sometimes the ending will be much different than originally planned and that is fine as long as it does something special for the reader. Flat or abrupt endings can kill an otherwise wonderful story.

Unfortunately, newspapers still put far less importance on the ending than the sacred lead. That's because newspapers traditionally cut off the end of stories when faced with a last minute space crunch. That happens fewer times now than in the past, but newspaper traditions, even bad ones, don't die easily. That's why often you will read newspaper stories and wonder why they didn't just take them a little further. Of course, that's better than asking the opposite question: God, when are they going to finish this thing?

And the answer, of course, always must be when the story has run its natural course and the writer has nothing else important left to say.

End Words

Afterthoughts: More Points to Remember

1. Some nonfiction writers are fine reporters, but their stories plod along. Just as bad are writers who turn a nice phrase, but have nothing to say. The art of feature writing requires that you both gather facts—that's reporting—and have a sense of what makes words flow.

2. Being a good writer and a good reporter don't happen overnight. Both skills have to be refined and then eventually merged. They take practice. Try all forms of writing. Sure, try some stories that don't need much reporting, such as a reminiscence. An essay. An opinion piece. A parody. You might even sell some. But don't stop there. Go out and report. Interview people, do research, and then write again. If it plods along, don't quit. Try again. Try merging your free-form styles with your reporting. Eventually you will write a story rich with facts that has your special style. And that will be a story that will sell.

3. Impressions from interviews are like dreams: when they're fresh in your mind, you think you'll remember them forever, but they fade. As soon after an interview as possible, record notes, atmosphere, and impressions in your computer, in your notebook, or somewhere you will not lose them.

4. Sometimes you will only get one chance to interview a person, but if you are doing an in-depth profile, chances are it will take a few interviews to get more than a surface understanding of your subject.

5. Every writer will find his or her own interview style, but most often the "tough cop" interview style will turn interviewees off and cause them to be suspicious of your motives. The best advice is to try a low-key approach, looking on the interview more as a conversation than an interrogation. Interview expert Kay Miller says interviewing, reduced to its simplest form, is good conversation — perhaps more carefully crafted than dinner table patter, and often, certainly, more intense.

6. Without tough questions, you will be limited to wishy-washy answers. However, save the "toughies" until late in the interview when both you and the interviewee are more at ease. If you don't quite understand something, ask about it, even if it makes you feel dumb to ask. Remember this advice from feature writer William Ruehlmann who wrote the book, *Stalking the Feature Story*: "The 'dumb' question may elicit a definite response. Should you avoid it, you may walk away with a hole in your story. The genuinely dumb question is the unasked one."

7. Tape recorders allow you to concentrate on the whole person

rather than just scribbling quotes. However, every reporter relies on handwritten notes for at least some of a story. In fact, many writers never use a tape recorder. First, learn to take notes. Practice it as much as possible. Then when you use a tape recorder, think of it as more of a backup than a primary or sole method of note collection. A couple of electronic or tape snafus will reinforce this advice.

8. Honesty is the best policy in interviewing. Don't try to deceive your interview subjects. Tell them who you are and where you plan to publish the story. Tell them you want to gather all the facts you can, which might include some negatives among the positives. Most importantly, emphasize that you will be fair, then *be* fair. Cheap shots work sometimes, but eventually you will have trouble getting entrée to future stories.

9. The best interviews are done face-to-face. Of course, phone interviews are fine for peripheral players or hard-to-get-at interviewees, such as those out of town. Indeed, all feature writers and freelancers spend a lot of time on the phone. The problem begins when they become office bound and never get more than talking heads in their stories.

10. Most professional journalists don't allow people being interviewed to read their stories before they are printed. If people want control over stories written about them, they should hire a public relations firm. Your job is to report accurately and fairly.

11. Never start a story without looking up past newspaper or magazine stories on the person you are writing about. If nothing else, it is a way to protect your integrity. Nothing is more embarrassing than to write about someone and then find he had a checkered past. Past stories are often rich with information and most often they are quick and easy to obtain.

12. Don't forget public documents such as probate files, divorce files, voter registration records, criminal and civil court records, traffic violation records and legal depositions. Anything that has been litigated will produce a wealth of information. In touchy cases where people refuse to talk, they may have already said plenty in public court documents. Go to the county, city and state court and ask for help in finding records.

13. Don't forget public information from government agencies

such as the Census Bureau and the National Weather Service. Indeed, the federal government is the biggest publisher in the world. Each major town has repositories of U.S. government pamphlets and documents. Ask a librarian for help.

14. Of course, there's also usually plenty of written material available locally. At some time every feature writer will have to search out old high school yearbooks for profile information and photos. Don't forget telephone books, city directories, reverse directories and business directories. The list is nearly endless.

15. The advent of computer databases has made available access to most major newspapers around the country and even around the world. Of course, this is not for free. Find out what it might cost before you start tapping into any electronic source. The cost could be prohibitive. Also, remember that most newspaper libraries only went electronic in the 1980s. If the sweet old grandma you are interviewing killed someone in 1970, you might not find out about it in the electronic clips.

16. When researching one story, always be alert to information that may be the seed for another story. Often the serendipitous finds make the best stories.

17. Have an idea of where your story is headed before you do the research. The better defined a story is, the easier it is to put parameters on your research. You don't want to become so overwhelmed with information that you can't figure out where or even when to start writing. This is most important for a freelancer, for whom lost time is lost money.

18. Here is advice from Jane Harrigan worth repeating in its entirety: "Writing is synthesizing, comparing, ordering—in short, writing is thinking. That's how writers are different from other people: Each of us wields our unique vision like a chisel, giving form to our raw observations."

19. Also from Jane Harrigan: "The story is not in my notes; the story is in my head." Of course, you must use your notes to support the facts and provide the details, but the story is what you make of those details—the connections and patterns you see and the way you arrange them to keep your story unfolding so readers can't stop reading.

20. To help you decide what your story is, try writing a headline or a summary sentence with a noun and an active verb. It should help give your story focus, and give you direction.

21. A story's lead should engage readers' attention and also make them want to read further. Adding a bit of mystery to the lead will help accomplish this goal. However, it is important that the lead does not deceive the reader. Don't make enticing promises that don't later materialize.

22. Don't be discouraged if you have trouble with your leads. Many writers are naturally intimidated by the blank page. Later in the story, a form of dialogue takes place between the words on the paper and the writer, and one sentence begins to play off another. If it helps you, start writing the body of your story and worry about the lead later.

23. You are better off saving complex information for the body of the story. When readers get to it, they've already made an investment and will be more likely to stay with your story. If the story starts out complex, they are likely to move on to something else.

Exercises

1. Sharpen your basic research skills. Go to the library and find the *New York Times Index*, the *Reader's Guide to Periodical Literature* and the *Encyclopedia of Associations*. These are just a beginning. Also become familiar with the electronic databases now available. There are hundreds of them and your librarian can help guide you in the right direction.

2. Take a well-written story, such as the avalanche story which follows, (How the Pros Do It—Writing Sample #3). Pretend you are a fact checker. Go through the story and see how many obviously gathered facts, bits of information, and quotes come from solid reporting. How long does it take you to reach the 100 mark?
Here are starred (*) examples from the first two paragraphs:

> "At about 20 minutes past 11* on a warm Sunday morning* in early February,* 6-year-old* Taylor Huddleston* and his cousins, Erwin Effler,* 6,* and Michael Effler,* 4,* were playing* in the snow.*

Below them*, in the driveway* of the Mountain Sunrise Condominiums,* the Efflers' father, Erwin,* was helping load luggage* in an
airport limousine van* as the families got ready to leave Mount Crested Butte.* They had expected to leave a couple days earlier,* on Friday,* Feb. 3,* but a heavy snowstorm had closed the airport* in nearby
Gunnison* for two days,* extending the Efflers' and Huddlestons'
skiing vacation.*

Notice all the wonderful details and facts that make those two
paragraphs work. There are more than 20 solid factual pieces of information. That's reporting. Continue with that story and check off
the places where solid information is woven in.

3. Next time you interview the main characters in your story
be sure to include time with them at home or at their place of work
or play — whatever habitat is central to the theme of your story. Interview, or at least watch, the teacher at her school, the firefighter at
the fire station, the industrial manager on the plant floor.

4. Next time you go out with a friend, pretend that you are
interviewing the person without taking notes. Don't force it. Keep it
in a conversational mode. Try not to let the person know what you
are doing. Try to get him or her to do all the talking. You listen and
ask interesting questions to keep the conversation going. Try the
simple "Why?" when you want to understand motivations, or "I'm
not sure what you mean" when something isn't entirely clear. If it
works with a friend, it should work with people you are interviewing.

5. Try Jane Harrigan's suggestion of taking a piece of writing
you especially enjoy, physically cutting it up, and shuffling the
pieces. Now try to put it back together again, noticing, as you fit the
pieces, the devices the writer used in giving the story structure.

6. When you have some time before your next story, try writing
the lead three or four dozen times. Some will be junkers, but you
might just see they improve as you delve for something more than
the obvious. Remember, leads are important because they can set
the tempo for the rest of the story.

Further Reading

1. *The Art and Craft of Feature Writing* by William E. Blundell
(Plume — New American Library, 1988). How feature writing is done

at the *Wall Street Journal*. An excellent book for novice and advanced writers.

2. *Stalking the Feature Story* by William Ruehlmann (Vintage Books, 1977). A nuts and bolts book on how to find, research and construct a feature story. Good advice, though some examples are a bit dated.

How the Pros Do It
Writing Sample Number 3

If you can master the kind of story Claire Martin of *The Denver Post* does in this example, you will have a fertile freelance or staff writing career anywhere you choose. This is a perfect example of writing about an issue and humanizing it.

The story concerns avalanches in Colorado. Martin uses the three boys in the story to humanize it, although it is not a story about them. If it were, we would have learned more about the boys, and probably less about avalanches. But we only know them in relation to how they were affected by the avalanche.

The novice writer may well have simply recounted the action sequences involving the boys because they're dramatic and heartrending. Some might even have thought putting in all the avalanche material would hurt their pure writing. But writing is information, and when you walk away from this story you will know about avalanches. You will know the human suffering they can cause, but primarily you will know a lot about avalanches.

As an experiment, take her story apart. Read just the parts about the rescue attempts and leave out all the background information about avalanches. The story moves by quickly, but lacks depth. Now do the opposite. Just read the background material about the avalanches. Pretty dry stuff. It lacks drama. Now put the two together as Martin did, and you have drama and information. You have a story that is difficult to put down. The structure demands that you read on to find out what happened to the boys.

You never sense the presence of the writer, but she is there. She times her breaks in the action sequences perfectly, she describes details, she makes scenes come alive, and she has done her research. This story took time. She obviously has read reports and news stories and interviewed tons of people, from experts to rescue crews who got to the scene immediately following the devastating accident.

So much information can swamp a novice, but this is the kind of story most writers can master—probably not the first time, but eventually. Study her style, look for similar stories in magazines and newspapers, and, of course, try them yourself. The more complex these stories become, the more important it is for you to have a good editor or teacher to help you through the morass of information. Incidentally, this story won a first prize in general excellence in feature writing from The American Association of Sunday and Feature Editors. (The original story was longer, but read extremely fast. We condense it here because we are using it primarily as a teaching guide.)

Living In the Danger Zone

By Claire Martin
The Denver Post

At about 20 minutes past 11 on a warm Sunday morning in early February, 6-year-old Taylor Huddleston and his cousins, Erwin Effler, 6, and Michael Effler, 4, were playing in the snow.

Below them, in the driveway of the Mountain Sunrise Condominiums, the Efflers' father, Erwin, was helping load luggage in an airport limousine van as the families got ready to leave Mount Crested Butte. They had expected to leave a couple days earlier, on Friday, Feb. 3, but a heavy snowstorm had closed the airport in nearby Gunnison for two days, extending the Efflers' and Huddlestons' skiing vacation.

Kib Crank, the van's driver, glanced at the boys. One was breaking a trail in the waist-deep new snow—34 inches had fallen since Friday—and the other two were following him. Crank had turned his attention back to the luggage when he heard the heavy sound of falling snow.

At first, Crank thought that snow had slid off the condominium's roof. When he looked up, he saw an enormous cloud of snow billowing toward the driveway. Suddenly, snow was moving under his feet. It didn't sink in until the snow cloud begin to settle: This was an avalanche.

"We've got kids in there!" Effler yelled. "Michael! Erwin! Taylor!"

The boys were nowhere in sight.

More than 10 feet of snow had buried the driveway. Crank panicked. He didn't know what to do first. He yelled

> Notice all the detail in her reconstruction, from where people were standing to who was driving the van. Though she doesn't dwell on it, you'll remember the role fate had in this tragedy.

> Of course, she got all this information for the reconstruction after the accident.

Easy to visualize images, like him running to place his hat, stick with readers long after they finish the piece.

at one of the mothers to call 911. He scrambled up on the settling snow and began digging frantically with his hands. Then he remembered something he'd learned from backcountry ski trips: Always mark the last place you saw someone before the avalanche. He ran to the place he thought he'd last seen the three boys, pulled off his hat and put it on the snow.

"The snow probably carried 'em down," said a voice down near his van. People were starting to gather. Many had brought shovels. Some were comforting the boys' parents, who were waiting at the edge of the slide, frightened and teary. Crank, shoveling snow, hardly heard the buzzing voices until one remark caught his attention.

"I looked up there the other day and I said to myself, 'Well, there's an avalanche ready to happen,' " said a man Crank didn't recognize.

This quote sets up the whole story . . .

. . . And it is the perfect transition for what the story is really about: developments in avalanche-prone areas.

"But still, you wouldn't expect that. You wouldn't expect the town to allow someone to build a condo right in an avalanche path."

But that is exactly what happened, and not only in Mount Crested Butte.

In Vail, you can still see the concrete foundation that the developers of the Kings Court complex were forced to abandon: It was sitting directly in front of a large avalanche chute. The Spring Gulch avalanche chute that hangs over Ophir, a suburb of Telluride, has in the past wrecked some homes and nudged others away from their original sites. In 1962, an avalanche rumbling down Mount Elbert killed seven residents of Twin Lakes and crushed mountain cabins as if they were shoe boxes.

These two graphs summarize the story's thrust.

There are newer developments—built over the last 20 years, when Colorado earnestly began courting tourists— that many geologists judge to be uncomfortably close to avalanche chutes. Yet developers in Crested Butte and other mountain towns compare the Feb. 5 avalanche at the Mountain Sunrise condominiums to a lightning strike—a wild card, a tragic but unique event, certainly not something that's likely to happen again.

The writer talks to many experts. They give the story credibility and help the writer understand her subject.

Or could it?

"The thing is, almost any area that has ideal ski terrain and climate has the potential for avalanches—they're kind of a built-in hazard," said Pat Rogers, a geologist for the Colorado Geological Survey.

"When we are asked now to look for hazards in lots of land being considered for developments, we are looking at land that tends to be more potentially troublesome. They're not the big lots we were looking at 10 or 12 years ago. By now, people have chosen the better tracts. Now, all that's left are lots that have been bypassed for various reasons, like being too close to runout zones of avalanche chutes or rock-fall areas."

The Mountain Sunrise condominium complex was built in 1979, one of dozens of similar developments popping up in mountain communities anxious to lure tourists. The resort town of Mount Crested Butte, just 3 miles from the old mining town of Crested Butte, was only 9 years old, but already it was attracting the young, upscale skiers who gladden developers' hearts. . . .

The building where the Huddlestons and the Efflers would spend their 1989 vacation was put on a slope whose incline measures between 30 and 35 degrees. Most avalanches begin on slopes with inclines of 30 to 45 degrees. A geological investigation of the hillside above the Mountain Sunrise condominiums would have included an evaluation of the avalanche hazard potential.

Had the Mountain Sunrise complex been built outside town limits, a 1973 law would have required the developers to do a geological investigation of the property. Whether they would have done it is another question: The law is toothless. If a developer fails to obey it, there is no penalty, according to Colorado State Geology Survey geologist Candace Jochim.

See how Mountain Sunrise is one example used to prove a larger point.

As it happens, the complex lies just within the town limits, and the town of Mount Crested Butte did not require developers to conduct geologic investigations. The zoning code did not even mention avalanches, and still doesn't, according to Bill Racek, the current town planner for Mount Crested Butte.

She had to check with officials or check official documents. It's best to do both.

"Part of the problem is that all those lots were plotted, divided, long before anyone ever really thought about doing any sort of survey with relationship to avalanches," he said.

Another part of the problem is that even though the slope behind the Mountain Sunrise condominiums did fit the profile of a potential avalanche hazard — an incline between 30 and 45 degrees, with a slope bare of trees — it was not a place where large avalanches often occurred.

More research.

The Colorado Avalanche Information Center describes the avalanche danger on that slope as "low intermittent," with several decades lapsing between substantial slides like the one that ran of Feb. 5.

Notice all the varying sources and interviews her information comes from.

"Because of their long return periods, (certain) avalanches are rarely observed, especially in areas that have been inhabited only a few years or decades," Art Mears wrote in the 1979 Colorado Snow-Avalanche Area Studies and Guidelines for Avalanche Hazard Planning.

Mears drove from his Gunnison home to inspect the Mount Crested Butte avalanche the day after it ran, and has returned to study it several times after that.

"Builders avoid where people see snow coming down regularly, where the avalanche hazard is obvious," Mears said.

"The problems arise where there are infrequent avalanches, avalanches where the average return period is a generation—30 years or so. If an avalanche comes down only every 30 years, chances are that people won't have observed that activity. Mount Crested Butte is relatively new, and not many people were up there until the mid-70s."

This coming back to the action sequence is a classical structure of this genre of writing.

The first radio call for help came at about 11:25 A.M. The dispatcher announced that she had received calls reporting children buried by a snow slide at the Mountain Sunrise condominiums. Any available emergency medical technicians were to go to 15 Marcellina Lane.

Again notice the use of details: from the time, 11:25 A.M., to the address, 15 Marcellina Lane.

Dave Siengo, an emergency medical technician and mayor pro tem of Mount Crested Butte, had heard the page. He looked out his window—he lives two blocks from the Mountain Sunrise condominiums—and saw the avalanche. He knew immediately it was more serious than the dispatcher realized.

Reconstructions like this are usually put together using interviews, news stories and official reports. The writer can't stretch the truth or make up details; the reconstruction must come from reliable sources.

By the time he got to the condominiums about two minutes later, a dozen people were already there, and more were arriving. Siengo was shaken at the size of the avalanche. There were slabs of snow 6 feet long, 6 feet wide and 4 feet deep—"slabs the size of Volkswagens" said Mark Helland, one of the rescue workers.

The growing crowd milled on the hardening snow of the avalanche runout. Most of the people were locals and tourists. Some clunked around in their ski boots. Many had brought shovels, broomsticks, mop handles, rakes and even skis to use as makeshift avalanche poles. They jabbed them into the snow, searching for the boys' bodies while Erwin and June Effler and Lauren and Rebecca Huddleston waited.

Suddenly, someone found a boot. Then a hat. People rushed over, digging with their hands. They pulled a small body out of the snow. It had been 10 minutes since the avalanche ran.

"We found one!" a woman yelled at Siengo. Someone thrust Michael Effler, limp and gray, at Siengo.

She writes in the past tense. Often these reconstructions are done in the present tense to give them even more immediacy.

Michael wasn't breathing. Siengo checked for a pulse. He found it. He put his mouth on the child's and forced air into the boy's lungs, a technique known as "rescue breathing," until suddenly the boy began breathing by himself.

By then, they had found Erwin Effler. Like Michael, Erwin had been buried under only about three feet of snow—in fact, he was found only a couple of feet from where his brother had been. Erwin wasn't breathing, either, but he had a pulse, and after another doctor performed rescue breathing, Erwin began to breathe, too.

The medical technicians and the Efflers, dizzy with relief, took the Effler boys inside to strip off their wet clothes, warm up and make sure they weren't hurt.

The Huddlestons stayed outside, tense and fearful. They stared at the broken snow gleaming under the warm sun. The volunteers prodded the settling chunks with a confidence that began dissolving as minutes passed—no more small boots or hats turned up.

Where was Taylor?

There is no leaving this story.

There are two kinds of avalanches. The one that trapped Taylor Huddleston was a slab avalanche. Slab avalanches are enormous blocks of snow that shatter almost as soon as they separate from the slope, raising clouds of fine snow. Powder avalanches form from dry, loose snow that gathers density and momentum—up to 200 miles an hour—as the avalanche runs.

What created this particular slab avalanche was a combination of conditions: a heavy storm that dumped 40 inches of snow in less than 48 hours; high winds that blew more snow on top of the load already burdening the lee

Remember this is a story about avalanches.

side of a steep hill; and a warm morning that made the new snow too heavy for the slope to bear.

Before the avalanche ran, a cornice — a lip of snow that the wind sculpted at the crest of the hill — had formed. The fracture line, where the slab broke off, is just below the cornice.

When the slab fractured, there was nothing to stop it but a fence that marks the boundary between the town of Mount Crested Butte and Gunnison County. The slope is utterly treeless. In the summer, cattle graze on the county side of the fence.

Avalanche expert Don Bachman measured the fracture later. It was 165 feet wide, and fell about 300 vertical feet to the Mountain Sunrise driveway, carrying about 500 cubic meters of snow. A small avalanche, by Bachman's standards. He considers a large avalanche to be like the one in Telluride that fell 2,000 vertical feet a few weeks after the Mount Crested Butte slide. Even a small avalanche can be deadly, though. As an avalanche advances, it accelerates and creates a dense core that picks up more snow as the avalanche gathers speed. A really fast-moving avalanche can become airborne, sailing over the snow at up to 200 miles per hour.

When an avalanche hits you, even at 10 miles per hour, it can strike as hard as a car, enveloping you in coalescing snow that can exert hundreds of pounds of pressure per square inch. Compressing snow closes around you, pushing against your chest. As it settles, it presses harder and harder, until you cannot breathe at all.

"It's similar to having wet cement poured on you," said Tom Mason, a physician at St. Mary's Hospital in Grand Junction, who has treated several avalanche victims.

"The snow is so crushing that people don't have the ability to expand their chests. They die of asphyxiation."

When Michael Helland, the assistant fire marshal for the Crested Butte Fire Protection District, heard the first radio call for help — the call Siengo had listened to — he thought it sounded as if they could use some extra help. He threw some shovels — the only avalanche equipment the fire district then owned — in the van and headed for Marcellina Lane, at the west edge of Mount Crested Butte.

Helland organized the chaotic crowd into an avalanche

probe line. A probe line is a single, slow-moving line of people with avalance probes—ideally, slender poles 12 feet long—followed by a second group of shovelers who dig at spots flagged by probers who suspect they've struck something unusual.

Helland's probe line with its makeshift probe poles swept the avalanche run twice. A few people thought they'd hit something, but the diggers found nothing but hardening snow. The impromptu probes couldn't strike down much more than 4 feet. When the ski patrol arrived from the Mount Crested Butte Ski Resort, carrying genuine avalanche probe poles 12 feet long, Helland gladly turned things over to them.

The ski patrol formed a practiced probe line, and slowly started over the runout. The snow was pitted where diggers had already searched. The ski patrol's probe line went over the runout once without finding anything. Then it went over the snow again, probing more deeply. This time, about 30 feet from where the Effler boys had been found, one of the patrol members found something.

A few minutes later, they uncovered Taylor Huddleston. He was unconscious. He was not breathing, and his heart had stopped. He had been buried for almost an hour under 10 feet of heavy, dense snow.

Both probe lines had passed over Taylor three times before he was found.

Usually, when people think of avalanches, they picture Colorado's backcountry, where plenty of avalanches happen. Last month's avalanche at Mount Crested Butte was one of 250 reported in Colorado's south and central mountains that weekend. Most of those were in the backcountry, but avalanches have hit towns, too.

> Back to information mode. This is the kind of statistic that shows depth of reporting.

In 1962, the small village of Twin Lakes, near Leadville, was hit by an avalanche that came crashing down from Mount Elbert. Seven people were killed. Some were in bed when the avalanche barged into their houses. Cabins were shattered. There are photographs of snow-filled kitchens and living rooms, of snowy mattresses with snow-glazed dolls lying on them, of pine trees snapped like asparagus.

> Obviously she studied the photographs. Use any medium that will help in your research from still photos to videotape to written reports.

For a while, people quit building their cabins in that part of town. Periodically the Colorado Geological Survey is asked to approve a proposal for a development on the site of the avalanche. The state rejects such proposals out of hand. A few years ago, a developer promised geologist Rogers that his proposed Twin Lakes cabins would be for summer occupation only. Rogers turned down that one, too.

Historical information puts recent tragedies into perspective.

In Ophir, a small town of about 30 just south of Telluride, residents have adapted their winter lives to accommodate the avalanches that routinely close the road between Ophir and Telluride. Until recently, when Ophir adopted an avalanche-control policy that involves triggering small avalanches to save the town from large ones, avalanches often tore into town.

"There's houses in Ophir that have been moved from where they were built to where they are now by snow and mud slides," said Dave Katz who, like most Ophir residents, commutes to a job in Telluride. His house sits just inside the Spring Gulch boundary line charted by the U.S. Geological Survey.

"Everyone here is very avalanche-aware," Katz said.

"Some people, before they leave Telluride, will call home and say, come get me if I don't get there by such-and-such a time. I know a ski patrolman who carries an avalanche transmitter with him in the winter. You carry a shovel and blankets in your car in the winter—although if one of the big avalanches hit you in your car, a blanket wouldn't really do much good. A transmitter might help 'em find your body faster, though." . . .

This last sentence makes this quote work.

When Taylor Huddleston was pulled out of the snow, Siengo looked at him and his heart sank.

"He had all the signs of death," Siengo said later.

"His skin was pale. It had a gray pallor. He wasn't breathing, nor was his heart beating. And the fact that he was under the snow for such a long time—well, in some hypothermia cases, people survive because their system slows down, but they can breathe. He'd been buried so deep, there was no way he could have been able to breathe. Without oxygen, you're clinically dead in four to six minutes, and after that, the brain begins to die. We managed to get his heart beating—hearts are incredible; they don't die for a long time after a person is clinically dead—but he never did breathe on his own."

An ambulance took Taylor to Dr. Dan Tullius at the

Crested Butte Medical Center, just down the road. Medical technicians were pushing air into Taylor's lungs, but they hadn't managed to persuade his heart to start beating. Tullius performed cardiopulmonary resuscitation on Taylor for 45 minutes with no success. He was about to give up and declare Taylor dead when Taylor's heart feebly began to beat.

Tullius called Joanie Dahlen, the Flight For Life nurse on duty at St. Mary's Hospital in Grand Junction. Dahlen had already been notified to stand by. Tullius told her to come get Taylor.

The Flight For Life helicopter landed at the ski-resort parking lot at 2:30 and flew Taylor out immediately. The Huddlestons followed in a plane chartered by Mountain Sunrise manager Paul Hird and Crested Butte Mountain Resort co-owner Ralph Walton, a longtime friend of the Huddlestons.

Taylor never began breathing independently, though. His eyes remained dilated and unfocused, an indication of brain-stem damage due to lack of oxygen. An examination found that he had internal bleeding.

At 10:11 P.M. that night, about 11 hours after the avalanche snatched him, Taylor Huddleston quietly died.

The story continues on from here, but by now you should have an idea of how to weave dramatic material with drier factual material. Taylor's death also shows the talk about zoning and avalanches is more than just an obtuse governmental issue.

CHAPTER FOUR

Elevating Mundane Writing to the Sublime

T oo many news stories are filled with talking heads. By that, Jack Hart of the *Oregonian* in Eugene, Oregon, means people are simply quoted without us learning any more about them. In straight news stories, that's fine. Often all we want are the facts, nothing more. But in features, and especially in profiles, the readers want more. Hart compares it with writing novels. In great fiction you have more than just people talking. You have characters being developed. The same is true in literary nonfiction and should be true in writing profiles.

Writing Profiles Means Going Beyond Talking Heads

Jack Hart

If we wanted to spend our time reading résumés, we'd all be personnel managers.

And yet, the conventional newspaper profile all too often consists of nothing more than a tedious recounting of biographical facts. "He was born near Linton," writes our profiler, "and attended high school in Corona."

Such profiles usually go beyond the list of basic job application stats, of course. They add the personnel office's screening interview, too. The nervous job applicant stands before the reader as quote after quote rolls out, each purely informational, each devoid of color or character, and each largely unrelated to the others. "I'm responsible for all shipping orders," says our applicant. "And I also like to jog."

Thus the personnel-office profile takes shape. A lead that identifies the subject. General biographical background with no particular focus. Then the chain of quotes, each joined to the next with a brief transition.

Such stories do justice to the word "profile" only in the first and second dictionary sense of the term — "a side view" or "an outline." They're holdovers from the antiquated view of the journalist as nothing more than a collector of bald facts, a recording device with no responsibility to serve readers by placing information in a meaningful context. They have nothing to do with what *Webster's New World* gives as a third definition of the profile — "a short, vivid biographical and character sketch."

Contrast the personnel-office approach with the form exploited by master profiler Gay Talese, whose more memorable character sketches were gathered in the 1970 anthology, *Fame and Obscurity* (reprinted in 1981 as a Dell paperback). When Talese tackles the likes of Frank Sinatra or Joe Louis, the subject lives on the page, breathing personality with all the intensity of a character by Larry McMurtry. When Talese finishes with his subject, the side view bores through the center of the subject, and the outline is fleshed out with human emotion, motivation and character. The resulting portrait meets the fundamental standard of success in profile writing: It explains why this particular human being ended up in this place, at this time, doing this thing.

Such a profile presents a theory of personality that persuades the reader through a careful recitation of evidence. In the end, it leaves the reader with new insight that goes far beyond bare biographical background and random utterances. It gives the why of a human being in a way that helps the reader understand the course of an individual life. A good profile leaves the reader confident that he could predict how the subject would act in a situation as yet unlived.

The key to that kind of profile lies in the tricks of characterization developed in 250 years of writing the novel. They work equally well whether the subject is a product of life or of imagination, and Talese uses them profusely to explore the truths of human behavior that often surface in the novel and remain hidden in the newspaper. Most of them show up in "Mr. Bad News," a classic profile of former *New York Times* obituary writer Alden Whitman. To construct his Whitman profile, which appears in *Fame and Obscurity*, Talese relied on a narrative line, vignettes and anecdotes, physical description and telling details.

A Narrative Line

A narrative line gives a novel its plot, but also serves as a vehicle for furthering characterization. Talese begins his portrait of Whitman as the obituary writer slips out of bed in the morning. The specifics of Whitman's early-morning habits tell more about his character than a volume of abstract observations. Talese could have described his subject as calm and measured. Instead, he revealed him as a morning tea-drinker and pipe-smoker.

Talese then followed Whitman through his morning routine, his daily commute to the *Times*, and his work in the newsroom, thereby pursuing a "day-in-the-life" action line common to newspaper and magazine profiles. The approach fits neatly into the limited space available for most newspaper profiles, but it allows readers a glimpse of the subject in a variety of personal and professional situations.

Still other narrative schemes can fit an expansive portrait into a tight frame. "The journalistic visit" takes the reader along on a trip to the subject's home or workplace. The extended anecdote breaks away from a revealing episode in the subject's life to slip in background and then returns to continue the action. Just about any story line with a beginning, a middle and an end will do:

> His real teeth, all thirty-two of them, were knocked out or loosened by three strong-arm men in an alley one night in 1936 in Alden Whitman's hometown, Bridgeport, Connecticut. He was twenty-three years old then, a year out of Harvard and full of verve, and his assailants apparently opposed opinions supported by Whitman. He bears no ill will toward those who attacked him, conceding they had their point of view, nor is he at all sentimental about his missing teeth. They were full of cavities, he says, a blessing to be rid of them.

As it develops character, a narrative line adds yet another element missing from all too many newspaper profiles — it adds the dramatic tension of a true story and makes readers eager to see how the episode comes out.

Vignettes and Anecdotes

"Mr. Bad News" contains more than a dozen anecdotes and at least that many vignettes. Each entertains in its own right, but each also reveals something of the theory Talese developed to explain Whitman's talent as an obituary writer. The subject emerges from the barrage of entertaining yarns as a fastidious, unflappable man, his "magpie mind" crammed with useful trivia. He has the romantic streak needed to appreciate the accomplishments of great artists and statesmen, the obsession with routine needed to love a sedentary assignment, and the passion for accuracy appropriate to the *New York Times*.

The tight focus displayed in Talese's anecdotes highlights two more attributes of the winning profile.

First, a short character sketch cannot hope to explain the complexities of an entire human being. So the successful profile writer concentrates on the one or two personality traits that seem central to the subject's newsworthy accomplishment. Virtually all of Talese's anecdotes relate to Whitman's personality and its contribution to his virtuosity as an obituary writer.

Second, Talese obviously culled the anecdotes he actually used from a much larger number. Focus grows out of careful selection, and anecdotes so perfectly focused suggest especially ruthless selection. And that, in turn, drives home the point that thorough, extensive reporting is an absolute requirement for each good profile. A quick interview and a couple of phone calls just won't yield the raw material needed for the sifting, winnowing and funneling that produce a controlled personality portrait.

Physical Description

By the time Talese wrote three lines of "Mr. Bad News" he'd launched an anecdote and told readers that Whitman is short, wears horn-rimmed glasses, and smokes a pipe. Other telling details follow within a page. Whitman has a full head of brown hair and a full bridge of false teeth. His face is round and his habitual expression is serious. He has surprisingly small blue eyes and a thick, reddish mustache.

An involved reader visualizes the profile subject acting out the action line as it unfolds. A few carefully chosen visual details allow readers to construct their own images. The photo that runs with the copy won't create that kind of active involvement, and the only details necessary to create an image are the three or four that set the subject apart from other human beings. Yet many newspaper profiles contain only mundane physical details of the sort shared by half the human race. Surprisingly often, they contain no physical description at all.

Telling Details

Alden Whitman owns two or three suits and wears a bow tie. He subscribes to the *New Statesman, Le Nouvel Observateur,* and "nearly every journal in the out-of-town newsstand in Times Square." He's seen *Casablanca* three dozen times.

Of such pieces human beings are made. The details are concrete, tangible attributes that readers recognize as signs of a particular style. They involve readers accustomed to reaching their own conclusions about other people on the basis of visible bits of information. They're the most persuasive possible evidence for a theory of personality because they make the case by showing, rather than telling.

But the temptation always is to tell. Too many profile writers draw their own conclusions — the subject is aggressive, diffident or cynical — and pass them along without substantiation. They risk not only the reader's willingness to believe, but his interest as well.

Tom Wolfe cites the special importance of a particular kind of telling detail, which he calls the status indicator. One of the main reasons we read (and why we read profiles in particular) is to gauge our place in the social fabric. What image do we project through our choices of possessions — clothing, furniture, automobiles and the like — and what does that say about our essential character? Observant profile writers focus on objects that are telling because they carry a status code shared by readers. Only a man of a certain stripe wears a bow tie and smokes a pipe.

The list hardly exhausts Talese's repertoire of literary devices. He unifies "Mr. Bad News" by weaving death metaphors throughout its narrative fabric. He maintains the narrative line by slipping in background with the techniques of exposition refined by short story writers. He begins his profile with a bit of dialogue that reveals character while generating a vignette.

In the end, we leave a familiar Alden Whitman leaning over his typewriter in the *Times* newsroom. We know something of his history and his style. We've seen him at work, on the subway, at a dinner party, and in his bedroom. We understand why he relishes a job that most reporters would shun.

With fewer than 5,000 words, Talese has defined the perfect obituary writer at a level of insight that goes far beyond the most detailed job description. No résumé, no battery of psychological tests, could reveal more about a potential employee.

In the final analysis, it seems talented profile writers have something in common with the best personnel managers. They buttress the biographical facts with insight and keen observation. They make their decisions by sifting through a broad array of often subtle clues to personality. And if they spotted another Alden Whitman standing in a line of applicants for an obituary writer's job, they'd hire him on the spot.

> Jack Hart is the *Oregonian's* staff development director and writing coach. Before taking his present job, he served as a general assignment reporter and as the editor of the paper's Sunday magazine, *Northwest*. He earned a B.A. in journalism from the University of Washington and a Ph.D. in mass communication from the University of Wisconsin. He has been a member of the journalism faculties at the University of Oregon and various other universities. He is a member of the Poynter Institute's visiting faculty and conducts writing workshops throughout the United States.

O ften the novice will ask: Why write description? After all, the story is more than likely going to have photographs. But often the photos just show what someone or something looks like. Written description can do that, but should also do much more. It should make connections between what we see and the theme of the story. Using active words like Kim Ode does in the last paragraph of this next essay not only tells how someplace looks, it also shows us how it feels to be there. Throughout the following essay on description, writer Bob Ehlert reminds us to make those connections and also that if we are going to describe that gun above the mantel, we had better well use it.

Using Description Effectively

Bob Ehlert

Several years ago photographer Marlin Levison and I decided to go on an impromptu feature story roundup in a remote area of Minnesota that the locals call the North Shore. We wanted to see who was holed up from life in this region that borders the northwest shore of Lake Superior, a place where a few thousand folks have the run of millions of acres.

Sure, it is peaceful and pretty up there. Tourists come from all over the Upper Midwest to hunt and fish and play along the North Shore in summer. All but the hardiest Shore dwellers leave when winter settles in along Cook and Lake counties.

What we wanted to know is what kind of folks were living there with the black flies and the black bears, at the ends of dirt roads through cabin fever cold spells, downshore from the Split Rock Lighthouse and along the inlets of the big lake they call "Giche-gume."

You get the picture: a dream assignment in a beautiful place. There was no deadline. No agenda. No preprinted text from a speech to fall back upon. It was like a free fall with nobody but the editor watching.

In Search of a Theme

After spending two weeks in the wilds up there, my mind, and more importantly my notebook, came back full of facts and tastes and smells and feelings.

I spent my first night on the Shore, for instance, in a roadside inn where there was a fire blazing in a great room that afforded a wonderful view of the lake. There, on a cool June night in the city of Two Harbors, I stayed up well past sunset reading about Lake Superior shipwrecks, geology and lore. That's because I believe every story needs a tone or a kind of theme.

I took notes about the unrelenting tides crashing on the rocky shores, about the wreck of the *Edmund Fitzgerald*, which left Two Harbors bound for the East in November of 1975.

Never to return.

I believe in getting steeped in what's around you.

Just as a news reporter takes notes about what goes on at a city council meeting or a fire, feature writers ought to be taking even more notes. That's because their job goes beyond the objective facts about what happened. They should also record what happened between the lines. I call that subjective reporting.

From that kind of mood research I fashioned one of the opening paragraphs about the lake which, by then, seemed like a friendly legend:

"Ever so slowly, Superior carves out coves and caves. She transforms cliffs and stout formations into pebble beaches. She goes where she wants and she takes what she will from the land and its people, the North Shore people."

Using the magical powers of a little description, the feature writer can take the reader along to the North Shore, the city council meeting — whatever it is — and make him feel as though he was there.

Since that was my goal on the North Shore trip, that's why I dug in and tried to learn the history and lore of the place — all the while taking notes. Sometimes I scribbled by hand and sometimes I dictated into a tape recorder.

Beyond my empirical observations I did things like taste the water or react to the cool temperature of the streams that fed it. I took notes of the bird, the wildlife and foliage.

Such research netted paragraphs such as this one, which is included in a section about hiking along a series of waterfalls:

Suddenly there is a sensation of walking through, or acting out a daydream on the trail. A daydream whose setting of swirling pools, rushing eddies, seagulls, robins, woodpeckers and silver birch forests is all so real.

I was convinced that I was in a very special place discovering it for others, perhaps for the first time, or rediscovering and defining it for those who had grown too familiar with it. All of this — call it data or whatever you like — became the bank from which I made withdrawals later when I wanted to describe things.

The First Draft

But what do you describe? When do you describe? And why do you describe in the first place?

I think we should describe anything out of the ordinary when we sit down to write a first draft. Subsequent editing will reveal what works best.

When we choose to describe depends upon how important the person or thing being described is to the story. In fiction writing, or general story telling, there is an old maxim that goes like this: Never describe the gun above the mantel unless you're going to use it. In other words, don't describe people or things that won't play into the theme of your story.

Once, when I was writing a profile of a former Minneapolis police chief, I wrote that the lines in his forehead went up and down like the slats in Venetian blinds.

I set that image up early in the story because I knew, later on, I was going to dramatize his reaction to a difficult question I had asked. When he gave his less-than-honest answer, the lines in his forehead seemed to go down—just like the blinds that are pulled when people want their privacy.

The answer to the question of why you describe is the simplest of all for me. I describe because it is fun. It is writing. Description breathes life into the copy. It is the reason I am a feature writer rather than a hard news writer.

In hard news, space is often at a premium. The facts are stacked at the top and, as a matter of course, often lopped from the bottom. Feature stories are more like a canvas. The space is still defined, but you can choose the colors and tones and shadings you like. However, just as you can't paint from an empty palette, you can't describe things out of thin air. When I talked to people on my North Shore sojourn, I listened to what they said and how they said it. I recorded where they said it. When they said it. And, perhaps most important-ly, why they said it.

Writers should never be passive tourists. They should always be actively engaged in life, describing how it looked and felt when they were there so they can recount it when they write.

After gathering a mass of objective facts and subjective impres-sions, a writer is ready to describe what it is he or she has experi-enced. Sometimes the descriptions themselves come almost word for word from recorded observations.

While watching an old commercial fisherman get his boat posi-tioned at his dock, Levison, my photographer companion on the North Shore trip, noted that it was just like a farmer bringing his cow home. Here's how that apt observation got into my story:

> And each night, Ragnvald Sve walks out on his water-worn pier to fetch his boat again. While the gulls watch from the rocky island just offshore, the old fisherman talks to the Viking (his boat) and leads it around with a rope as if it were an old cow.

The North Shore feature story excursion was a wonderful trip.

I filled up my notebooks and cassette tapes with hundreds of observations. And when it came time to write, I was not only ready to describe things, I was anxious.

One of my favorite bits of descriptive writing came in the introduction of a story about a man and his daughter. He had "rescued" her from an ugly custody battle and now was raising her in a very liberal fashion. He was her teacher, her friend, her parent.

Home was a sorry-looking place in a miniature junkyard of art and decaying wood. They lived off the main road of the North Shore and far from the mainstream of a normal life. After talking to the man and his daughter and recalling the dilapidated structures in the area and the ramshackle nature of his own house, I made this connection between him and those deteriorating buildings:

> He has a face like an abandoned house. His eyes are deep-set and empty like dark rooms on the second floor. His teeth are here and there like boarded up and broken windows . . .

There was plenty more where that came from on the North Shore. There is plenty more wherever a keen observer travels. As writers, our job is to take mental pictures and literal notes — the results of which can make for wonderful description.

This last bit of description comes from Kim Ode, a feature writer at the *Star Tribune* in Minneapolis who, obviously, has come to know the Badlands in South Dakota:

> The sun drops like a coin into a slot on the horizon, triggering a jukebox of coyotes. The full moon rises so huge and fast, you unconsciously brace yourself against the rotation of the Earth. Stars burst into view. You wouldn't be anywhere else. There is nowhere else.

Bob Ehlert is a staff writer on the *Star Tribune*'s Sunday magazine. In 1989 he was a finalist for the Pulitzer Prize in feature writing. He has won several other state and regional awards for his writing. He came to the *Star Tribune* from *The Virginian-Pilot* and *The Ledger-Star* newspapers in Norfolk, Virginia, where he was a feature writer and arts and entertainment editor.

M ark Patinkin is a columnist who makes his living by writing in the first person. Most of us will only do the occasional first-person piece. For it to work, it will have to be about an unusual experience or an experience so common that many readers can empathize with it. The more perceptive you are, the stronger your writing will be. Occasionally in a first-person piece you can get away without doing research, but as with all writing, the more information and knowledge you bring to it, the richer it will be. One further thing: Few writers find immediate success by writing first-person pieces. Usually they learn the fundamentals of writing and reporting and then come to first-person writing with all their skills fully polished.

Writing in the First Person

Mark Patinkin

I'd just returned home from a two-month assignment writing about religious violence in Belfast, India, and Beirut. I was at a local restaurant, handing my VISA card to the waitress. She paused when she saw the name.

"Are you the Mark Patinkin who writes for the paypa?" she said.

In Rhode Island, my home state, that's how "paper" is pronounced. She was referring to my column, which I'd been writing four times a week for the Providence *Journal-Bulletin* for several years.

I told her I was. As someone who often writes about light, personal subjects, I was proud to be recognized after just completing a lengthy series on the world's war zones. At the time, mid-1986, I'd been the only American journalist to make it to the Moslem side of Beirut in months. I waited for the waitress to say something about my accounts of sneaking across the Green Line, of Sikh-Hindu violence in India, of Catholic-Protestant hatred in Northern Ireland.

Instead, she said this:

"I really like your stories about how you and your brothas used to eat red licorice for breakfast and stuff."

Brothas is Rhode Island for brothers.

And her comment showed one of the burdens of being a first-person journalist.

No matter how often you strive for substance, readers will remember you not for your insights on the drug problem, or the Warsaw Pact, but for the time you had a babysitter crisis, about your admission that you now have to ask your wife what you like to eat at restaurants, about being so "houseblind" you no longer see the piles of clutter around your living room.

A story about the trade deficit—possibly the nation's most serious long-term problem—will, if you're lucky, bring a single letter from an assistant lecturer on economic history. A column about the trauma of doing home repairs—and how the most difficult phrase in the language is "while we're at it"—will likely bring a dozen.

I've been a columnist now for 10 years. In addition to the series I did on religious violence, I also spent a month in Africa writing about famine. And a month in Eastern Europe just after the Berlin Wall fell—in both cases writing daily.

But a single column I did on how my parents met got more response than either of those two global projects. So did a column suggesting that, in my view, cats could best be used as skeet on rifle ranges.

The point of all this is that few things tend to engage readers as much as writing about yourself, and how you see the commonalities of everyday life. The letter "I" is a powerful means of connection.

Living Out Loud

It took me a while to get comfortable with "I." I tended to avoid it, writing feature stories with my picture on top rather than columns. I was wary of being too exposed. Write a mediocre third-person feature and people will turn the page. Write a mediocre first-person column, and people will say, "What an imbecile."

My initial attempts at first person were the most blatant kind: the personal participation category. Instead of covering an event, I *did* the event.

I joined an annual two-mile swim across Rhode Island's Narragansett Bay, managing to finish about ten minutes behind a 70-year-old man. Later, I registered to be part of a male bodybuilding contest. My preparation was doing a set of 15 push-ups the day before. I arrived to find the other entrants shaved, oiled and pumped. I was thin and pasty. When it was my turn, they played the theme from Rocky and told me to go onstage and strike poses.

"Flex your pecs," a female audience member shouted at one point.

I already was.

I quickly learned that participation can be embarrassing.

But it led me to another, subtler category of the first-person journalist: writing about your own day-to-day life. It's what Anna

Quindlen, the *New York Times* columnist, has called, "Living out loud."

Ask yourself: Have you gone through anything recently that might make a first-person piece?

Not long ago, my doctor gave me a checklist to fill out, a mundane exercise, but when I was done, I saw the seed of a column. I realized that I was fudging my answers. It helped explain why so many Americans have medical problems: we lie on health forms. How often did I drink? Hardly ever, I said. Eat fatty foods? Oh, rarely. Exercise? Daily, of course. To impress my doctor, I'd trumped up half my responses.

Another time, I was with my wife when I pulled out my driver's license. She noticed I listed my height at 5-feet, 10½ inches. She asked why men always do that: add that extra half inch to our height? I insisted it was for the sake of accuracy. At that point, she took out a tape and measured me. I stretched my neck for all I was worth, but I only came out 5-10. I was crestfallen. She told me not to worry about it, since all that was important was that I had a good personality. That's like telling a woman she shouldn't worry about being ugly since she's fun to be with.

Again, it was the seed of a column: It helped me realize that men are more sensitive about one physical measurement than any other: height. I'm still angry at my parents for not making me at least 6 feet. When I'm barefoot and my wife's in heels, I walk around the house on tiptoes. And yes, tape measurements aside, I do plan to keep listing myself as 5-feet, 10½.

Commentary on Daily Events

A technique I often use to come up with ideas is to simply study each day's news stories and ask how they relate to my own life. I remember reading an article about a child who'd saved a choking playmate with the Heimlich Maneuver. The child, only about 7, referred to it as the Time-Life Remover. It got me thinking about all the words I'd mangled myself as a child. For years, I used to catch butterflies in the "bacon lot" at the corner. I also enjoyed eating "cold" slaw, and liked putting "catch-up" on everything from burgers to chicken. I had "romantic fever" when I was 6, and needed a "tennis shot" after cutting my leg on a rusty slide.

The technique of perusing newspapers also brings up another

key first-person category: serious commentary on daily events. Many writers shy from taking on global issues, feeling they have to be experts. But if you talk about how your own experience relates to such issues, you're always an expert.

A few months ago, I was reading about Wilson sporting goods being sold to a Helsinki firm. I began to think: "What does that mean to me?" While others wrote of what such foreign takeovers would do to our trade deficit, I decided to take a personal tack. I began to write about how Wilson was a big part of my childhood. I used to sleep with my Wilson baseball mitt under my pillow. I'd try wearing it to dinner. The mitt meant summer to me. It meant growing up in America. Now that symbol had become foreign owned. As was Bantam Books, publisher of Edgar Rice Burroughs' *John Carter of Mars* series — another staple of my childhood. As was the A&P, where I used to grocery shop with my mother. I continued the list: RCA televisions, Brooks Brothers clothing, Sylvania electronics. Things that were all part of growing up in the United States were being taken over by our overseas competition. "I'm sure I'll still buy Wilson from time to time," I said in ending, "but now, when I do, I'll be more likely to think of what's happening to our heritage than of treasured boyhood summers."

Inner Lives of Friends

Endings, I find, can be one of the hardest parts of a first-person piece, chiefly because when you use the letter "I," it's somehow not quite enough to end with a simple wrap-up quote; you're expected to come up with a wise — or at least conclusive — thought. I find that two simple questions sometimes can help. Sit back, look over the piece, and first ask yourself, "What, really, is going on here?" Then: "And how do I feel about it?"

Conversations with friends and family can also be a rich source of first-person material. Writers like Ellen Goodman have shown how the inner lives of friends can be a unique glimpse into forces shaping our time. Recounting a talk with an acquaintance about his or her divorce, job frustration or rediscovery of religion can end up saying as much about the subject as a set of interviews with sociologists. A weekend at my fifteenth college reunion helped show me an interesting shift in the outlook of many women. Five years before, at my tenth, few were at home with children; career was everything.

This time, one of the most frequent questions asked was, "Are you staying at home?" The answer, in more cases than not, was yes. You can always rebuild a career, one woman said, but you can't rebuild your children's childhood. One woman had decided to have a baby on her own and move in with her parents so she could stay home to raise it. I'd seen a number of studies on this kind of shift in women's choices, but an anecdotal first-person column on the subject, I think, helped bring it alive more than most third-person analysis pieces.

I should admit something here. While talking to those women at that reunion, I didn't instantly think it would make a column. Even when the weekend was over, I never connected the conversations as the seed of an idea. It only occurred to me the following Monday when I got to work and faced a blank page. By mid-morning, still lacking an idea, I began to brainstorm hard for ideas. What had I been through recently? The reunion, of course, had been my most marked recent experience. But what about the reunion? I began to sketch out notes, remembrances of talks, and then a pattern began to come together — the pattern of women's choices.

Deadline Inspirations

What I'm trying to say, I think, is that just because first-person ideas are, well, personal, it doesn't automatically mean they grow out of inspiration. Like most story ideas, they best grow out of desperation. If I didn't have to write four columns a week, I'd write one a month. Three-quarters of the time, I arrive at my office having no idea what I'm going to write for the next day's paper. It's taught me that the most prolific first-person writers aren't those with a fertile imagination, but those with regular deadlines. It's not enough to wait for ideas to present themselves; you have to set aside time, every day if possible, to pace, to brainstorm, to grope. Ideally, get yourself locked into steady deadlines. There's nothing like a dynamite stick beneath the seat with the fuse lit.

First-person writing can take on one other form, a hybrid form. It can be a combination of personal column and reportage. I've tried this most pointedly on a number of foreign assignments I've been given. At first, I was surprised when my editors suggested sending me abroad — as a columnist. The idea was to write about the African famine of 1985.

Why not send a feature writer? I asked.

They explained they wanted to try personalizing a faraway event by chronicling it through a voice familiar to our readers. It was the same idea behind the reporting of Charles Kuralt — or Ernie Pyle. So I went, as much a columnist as a reporter.

One of my first stops was Korem, Ethiopia's biggest famine camp. When I sat down afterward to write the lead, I tried to think not just of what was in my notebook, but how I reacted personally. I wrote:

> The first thing that struck me was the sound, except it was not sound. It was the absence of sound. People everywhere, and so little sound. Starvation does make a noise. It is silence. And it is very loud. Then I noticed the flies. They covered the eyes of the weaker children. And the weaker men, too, and the weaker women. I once worked on a farm. The flies on the cattle were not as bad as the flies I saw now.

When I got to the end of the piece, I tried asking myself the same question I do at the end of columns: "What, underneath, was going on here?"

I wrote:

> On our way out, we pass lines for everything. Water, medical help, food, of course. The lines stretch hours long.
>
> No one complains. No one jostles.
>
> The people crowd around as we climb into the car. They smile and reach out.
>
> "Ferengee," they say. Foreigner.
>
> Other than that, there is no sound.
>
> We drive away in silence. I look back, watching them begin their day: 55,000 of the most desperate of people, living in near-impossible conditions.
>
> And it occurs to me that there are no police in this city of refugees. And no crime.
>
> I had never before been to a place so inhuman. Or more civilized.

The same technique, of course, can be used on a more local plane: a visit to a press conference, a criminal trial, or a simple interview. I recently profiled the victim of a drunk driver. I began with the phrase, "He met me at the door in his wheelchair." That kind of image, I think, allows a reader to feel more of a connection.

It's also a writing technique I borrowed from another columnist — Bob Greene of the *Chicago Tribune*. While still a general assignment reporter, Greene once wrote, he used to get together with his colleagues after work. Over drinks, they'd ask each other about their day's assignments.

"What really happened?" they'd say.

When Greene began writing his column, he made himself a vow: He'd write to his readers the way he talked with his colleagues after work—a conversational telling of what really happened. It's a technique that can work as effectively in a story about a college reunion as one about the fighting in Beirut.

But once again, be ready for columns of such substance to fade more quickly in the minds of the reader than the ones where you confess that you're utterly dependent on your wife to pick out your clothes in the morning. Be ready, in other words, to be remembered for light instead of heavy.

Be ready, also, to be judged.

When you use the letter "I," for every supportive letter you get from someone who related to your one year old having a scene at a restaurant, you'll get another from a reader tired of hearing about your kid.

Be ready for the rewards, and the price, of having yourself as a subject.

Mark Patinkin has spent more than 10 years writing a four-times-a-week column for the Providence *Journal-Bulletin*. His column is syndicated by the Scripps-Howard News Service. In 1986, he was a finalist for the Pulitzer Prize in international reporting for a series he did on religious violence in Northern Ireland, India, and Beirut. In December of 1984, he spent a month traveling to five African countries to chronicle famine, later publishing a book about the experience called *An African Journey*. In 1990, Random House published *The Silent War*, a book Patinkin co-authored on the global business battles shaping America's future.

In the preceding article, Mark Patinkin's own experiences are the essence of his first-person stories. In newspapers, columnists often are given the latitude to write about themselves. But the first person is banned in most news stories. The objective reporter keeps himself out of the story. However, some would argue, since the reporter is writing the story, he *is* in the story; why hide it? Walt Harrington of *The Washington Post Magazine* introduces himself in stories that are essentially about other people. If newspapers are reluctant to use this method, magazines are not. Often the writer becomes an active participant in the story. *Vanity Fair* uses the technique, as do many magazines that value writers with distinct personalities. As a freelancer you should define these markets and use the technique when appropriate. But use it sparingly, for you don't want to switch the balance and cause a story about someone else to become a story about you.

When a Reporter Becomes
Part of the Story

Walt Harrington

I started appearing in my own stories when an occasional "I said" would replace "a reporter said," or an infrequent "I asked" would replace "a visitor inquired." But before long I'd gone all the way and interjected myself as a character in my *Washington Post Magazine* profiles of Vice President George Bush and Jesse Jackson.

It was a surprisingly painless transformation. The sky didn't fall, old journalism professors didn't threaten to revoke my degree, Hunter Thompson didn't invite me to his place for the weekend. In fact, I came away with a refreshing sense that readers know intuitively that it isn't always self-aggrandizing to become a part of our own stories, and what counts is how and why we put ourselves into our articles. Readers know this, I suspect, because they are on to us: They know that our reporters' claim to third-person omniscience is bunk, and that third person can be far more pretentious and misleading than acknowledging through first person that our personal insights are simply that, personal insights.

I got to this place after more than a decade of news and feature writing and editing. I'd written any number of first-person articles over the years, stories about my childhood, my marriage, my father and my son. I knew that saying "I" in print wasn't necessarily an ego trip, as is so often pounded into the heads of young reporters, but simply one vantage from which to tell a story.

If I could recognize in my own life the kinds of intimate details that make for a good story, I reasoned, then I also would be more attuned to those details in telling the stories of other people's lives. I also figured this sensitivity would help me develop a better reporter's eye for anecdotal detail. All of these things turned out to be true, and I'm convinced now that if you can't tell an honest story about yourself, you're a long way from telling an honest story about someone else.

Yet in writing about other people, there's an obstacle that can't be overcome: The observer can never become his subject. So try as we will to feel or think or imagine what another person feels or thinks or imagines, we can't ultimately do it. We are not in his skin. Sure, any decent feature writer today knows the Tom Wolfe checklist of methods used to capture the tone of naturalistic fiction in their stories — use actual dialogue, re-create scenes, watch for little details that speak volumes, spend time with your subject in varied settings. But what's left out of this list is you, the reporter. Because right in the middle of all of this observing and gathering and re-creating is you, asking the questions, collating the anecdotes, determining the order of events that will determine conclusions. And if your subject is at all media savvy, the odds are he's bending and massaging what you're learning based on what he knows or perceives to be your biases or reportorial needs. In short, you aren't a bystander at this dance, but a partner.

Reporters know that this relationship between reporter and subject is often a wonderful source of insight about people, particularly the way they cajole, flatter, harangue and, in general, treat us while hanging out with them. I've also learned that after writing about somebody with a public image, my friends, neighbors, even colleagues inevitably ask, "So what did you really think of him?" They assume I haven't already told them in my story what I really think. Eventually, I vowed to be more up-front about how my beliefs and biases were shaping my stories, since that's what readers seemed most interested in, anyway.

I had a recent test of my theories when the *Washington Post National Weekly* reprinted a version of my free-wheeling *Post Magazine* profile of Jesse Jackson. The weekly denuded my article of its first-person references and anything even close to an opinion. The rewrite made the story a straight third-person piece. I soon received an angry letter, the likes of which I hadn't gotten when the story ran in the magazine earlier. The writer said of me: "He has not the courage to express his own opinions forthrightly." As I said, readers are on to us when it comes to the idea that a third-person story is objective.

Finally, one more kind of journalism, typified by the *Playboy* interview and the Mike Wallace interrogational style, also shaped my thinking. I'd always enjoyed the give-and-take of the interview format, its tension and unpredictability, its quality of unbridled debate. In standard third-person profiles, these qualities are lost because the reporter strips his questions, often obnoxiously direct questions, from the telling and leaves only the subject's answers. The writer sets up the answer one way or another, often using convoluted constructions such as "a visitor asked" or relying on a third-person rhetorical question—a question rarely in quotation marks. The unspoken message here is that the writer has fudged the reconstruction of his own question, probably to make it look more forceful or thoughtful than it actually was. The subject, of course, gets no second chance.

Besides playing straight with readers, using the real give-and-take between reporter and subject in an article captures the best qualities of a *Playboy* or Mike Wallace interview. In a feature piece it also takes on the tone of dialogue. It's just that you, the reporter, are half of the dialogue. To the reader, the story becomes more personalized, allowing the reader to identify with the reporter or the subject. Either way, the story gives the sense of two people talking, whether they are clashing or enjoying each other.

Now the big question: When is enough of me in a story enough? The test I've used whenever I've gotten the urge to become a character is to ask myself whether my being in the article at any given point sheds light on my subject, or on me. The answer should always be "the subject." That's because these aren't true first-person pieces, but rather pieces that borrow some of the advantages of first-person stories to make a more compelling, intimate and exciting read. The reporter is in the story only as a vehicle for saying something about the subject, never the reverse. Please note: References such as "he told me" instead of "he said" are gratuitous; they add nothing about the subject.

All of this said, it's important to realize that every story will not come down this way, nor should it, certainly not on the front page and not even on the features pages. It's not an approach for the inexperienced. But I do think we too often assume that is grandstanding for a writer to enter his own story. It's not. Often it's much closer to the truth than staying out.

Walt Harrington is a staff writer for *The Washington Post Magazine*. He worked previously as an assistant editor on the *Post* Metro desk and as a reporter and editor at other newspapers, including *The Allentown Morning Call*. He has won two recent Sunday magazine writing awards, and he holds master's degrees in journalism and sociology from the University of Missouri-Columbia.

I n putting together this book, I was struck by the varying voices of the authors. Some are serious, get-down-to-work voices; others, like those of critics Dan Sullivan and Stephen Hunter, are light-hearted. Of course, for most of them, it's precisely that individual voice that has helped move them to the top of their fields. If they sounded like everyone else, they would no longer be exceptional writers. And the point of this book is to help make you an exceptional writer because the way the communications industry is evolving, only the exceptional writers will be free to be individuals. The rest will be treated like interchangeable parts. Only those with a voice heard apart from the rest will prosper. So listen as Andy Merton explains how to develop, use, and control the writer's unique voice.

Finding a Writing Voice That's Yours Alone

Andy Merton

I am going to tell you a secret about feature writing. It is a secret so basic that you will wonder why you didn't think of it yourself, so simple that you will be able to use it to your advantage immediately. And yet, it is often ignored, misunderstood, even shunned, in newsrooms across America.

Before I tell you the secret, let me show you part of a feature by *The Boston Globe* writer Nathan Cobb:

> The Day-Glo orange tyrannosaur appears to be starring in a Japanese movie entitled *The Beast That Ate Chisholm's Motel*. Rearing on its hind legs above the sixth hole of Route 1 Miniature Golf, the 12-foot metal statue bares its spotless white teeth casting a fearsome green eye across six lanes of traffic at its one-story target. You can almost hear the screams of the hapless couple inside room 18 as this Sunkist Godzilla hurdles the median strip and mercilessly drowns them amidst the waterbed, whirlpool and steam bath they have rented for the night at $39 plus tax.
>
> "It used to be hollow," says Joe Hallinan, a portly employee of the miniature golf course who is standing shirtless while admiring the

dinosaur's gaudy presence. "Some kids tried to steal it once, but all they did was turn it over. Still, we filled it with cement. Heh. I'd like to see somebody steal it now."

Where else would a Day-Glo tyrannosaur look so . . . so . . . perfectly at home? Certainly it has found suitable surroundings here on Route 1, beside the southbound lanes of this 7.6 mile ribbon of blacktop and neon which stretches from the confluence of the Malden/Melrose/ Saugus to the Route I-95 turnoff in Peabody. Like the garishness of the strip itself, the bizarre orange figure oozes grotesque charm which is at once both appealing and repelling.

There is very little that is subtle about the strip.

Probably you don't know Nathan Cobb. I don't know Nathan Cobb. But we can guess some things about Nathan Cobb from this piece of writing. We can guess, for example, that his better judgment tells him he should be appalled by the excesses of the Strip. And we can tell that, against this better judgment, he admires the dinosaur, admires the whole strip, even while acknowledging that it is kitsch. Views it, tongue-in-cheek, as the best of its kind.

And we can tell that he has chosen to approach the whole thing as an innocent pilgrim, Pinocchio on Pleasure Island.

How do we know these things? From the sound of his voice. From his glorious fantasizing ("You can almost hear the screams . . .") to that little catch in his voice as he pauses for words, overwhelmed, nearly speechless: "Where else would a Day-Glo tyrannosaur look so . . . so . . . perfectly at home?"

Here, try another one. This is a story from the Cincinnati *Post* about the C.I.A. in Cincinnati. Writer Paul H. Harasim went out to uncover the real poop on what, exactly, the C.I.A. does in Cincinnati. He failed, but that's beside the point.

Gunn sat there in a gray suit. He talked from behind a cloud of cigarette smoke.

"I can't tell you," he said, "what else the CIA does in Cincinnati."

It was 1345 hours – 1:45 p.m. to most Cincinnatians – and Stephen Gunn, an agent of the Central Intelligence Agency in Cincinnati – had clammed up.

"How many people have you recruited for the CIA in Cincinnati?"

"I can't tell you that."

"Where were you stationed as an agent overseas?"

"That's confidential."

"How many people work for the CIA?"

"That's classified."

"Where is the other CIA office in Cincinnati?"

"I can't tell you that."

There was a pause, a long pause, as the visitor checked through his notes. Gunn—"yes, that's my real name"—was smiling . . .

. . . The conversation with Gunn made it easier for the visitor to find this truth self-evident: The interview—supposedly set up through the CIA's main office in Virginia to discuss the activities of the intelligence agency's two offices in Cincinnati—wasn't operative.

Harasim got nothing, right? A lot of reporters would go back to the editor and say, "I got nothing. He wouldn't talk." Not Harasim though. He turned a stonewall interview into a terrific story.

He did it by relying on his own persona, the persona he projects with his voice. He set himself up as a dupe, some dumb reporter hopelessly trying to acquire information far beyond his grasp. He also mocked the CIA milieu, the whole cloak-and-dagger atmosphere, with his dime-novel dialogue. And in so doing he got across his sense of the CIA operation in Cincinnati.

By now you are closing in on the secret. Here, try two more:

PARRIS ISLAND, S.C.—He is seething, he is rabid, he is wound up tight as a golf ball, with more adrenalin surging through his hypothalamus than a cornered slum rat; he is everything these Marine recruits with their heads shaved to dirty nubs have ever feared or ever hoped a drill instructor might be.

He is Staff Sgt. Douglas Berry and he is rushing down the squad bay of Receiving Barracks to leap onto a table and brace at parade rest in which none of the recruits, daring glances from the position of attention, can see any more of him under the rake of his campaign hat than his lipless mouth chopping at them like a disaster teletype: WHEN I GIVE THE WORD YOU WILL WALK NOT RUN DOWN THESE STEPS WHERE YOU WILL RUN YOU WILL NOT WALK TO THE YELLOW FOOTMARKS . . .

That's Henry Allen in the *Washington Post*. I don't know what Henry Allen is like in everyday life. But I do know that when Henry Allen takes on the persona of a drill instructor I am going to listen to him and pay attention to what he says. Because, like every good writer, Henry Allen has used his voice to set up a relationship between himself and his reader. In this case, Allen's voice is as hard-driving as a drill instructor, and the reader is the recruit, who had *well better* LISTEN.

It is clear that Allen admires the drill instructor. But it is also possible to use a writer's voice to show disapproval. Back a few years ago, when former Miss America Phyllis George had a brief run as co-host on the CBS Morning News, *The Boston Globe* writer Ed Siegel reacted as follows:

> I like "The CBS Morning News."
>
> I like Phyllis George. I like the way she smiles. I like the way she's always smiling. It's like a long, refreshing glass of Anita Bryant orange juice. I like the way she says, "It's 12 below zee-ro on the top of Mt. Washington." It makes me feel warm all over, just the way Miss Frances used to make me feel when she rang her bell every day on "Ding Dong School."
>
> I like the way Miss Phyllis is nice to her guests all the time. Like when Jim Valvano, the coach for North Carolina State, was showing clips of Indiana basketball coach Bobby Knight acting up on the sidelines. "More people should do the kind of things that Bob Knight does," Valvano said. I bet Bryant Gumbel or Jane Pauley would have been rude and challenged him on that. Miss Phyllis smiled. That's because she's a sports fan. That's because she used to be on "The NFL Today."
>
> I like the way she asks questions nobody else would ask. "Has Fernando Lamas ever told you what he thinks of your imitation of him?" she asked Billy Crystal of "Saturday Night Live." It isn't Miss Phyllis' fault that Fernando Lamas died in 1982.

The main character in the story is Phyllis George. But Phyllis George is not the only character in the story. The narrator is a character, too. The narrator sets up a relationship with Phyllis George (and if she doesn't like it, too bad), and also a relationship with the reader.

Which is my point.

Which is, in fact, the essence of the secret I promised to tell you — the secret buried deep in the soul of every successful feature writer.

The secret is this:

You, the writer, are a character in your own stories.

No, that doesn't mean you have to use the first person singular, although that is not a terrible thing to do on occasion. What it does mean is that you, as narrator, must convey a persona through your voice which will provide the reader with an emotional and intellectual context in which to read the piece.

I see that look in your eye. It is the look of a deer startled by headlights, and I know what you are thinking if you went to journalism school: *Easy for him to say. All through school they taught me to keep myself out of my stories. Once when I let my attitude slip into a piece about the quality of the food in the college dining hall my instructor prescribed three Hail Marys and a week of cold showers. I am so conditioned to writing neutrally—neutered, you might say—that I don't know* how *to find my voice. I don't even know if I* have *one.*

I have good news for you. You have a voice. It is there in that italicized stuff you were thinking just now. At the moment it is a plaintive voice, argumentative, mildly cynical and laced with a touch of self-pity. Take note of it—it may come in handy when you are asked to write a piece about the food in the local high school.

But—and this is important—it's not your only voice. You have others.

Like the one you use when you talk to your parents. And the one you use when you talk with your friends. You have another voice for your lover, and others for the people you work with.

So when you write, you have a lot of voices to choose from. Dozens. Each one reflects a different aspect of you.

Which one do you choose when you sit down to write? You choose the one that fits the situation—the one that best conveys the material at hand, along with your attitude toward that material.

When Michael Winerip of the *New York Times* sought to convey the spirit of the first day of kindergarten at a Long Island school, he allowed the child in himself to emerge through his voice:

> "My name is Mrs. Zimmerman," said the full-grown person standing in front of the Park Avenue School. "You probably don't know who I am, since this is the very first day. I want it to be a very special day. Don't you?"
>
> "Yes!"
>
> "Good," Mrs. Zimmerman said. It was time to sing "God Bless America." Piece of cake. They learned it last year in pre-K. No one's voice was louder than Anika Davis's as she sang, "From the mountains, to the fairy."
>
> "Lovely," Mrs. Zimmerman said, "such lovely singing." And they all followed Mrs. Zimmerman into the building, walking along the line in the middle of the corridor, so they wouldn't get crooked.

Probably in his everyday conversation Michael Winerip does not use phrases like "so they wouldn't get crooked." Does that mean Winerip is faking his voice in the story? No, because Winerip was a child once, and to his credit he is not ashamed of it. So for this story he was able to reach back and retrieve his child's voice, the voice from when he was little Mikey, excited and confused on the first day of school.

Once you get used to the idea that you have a voice, you will start doing wonderful things with it. For example, you will begin to play your voice off the voices of the people you are writing about. Wendy Fox of *The Boston Globe* did a magnificent job of this a few years ago after interviewing a small-time scam artist named William Masiello:

> A touch of hurt and child-like bafflement creeps into the voice of William V. Masiello — admitted briber and perjurer and contract-fixer — as he laments his most recent predicament.
>
> "Oh what another mess I'm in," he moans, resting his head in thick, heavy hands and rubbing his tired eyes. "My wife is gonna kill me."
>
> Another mess indeed. For the 19th time he can remember, the portly Masiello has failed a lie-detector test. And for the umpteenth time in anyone's memory, his name is publicly associated with lying and trouble.

The tongue-in-cheek attitude Fox sets up here is something like that of a mother, sadly shaking her head over the misdeeds of a slow, dumb son who just doesn't get it. The key sentence here is three words long: "Another mess indeed."

Now, isn't that more fun to read than the traditional, stale, quote-paraphrase-quote formula that passes for feature writing in so many newspapers these days? You're not sure yet? Come on. Would you really rather read:

> Admitted contract-fixer William V. Masiello said yesterday he regret-ted the controversy his recent activities have caused.
>
> Acknowledging that he was in "another mess," Masiello indicated that he has caused his family undue suffering.

And so on *ad nauseam*.

No, you would not.

And if you don't want to read it, why in the world do you go on writing it?

I'll tell you why. Because it's safe. Because it's the devil you know.

Get to know some other devils. And angels. And all the characters in between—the ones that collectively make up the person who is you.

Listen to them. Learn to trust their voices. And when you deal with feature material, allow them to take over.

Listen to Other Writers' Voices

If you have trouble getting started, imitate somebody else's voice. Find a writer you like, a writer with a strong voice. Nonfiction, fiction, poetry, it doesn't matter. Read for a while. Get that writer's voice inside your head. The sound, the rhythm, the sensibility.

Then try using that voice on your own material. Write a feature the way, say, Kurt Vonnegut would, or Joan Didion, or Norman Mailer, or Nora Ephron, or Hemingway or Dorothy Parker.

This is not cheating or plagiarizing. It's *your* stuff. Besides, there isn't a writer in the world who hasn't learned from other writers.

And probably after a few paragraphs you will notice a subtle, wonderful thing happening. You will notice that you are no longer Hemingway or whoever; you are you. But a much more natural, at-ease you than that other you, the you who was trying to handle feature material with a hard-news style.

You will also notice that you are having fun.

(Here is a bonus secret: If you have fun writing something, your reader will probably have fun reading it.)

And if your internal censor kicks in—the one that intones, "Thou shalt not feel, let alone allow thy feelings into thy voice"—kick it out again.

And go back to writing.

In your own voice.

Because you have got something to say.

Andy Merton is a journalism professor at the University of New Hampshire. He writes a column for *The Boston Globe* and his feature stories appeared in many national publications, including *Esquire* magazine. He is author of the book *Enemies of Choice: The Right to Life Movement and Its Threats to Abortion*.

End Words

Afterthoughts: More Points to Remember

1. A full-blown profile is more than just talking heads answering questions. As in a novel, it requires developing the main character

and following him or her through sequences of action. It often works best with a beginning, a middle and an end. As in a novel, the profile includes description that helps us see the character, and telling details of the person's mannerisms. We watch as the person comes alive on the page. Of course, unlike a novel, all the details, action sequences, quotes and mannerisms have to be real. There is no tolerance for fudging on the facts.

2. An in-depth profile, as opposed to a simple interview story, requires much more than a quick visit and a couple of phone calls. You need initial research, interviews and time to watch the person function in his everyday life or specialty. All this is rounded out by interviewing people who know your subject best and who might provide information he might not reveal — or even recognize — about himself.

3. Writers new to features will often say, "But there is a photo running along with the story. Why should I describe my subject in my story?" Because a photo is only an image of the person, it often does not make the connections a writer should be seeking. As Jack Hart reminds us, in developing a personality portrait, look for telling details. For example: "Only a man of a certain stripe wears a bow tie and smokes a pipe." If in the story you show he also subscribes to the *New Statesman, Le Nouvel Observateur,* and "nearly every journal in the out-of-town newsstand in Times Square," and that he's seen *Casablanca* three dozen times, you have provided a lot more, or at least a lot different, information than a photograph might.

4. Avoid gratuitous detail. The best description gives us a mental picture of a person or place, and usually helps move the story forward by adding information to the main theme we are developing. After you've finished Madeleine Blais's piece on page 252, reread the ending. If Frank hadn't been dead, saying the sky was cloudy and still would have been nice, but would not have taken the reader anywhere. Placed in the context of Frank's death and Vivian's memories of him, the short description of the sky helps make this story a great one.

5. Deadlines are extremely important. By meeting them you will ensure that editors have the proper time to give your story a thoughtful edit. Deadlines also help you become more focused on your work. Without them you will have no pressure to get things

done. Besides, deadlines are the best way to break writers' block. You have no choice but to write.

6. First-person writing has its place in feature writing, but it only plays a small part in magazine and newspapers. On rare occasions, writers produce intimate, sometimes heartrending stories that only the person who lived through them can write. But every editor sees far too many thinly written first-person pieces from freelancers. Most writers have too few dramatic highlights in their lives to produce a wealth of first-person pieces. Your chances for success will be greater if you look beyond yourself and write about other people's lives.

7. Occasionally you might want to insert yourself in stories that are not first-person pieces. You will want to do this sparingly, but when the time is right and the interaction between you and your subjects adds to the body of information, then add yourself. See in the example at the end of this chapter how well Walt Harrington has done it.

8. You have a writer's voice. Practice using it in your writing. But you have to learn to control it as well as use it. At a football game being loud and boisterous is just fine. At a dinner party it would be rude. Each subject and story will dictate your writing voice as much as the "internal you" will control it. Just as you have learned which voice is appropriate in social situations, in time, you will learn which is appropriate in your writing.

9. Not only will you have a voice, but in time you will have a style that is all your own. In the beginning you will, and probably should, play around with many styles until you find your own. Then it will be yours alone and your reading audience will recognize it even if your name is not on it. Just as you could quickly tell Hemingway from Fitzgerald, people will notice your style. It might be the slightly frenetic style of *Sports Illustrated* or the methodical but rich style of *The New Yorker*, but it will be yours.

10. Writers who care about their writing and keep striving to grow will have a style that gets richer and more complex as they mature in their craft. This does not mean they should switch styles and mediums. In sports there is no need for a baseball player to feel he must also be great in soccer, basketball or football or even for a shortstop to ever pitch or

play the outfield. Writers, similarly, usually find a particular niche, but that doesn't mean growth can't take them to new heights and new directions. It only means a writer doesn't have to be all things . . . unless of course, he or she wants to be.

Exercises

1. Think of some of your friends as if you were an artist who draws caricatures. What are a few characteristics that would give someone who doesn't know your friends quick insights into who they are?

2. Turn to "A Boy of Unusual Vision," which is the "How the Pros Do It" example in chapter 2. Study the description in the first paragraph. The writer describes Calvin's eyes, description that is central to the story. She is a writer who uses description sparingly, and always with a point. Using the examples in this book, take some time to see how each writer uses description, then look for description in all the reading you do. Make notes on how the writers use description. What details do they mention? Is it description for description's sake or does it move the story along?

3. Read closely and then imitate the styles of some of your favorite fiction and nonfiction writers. Listen for their writing voices. Play with their rhythm and the way they pace themselves.

4. Forget about writing for a while. Think about all the things that make up your own life-style. How do you dress: conservatively, flamboyantly? Are you a risk-taker or do you play only when the odds are in your favor? What kinds of people do you like to be around? Are you loud or quiet? Make a long list and add explanations if possible of all the things that make you an individual with a personal style.

5. After doing exercise 4 above, do the same with a piece of writing by your favorite author or authors. Is the style conservative or flamboyant? How does the writer's voice sound? Can you hear it? How are the sentences structured: mostly long, short, or are they varied? How does he or she use description: sparingly or lavishly? Is there humor? Does the author make connections between his obser-

vations and the theme of the story? Just as you recognized a personal life-style, did you recognize a personal writing style for the author you chose? Is the writer loud, quiet? Is he a risk-taker or a conservative? Now do the same analysis of your own writing style.

6. When you read different writers, become aware of what makes each unique. Read several pieces by one writer and then several pieces by another. Try to identify their styles. See how they differ. Make notes on everything from difference in voice, to use of description, to use of dialogue, to humor, to apparent research, to rhythm, and even to sentence structure.

7. Write two first-person pieces. Write one in an armchair style with the facts you know, independent of any research. Remember to incorporate anecdotes, humor, description, all the elements of good story telling. Now do the same thing with another first-person piece. This time do research. Back up your assumptions with specific details. Remember, the more information you bring to a piece, the better it will be. Here's an example: Suppose you write about your first high school dance. In the first piece just use your memory. Then do research. Find your old high school yearbook. Call some friends and ask them what they remember about the dances and about you. Look at old magazines to see the clothing styles of the time, read newspapers to see what was happening in the world as you worried about the dance. Talk to a present-day student to find out how dances have changed over the years. Which story in the end do you feel is the stronger?

Further Reading

1. *The New Journalism* edited by Tom Wolfe (Harper & Row, 1973). An anthology of the wonderfully innovative pieces written in the late sixties and early seventies that helped change nonfiction writing in the second half of the 20th century. Includes an introduction by Tom Wolfe. Must reading to appreciate the possibilities in nonfiction writing.

2. *Pieces of the Frame* by John McPhee (Farrar, Straus & Giroux, 1975). An anthology of pieces written by perhaps America's best

nonfiction writer. Read this one or any of the more than 20 other books he has in print.

    3. *In Cold Blood* by Truman Capote (New American Library, 1967). A classic in nonfiction writing. Capote demonstrates how many of the techniques of fiction can be incorporated into nonfiction writing.

How the Pros Do It
Writing Sample Number 4

This small excerpt from *The Washington Post Magazine* shows what Walt Harrington wrote about earlier in the chapter. He appears in a story which is really not a first-person story—it's about George Bush when he was vice president. You see a reporter on assignment caught in give-and-take. You see he is not simply out there asking one prepared question after another. This is conversation. Confrontational for sure, but it goes far beyond a reporter just asking question after question without interacting with his subject. Even if you do not write about yourself, read this just to get a feel for how an interview can be done.

A Class Struggle

By Walt Harrington

As George Bush, his 40-year-old son George Jr. and I bob lazily on the Saco River, the vice president becomes suddenly reflective.

    "I think you think 'class' is more important than I do," he says.

    I suggest—I'm smiling when I say this—that people at the bottom of society often think social class is more important than do people at the top. But Bush will not be deterred. What did I mean when I said he was a product of America's upper class? Bush believes "class" is the snottiness and arrogance found in some rich people, those who think they are "better" than the less well-off. He says he has never felt that way. Exactly what does the word "class" mean to me?

    This is an uncomfortable turning of the reportorial ta-

The description in the first sentence is written with verbs, not adjectives. It makes writing come alive. The reporter is not asking questions, but he is definitely gathering good material for his profile.

The reporter is in the story, but it certainly isn't about him.

bles, and I am less than eloquent. But in fits and starts I say that "social class" is all about family connections and money and expectations and training, and what those can mean. I say the sons of fathers in high-level jobs end up in high-level jobs about half the time, while the sons of manual workers end up in high-level jobs about 20 percent of the time. I say that social class shapes everything from our self-esteem to our child-rearing to our sense of control over our lives. I say that education is the great American leveler—but that rich kids get more of it. And that families like the Bushes often send their kids to expensive private schools to ensure their leg up.

Reporter makes his statement and pulls it off, but it wouldn't take much to turn the focus away from the Bushes to the reporter. Use this style sparingly.

This sounds, well, un-American to George Jr., and he rages that it is crap from the '60s. Nobody thinks that way anymore! But his father cuts him off. "No, I want to understand what he's saying." He seems genuinely interested—and relieved that I don't plan to call him snotty. But the amazing thing is that Bush finds these ideas so novel. He seems baffled that I could see America in this way. People who work the hardest—even though some have a head start—will usually get ahead, he says. To see it otherwise is divisive.

I confess: I think a lot of Americans see it otherwise.

Excerpt from Walt Harrington's first-person profile of Vice President George Bush in The Washington Post Magazine, *Sept. 28, 1986.*

CHAPTER FIVE

Feature Section Specialties

J im Molnar, a travel editor at *The Seattle Times*, makes a distinction between travel writing and travel guide writing. The 1980s brought us the resurgence of travel writing, which at its best is feature writing that makes the leap to great literature. Just as in any other kind of writing, it demands hard work and research, plus an extra dose of integrity in a field where special interests are constantly trying to exchange freebies for favorable writing. Of course, the best guard against this is to reject the freebies and write it as you see it.

The Art of Travel Writing

Jim Molnar

Of all the romantic myths surrounding the role and work of the travel writer, the most mistaken is the one that supposes that she or he is somehow exempt from the responsibilities of other journalists and from the travails of other travelers.

While travel writing does allow — in fact, demand — greater flexibility in form and style than, say, conventional feature writing in most contemporary newspapers, it's bound by the same compulsions: accuracy and fairness, thoroughness of observation and research, and conciseness of expression.

And while travel writers with legitimate markets may find more doors open to them than average tourists — government bureaus and the tourism industry are only too willing to curry good press — the best writers find that only by traveling as their readers do, or would like to, can they develop the kinds of features that meet the highest standards of their craft: the kinds of features that sell.

Successful travel writers must realize that the avocation requires two basic skills, neither of which is easy to master and the effective combination of which is rare.

First, and truly foremost, they must know how to travel. That doesn't mean just going on vacation. It doesn't mean just finding a good hotel or restaurant in a foreign capital. It doesn't mean simply venturing off the beaten track any more than it means toeing the line that tourism promoters have drawn to standard and manufactured attractions. It doesn't mean insisting that the world meet one's expectations. It doesn't mean sifting, like some itinerant miller, the wheat of a trip from the chaff, then baking it into some idealized memory for a movable feast.

Traveling is a way of thinking and seeing, a way of relating honestly to the world and the people in it, a way of accepting the world on its own terms.

Second, obviously, travel writers must know how to write — not just gather information, not just observe, not just describe, and not just put together a lucid sentence.

Writing, travel writing in particular, is a way of evoking an experience in the world. It's a way of re-creating in literate and literary prose not a place, but a thoughtful and intimate appreciation of a place, and the physical, social, political and cultural forces that form it and distinguish it.

All good writing implies an intensely personal relationship with a reader, an acknowledgment at least of the writer's and reader's mutual humanity. A good travel narrative focuses that consanguinity on a shared desire to understand not just a particular destination, but our place in the world at large.

Any travel writing undertaken without those skills and that sense of responsibility, I think, is doomed to disappointment.

Freelance Opportunities

Certainly, making a living as a travel writer is easier when you can arrange and finance your trips from a desk at an established magazine or metropolitan newspaper. Especially now, as more publications ascribe to ethics policies that preclude features subsidized to any degree by a tourism bureau or the tourism industry, the freelancer faces an uphill journey.

But why should a travel writer, any more than any other professional in literature or journalism, expect an easy, uncomplicated or lucrative future? This is a tough way to make a living—a tough field to break into.

I was a writer long before I could afford to become a traveler. I struggled academically with poetry and prose, playwrighting and story telling, then taught literature and writing part-time. I stumbled accidentally into journalism as a way of financing the peanut butter and beans I needed to stave off starvation. After working at a series of small daily newspapers as a reporter covering education, politics, the arts and general features, I became a city editor and a writing coach. A couple of years on a metropolitan newspaper's copy desk put me in position to compete for a rare opening in a travel department with a staff of three.

Making proposals for perhaps a half-dozen major trips a year, I can expect assignments for two or three of from two to three weeks' duration each, based on the needs of my newspaper, schedules and budgets. Each trip yields from two to four lead articles accompanied by color photographs, plus any number of secondary features and columns. Turnaround time, from the date of my return until a story's publication, can range from a few days to several months.

In any given week at *The Seattle Times* travel desk, we receive more than 30 unsolicited manuscripts from freelance travel writers. Some are trying to make their living at the craft; most are casual, at best occasional, writers and photographers who have packaged the events of a vacation for sale. *The Times*, with its two travel sections a week, represents a standard market in metropolitan dailies of regional scope. We publish an average of three to six freelance features a month, including those by our own staff reporters from other news and features departments—about 3 percent of what we receive. The pay, based on onetime publication rights, is competitive: generally from $200 to $375, extra for photographs.

To understand what *The Times*—and most other publications—are looking for, it can be helpful to look at travel writing in an historical and literary context.

Historical Roots of Travel Writing

A hundred years ago, in the 19th and early 20th centuries, travel writing was one of the most respectable, distinctive and distinguished forms of popular literature. As both a journalistic and literary form, it reflected a new energy flowing through Western civilization. For the first time, traveling was the province of not only the upper classes and of explorers patronized by aristocrats and merchants and colonial powers, but of an increasingly affluent middle class with leisure time flowing from society's democratization and industrialization.

The most respected poets, novelists and essayists of the day were among its practitioners, and created what still rank as classics of the travel-writing genre: Lord Byron, Charles Dickens, Ralph Waldo Emerson, Robert Louis Stevenson, Henry James, D.H. Lawrence.

Like Tennyson, in the voice of Ulysses, these writers were possessed of a need to fling themselves and their readers into a wide world newly vulnerable to general inquiry and observation—"I cannot rest from travel: I will drink / Life to the lees: all times I have enjoyed life / Greatly . . . "

Like Mark Twain, the common people found themselves in the role of "Innocents Abroad." Both from their libraries and living rooms and in the embrace of tour groups devised by Thomas Cook and other entrepreneurs in the vanguard of mass tourism, they could experience a world that previously was a realm of fantasy. Honest shock and enthusiasm were common tones in the "literature of place," as in this passage narrating Twain's cruise into the Golden Horn and his first impressions of Constantinople:

> Ashore, it was—well, it was an eternal circus. People were thicker than bees, in those narrow streets, and the men were dressed in all the outlandish, idolatrous, extravagant, thunder-and-lightning costumes that a tailor with the delirium tremens and seven devils could conceive of. . . .
>
> The shops here are mere coops, mere boxes, bathrooms, closets— anything you please to call them—on the first floor. The Turks sit cross-legged in them, and work and trade and smoke long pipes, and smell like—like Turks. That covers the ground. Crowding the narrow streets in front of them are beggars, who beg forever, yet never collect anything; and wonderful cripples, distorted out of all semblance of

humanity, almost; vagabonds driving laden asses; porters carrying dry-goods boxes as large as cottages on their backs; pedlars of grapes, hot corn, pumpkin seeds, and a hundred other things, yelling like fiends; and sleeping happily, comfortably, serenely, among the hurrying feet, are the famed dogs of Constantinople; drifting noiselessly about are squads of Turkish women, draped from chin to feet in flowing robes, and with snowy veils bound about their heads, that disclose only the eyes and a vague, shadowy notion of their features. . . . A street in Constantinople is a picture which one ought to see once — not oftener.

In that so-called Golden Age, the Western travel writer's voice came to carry exotic sights and sounds and odors from the perspective of a culture settling into a world it had just about finished colonizing. The writer didn't simply observe and reflect, she or he tended to evaluate, compare and judge. The writer sometimes became a contentious and aggressive consumer of foreign places and cultures — someone at often uncomfortable odds with a new and very big world.

From the mid-1940s through the mid-1960s, mass tourism began to shrink the world. Guidebooks proliferated: Baedeker and Fielding, Fodor and Frommer. But these presented less travel writing than catalog journalism: lists of attractions, hotels and restaurants with a tad of history and a smattering of practical advice for tourists who were starting to leave the tour buses but still covering the same old ground.

As tools for tourists they had — and still have — their merits, but guidebooks never have been the medium for true travel writing. They simulate travel writing, as, says historian/essayist Paul Fussell, tourism simulates travel ("It is to travel as plastic is to wood."). Guidebook prose doesn't evoke a sense of place; it tends to subordinate the individual, both the traveler and the native of the host culture, and the ideal of personal experience to broad-brush, panoramic description; it tends to elevate the familiar, the conventional, the common experience.

As tourism became more subject to the exigencies of mass marketing, only a relative few practitioners of the travel-writing craft persisted, writers such as Hemingway, Capote, Kazantzakis, Lawrence Durrell, and Jan Morris — and they found only a limited outlet in a handful of magazines.

Whereas travel dispatches had been a staple feature of major newspapers before World War II, from the late 1950s through the early 1970s newspaper travel sections became extensions of advertising departments. The stories became largely promotional pieces wrapped around ads and often subsidized by airlines, hotel chains and tourist bureaus.

But all that has been changing. The successful travel writer is one who is responding to those changes, and in some senses leading them.

Surveys during the past several years have indicated a number of trends: Travel and tourism have become one of the largest, if not the largest, industry in the world—employing one in every 16 workers in the world and accounting for more than $3 trillion in revenues annually, according to the World Tourism Organization.

More people are traveling independently than ever before, choosing more adventurous itineraries to more remote and exotic destinations as Third World nations open their doors to visitors. Domestically, the affluence of middle-class professionals who compose the bulk of the traveling public, combined with their more stringent schedules, has created a trend toward more, albeit shorter, holidays. Americans are more often turning away from urban destinations toward beaches and less-developed areas, such as national parks and forests.

At the same time, more high-quality travel writing is being published now than perhaps ever before, both for tourists and armchair travelers. Travel books—novels and personal narratives—are a booming trend. And, with a raft of new travel-oriented magazines and the refocusing of many newspaper travel sections, travel writers are starting to find a more active marketplace. As author and travel writer J.D. Brown puts it: " . . . the '80s may well be remembered as both the Era of Travel and the Era of Literary Travel."

Travel Writing Guidelines

What does all this mean for the would-be travel writer? How can she or he catch a corner of the wave? To what are publishers, editors and readers responding?

Here are some guidelines:

First, remember that your writing must be very good. Standards are high these days, in part because there is so much writing to choose from.

Quintessential practitioners such as Jan Morris, Paul Theroux and the late Bruce Chatwin have gone to lengths to disassociate themselves from the term "travel writer," hoping to distance themselves from the standards and guidebook formulas of the 1950s and 1960s. They want to be known and judged simply as writers who employ the devices and conventions of the novelist and storyteller in the "literature of place."

A good travel story is just that: a story, with all the plot and tensions and sophistication that it implies. A story is, for all that, a simple thing. It generally is about a person reacting to circumstance, to a place, to other people. For the travel writer, that main character is often her- or himself. It is through the writer's emotional response to a place that the reader becomes involved, gains insight, and is able to savor a taste of a destination.

Travel writers who overreach, who attempt to define a place based on a few days or even weeks of observation and experience, tend to lose their own perspective—not to mention the reader—in a bog of generalizations. Just tell what happened, what you saw and felt. As in the Twain passage on Constantinople, that means using detail to evoke rather than simply describe: to show rather than tell. As any good writer knows, the successful travel writer learns that his most effective tool is the verb, not the adjective.

Take this passage from a piece on Ireland by Mike Nichols, humor columnist with the *Fort Worth Star-Telegram*:

> Geographically, Ireland is an island rumpled and ridged. It is an island of sharps and flats—the topography rises and falls, like the notes of an Irish jig. . . . You can drive north to south, tip to tip, in a day.
>
> But that would be living on American time. On Irish time, the same trip takes longer. So slow down. Match your metabolism to the pace of a gray old squire as he strolls along some village high road, walking cane in hand, glen-plaid cap on head. Match your heartbeat to the 4/4 time of an Irish ballad. . . .

Pack a poet's paraphernalia in your bags when you go. Take a trope or two for the road: Metaphor, simile, eponym, metonymy, even a judicious hyperbole now and then—they all have their place in this literary journalism. Let a single detail create an entire panorama.

Because a story without people in it usually isn't much of a story, the travel narrative that depends on descriptions of buildings and landscapes, city streets and bus routes, becomes plodding. Populate your stories with the people you meet along the way.

Often, the most successful travel feature is a simple account of a serendipitous encounter with a character you have met – a dialogue that encapsulates and illustrates your impressions of a place, evoking an emotion or spirit that lets the reader share your relationship with a land or culture.

Bob O'Sullivan, a highly successful travel writer frequently published in the *Los Angeles Times*, *The Seattle Times* and other newspapers, focuses his narratives on other tourists. The technique, applied sensitively, gently, emphatically, can allow readers to see themselves – their virtures and their foibles – in relation to places they travel.

Most of my trips for *The Times* have been to Europe. The stories I've been happiest with have centered on people: the peasants I stopped to talk with in a sugar-beet field in Romania, who shared their lunch with us under the chestnut trees that lined a dusty Moldavian road, who gave my young son a ride on the back of an ox; the Gypsy women in Sofia, Bulgaria, who, keening wildly, chased me several blocks through the marketplace for suggesting that I take their photograph; Shamus, the grizzled, pipe-chewing Irishman who explained that it could take as long as a day to contemplate the perfect stone to fit into the wall he was building along a County Mayo pasture; the Greek olive farmer on the slopes of Mount Parnassus who insisted on giving me a ride back to town on his tractor because he couldn't understand why anyone would choose to walk for recreation.

Finally, be aware that, especially now as tourism assumes a greater economic profile in the world, travel is surrounded with issues that reach beyond the sphere of the individual tourist. Tourism has profound impacts on the social, natural, cultural and economic environments of the places that embrace it. Deforestation, waste and pollution, energy depletion, exploitation and erosion of native traditions – they all are issues that the tourism industry and individual travelers are just beginning to be aware of and that the travel writer should not ignore.

A travel writer must pay close attention to the environment she or he is writing about. The days of composing idealistic travelogues that foster tourists' sense of isolation from the complexities of the often dark and desperate lives that swirl about them seem to be drawing to a close.

Readers can sense shallowness in a story, just as editors can sense a writer's ignorance and lack of perspective. I usually spend triple or quadruple the time researching the culture, history, politics, economy and environment of a destination that I spend on the trip itself.

A 1,500- to 2,000-word feature—the longest stories that will find a warm reception from most newspaper and magazine editors—should have a veritable library of research to support them and give them context.

In the end, travel is hard work. Travel writing, I think, is even harder work. And both, for our readers, touch the same chords.

As Paul Fussell says: Travel has a touch of the illicit to it; it "triggers the thrill of escape from the constrictions of the daily . . . from the traveler's domestic identity." But it is no less a humbling experience, a desire for growth and a pursuit of understanding: "It is as learners that explorers, tourists and genuine travelers . . . come together."

Jim Molnar has been an editor and writer with *The Seattle Times* travel department for more than six years. He's worked as a reporter, feature writer, copyeditor, news editor and writing coach in California and the Pacific Northwest for some 20 years. He has also taught writing, editing and the oral interpretation of literature part-time at several colleges and universities.

P | erhaps the biggest revolution in the United States during the last 30 years has been in what we eat. In the 1950s we were primarily a white bread, meat loaf nation with the occasional take-out container of chow mein. As we became more of a polyglot nation and a better traveled one, thoughtful food writing became a necessity for readers. How else would we know what was being served to us each day? We learned to eat with chopsticks and how to make our own pasta. At the same time we were all paying attention to our health. Again we turned to the food pages to find out what was best for us. During this time there emerged a host of food writing superstars and among them is Mimi Sheraton. Here, using her years of experience, she provides advice for the novices who wonder if food writing is right for them.

Eating My Words: What It Takes to Be a Good Food Writer

Mimi Sheraton

Now that eating is "in" and chefs so often achieve the status of superstars, food writing has become a glamorous profession. Barely a month goes by during which I do not receive two or three letters from young (and not so young) hopefuls each asking, "How can I learn about food?" It is a temptation to answer, "If you have to ask, you're never going to make it." But remembering what it felt like to be young and hopeful, I resist and instead write an expanded version of, "You have to know how to write well and you must know food."

In fact, the first answer would be more accurate, for I really believe that a passionate love of food is essential to success. The best practitioners in the field are those who ate first and wrote later, who followed a natural inclination to learn all about dishes and ingredients, who loved visiting food markets and buying cooking utensils and who found their way to the literature of food, all at considerable expense of time and money. Finally, such dedicated eaters came to their rewards: They were paid to do what they like to do best.

All would be to no avail, of course, if these blessedly obsessed buffs were not able to transmit their enthusiams and findings to readers. That is where writing well comes in, but that is the talent most easily understood by anyone who will be reading this, and so needs no elaboration.

Passion, then, is the first essential and to that add a lively curiosity that drives a reporter to eyes-on research. "How do they make smoked salmon anyway?" he or she might wonder, just enough to find out, thereby learning the different quality points. Originality and ideas are needed because believe it or not, with all of the food articles around, there are hundreds of ideas that have never been explored.

Add to the above generous handfuls of cynicism and skepticism, the twin allies of any good reporter, and the dish known as a food writer begins to jell. With luck there will be a healthy sprinkling of personal disinterest, prompting the writer to report on findings, letting the chips fall where they may. Too many food writers are corrupted not by money, but by the desire to be popular with each other, or with restaurant owners and shopkeepers and anyone else who can ease their paths with plenty of cushioned red carpet.

In fairness to writers, it should be said that too often their editors and publishers are susceptible to the same blandishments and so short-circuit or discourage copy that tells the whole, ungarnished truth. Which brings us to the subject of advertisers and their role in all of this, which should be no role at all. They should just pay the bills and go away quietly. Reviews and reports slanted for advertisers lose credibility, and it takes a few bad reviews to make the good ones believable.

In hiring young food writers, editors should restrict them to the stories they are equipped to cover. On-the-job training has no place in criticism, for example. Too much is at stake both for the food industry and for the readers. Few writers are interested in and capable of covering all aspects of the food scene. The nutrition-minded reporter has her place but it is rarely as a restaurant critic or as a judge of fancy foods. Criteria applied would not be fair or valid and many a restaurant owner would be given a bum rap. Unless the writer is interested in the subject, the article will not be convincing. Good writers write what they want to read but cannot find, not what they think their peers, their publishers or their public wants to see.

With it all, the successful food writer makes it seem like fun, always aware that this most human of subjects is part spiritual, part scientific, part physical, part psychological. Food is all things to all people and the food writer is its champion.

> Food has always been a hobby for Mimi Sheraton, who for seven years was a writer for the *New York Times*. She is now under contract to *Condé Nast Traveler*, where she travels around the world as the magazine's food editor. She also publishes *Mimi Sheraton's Taste*, a newsletter that primarily reviews New York restaurants. *Mimi Sheraton's Favorite New York Restaurants* is scheduled for publication by Prentice Hall Press in 1991. In spring, 1992, a similar guide to dining out in the United States will come out. Other books in print include *The German Cookbook* and a new edition of *From My Mother's Kitchen*.

I f I remember the statistics correctly, the average American watches some 27 hours of television a week. With cable and the reruns, we can see just about everything that ever appeared on this relatively new medium. So if you are a TV addict you may already be an expert of sorts and have as good a chance as anyone of breaking into the field of television criticism. The tack you want to take is up to you, but since we are all experts you had better be clever, wise, and write well.

On Being a TV Critic

John Voorhees

The secret of being a TV critic is that it's a position that's still in the process of being defined — and that's partly due to the nature of TV itself.

Whatever your interest is, chances are that interest is prominent on television in some form or another, be it sports, music, drama, news, personalities, history, humor, religion—you'll find 'em all on TV and in a great variety of formats, from the inspirational to the silly.

In some ways, writing about TV is like that group of blind men describing an elephant. And because of the all-encompassing nature of the medium, it pretty much allows the individual critic to define the job as he or she sees it.

Television may take a drubbing—like the weather, everyone complains about it—but nevertheless if you write about TV, you'll not want for readers. Everyone is interested in and aware of TV and while just as many may disagree with your opinion as will agree with you, they'll still be interested in what you have to say.

The best TV critic wants to do it all, even while recognizing that's impossible. In the earliest days, TV criticism was limited to writing about what people saw the previous night on a couple of networks. Today, TV includes not only the three commercial networks but public TV, cable TV, pay TV, public access TV, as well as videocassettes, and the emphasis has changed to previewing programs.

But because of the wealth of TV that exists, TV criticism can handle any number of approaches and I find, as I survey my colleagues, that the best TV criticism is related to the characteristics of the individual practicing it. If that individual is intelligent, perceptive, has curiosity, an active mind, and can write, it's likely his or her criticism will reflect those qualities—and be interesting and thoughtful to read.

Pick Your Own Approach

Some TV critics are more fascinated by the inner workings of the industry than that product it creates—the *People* magazine approach. Some like to ponder Whither Goest TV?, since, after all, it is one of the most pervasive and powerful mediums of communication yet devised.

Others, and I number myself among them, like to think of newspaper TV criticism as a useful service for the reader—and one, incidentally, unavailable elsewhere on a daily basis. All of us, I'm sure, try to include aspects I just mentioned, but I see TV as yet one more aspect of our culture clamoring for our time and thus I see my primary function as a surrogate viewer checking out what's happening across the board and offering recommendations, always qualified, of course, with one's own prejudices and interests.

TV criticism will undoubtedly reflect the publication itself. *USA Today*'s TV reviews are very much in the vein of that newspaper — brief, to the point, and without much chance of subtlety, either in writing or thought. The *New York Times*, on the other hand, has several critics — one concentrates on documentaries and news-oriented programming, while another reviewer concentrates solely on entertainment programs. Here there is space available — and a chance for the writer to ruminate on the topic at hand.

One of the very best TV writers is the *Washington Post*'s Tom Shales, who manages to be entertaining while also providing a good deal of information and a thoughtful examination, whatever the subject. But a newcomer would probably be best advised to concentrate on communicating information to the reader, letting style develop over time.

After you've been writing for a period, readers begin to know your weaknesses and strengths, your likes and dislikes, and behave accordingly. If you recommend something, readers who generally agree with you will try to see it; others, who know your tastes are dissimilar, will avoid it — and make a point of seeing something you have dismissed as trivial.

The key to TV program criticism, as I see it, is to try and discern how successfully any program — newscast, TV drama, comedy, sports, children's show — has achieved what it set out to do, and judge it accordingly.

Sure, sometimes it may be just another cop show or sitcom — but within each programming genre there are highs and lows, successes and failures. And the readers, in order to make up their minds whether to invest valuable time in watching it, need this kind of information. You need to ascertain what you think the producers were aiming for — and whether they succeeded or not.

Reaching Your Goals

So far we've been talking optimum conditions but if you begin to write in this area, you'll soon become aware of how seldom you feel you've reached your goal.

First of all, there's the simple problem of time. Forget 40 hours a week. If you're trying to keep track of what is happening in all areas of the medium, you're going to be spending a lot more time than that looking at cassettes of everything from children's cartoons to adult dramas for cable. If you don't *like* watching TV, this is not the career for you. And if you try to write about it without really looking at it, you can find yourself in trouble. We may be told people don't watch TV that closely, but make one mistake and someone will call you on it. Writing about that movie you didn't finish seeing is just asking for trouble.

The second major problem after time is space. If you like writing about TV and watch a lot of it, you'll never have as much space as you'd like.

Most newspapers allot a set amount of space to the subject, and it's up to the critic to decide how to use it. One of the biggest dilemmas is the choice between the long review or article and one containing a number of short pieces of information. I can't say that I've necessarily resolved this question. It can be very rewarding to write in depth about a certain topic but you're also left with the nagging feeling: What about the programs I didn't mention? If viewers miss them because you didn't write about them, even briefly, preferring to write at length about one, have you served the reader to the best of your ability? Who wins?

Writing TV criticism is one of the best ways to learn to write concisely. True, there are frustrating moments when you'd like to write just one more paragraph to call attention to some subtlety, some fascinating inside information you'd like to pass along. But there's also a satisfaction in re-reading a column in which you may have had to leave out certain details but which still communicates essential information that will help as wide a range of readers as possible. And as you agonize over what to leave out, you'll discover new ways, shorter ways, to deliver the information. A good sentence can sometimes be as on the money about what you want to say as a paragraph—and remember that readers are as pressed for time when reading a newspaper as they are for watching TV.

My response convinces me that readers appreciate concise information they can trust.

One of the best ways to get into writing about TV, if you are not already working for a newspaper, would be to attempt to make contact with a community or area weekly newspaper or even monthly magazine.

This in turn, would allow you to contact your local TV stations and make arrangements to view upcoming programs, either via cassette or at the station. All TV stations, network or independent, are eager for more publicity and they are likely to be sympathetic to your requests — especially if you can soon show them some examples of your work. You can also get a foot in the door by asking to write about their local programming. Each station does some local programming, in addition to the news, whether it be religious programs or children's programs. This kind of programming too often gets lost, when it comes to the major newspapers, and a station will probably take kindly to your interest along these lines.

Beyond Just TV Watching

Thus far we've been pretending the job consists mostly of viewing cassettes and writing about them. Wrong. Those are the things you sandwich in between other things, such as reading news reports about TV, dealing with mountains of publicity mail, fax reports and phone calls from producers, networks and agents. You'll be bombarded by calls wanting to know if you wouldn't love to interview almost anyone connected with a program. (I make it a rule never to talk with anyone unless I've been able to see the program prior to the interview.)

Then there's the public that calls to (a) chat, (b) complain, (c) ask questions, (d) accuse you of taking their favorite program off the air, (e) ask how that movie ended last night because they fell asleep before it was over, (f) tell you how stupid you are because you don't like their favorite series, possibly even accuse you of racism, and (g) occasionally even say they like your work and read you every day — even when they don't always agree with you.

The latter calls are the best, of course, and make it all worthwhile.

Readers are more prone to call than write — remember their time is precious, too — and more likely to write when unhappy than when they approve of what you're doing. How many of us write letters of commendation but are quick to fire off a note when annoyed or angry? I take the small amount of personal mail I receive as an indication most readers are reasonably happy with the quality of my work.

In addition to convincing your superiors that your approach to TV criticism is the best one—especially if a competing newspaper might take a different one—there's still one more problem: TV schedules. Every day you have dozens of chances to make mistakes, to write about a program and place it on the wrong day at the wrong time on the wrong network—or any combination of the three. It may not be your primary responsibility to worry about schedules but it's still a necessary chore. Nothing can make you look stupid faster than making mundane errors involving schedules and nothing angers a reader more quickly than to interest him in a program—and then give him the wrong information about when to view it.

After all, how are they going to believe you know what the program is about, or whether it is good or bad, if you can't even get the date, the time and the channel right?

That dad-blamed TV critic . . .

John Voorhees reviewed television full-time for *The Seattle Times* from 1971 until 1990. He started at the *Seattle Post-Intelligencer* in 1953 where he reviewed art, music, film, theater and TV.

I n music criticism there is no faking it. Either you know music or you don't. Just being a great writer is not enough. Besides, we know great writing is built on information, and if you are not informed about music you can't be a very good music critic. Of course, there are various levels of music criticism. A rock critic needs less training than someone reviewing classical music, and a local weekly will require less training than the *New York Times* does, but all writers should strive to know all they can about the subject matter they are covering. Daniel Cariaga is a classical music critic at the *Los Angeles Times*, but much of what he says can be transferred to all forms of music criticism.

Being a Music Critic

Daniel Cariaga

A lifetime of intelligent listening is the first and inescapable requirement for one who wants to be a music critic. Nothing less will do, and much more may be needed.

Being a music critic means being an interested and analytical listener, an observant member of the audience, a well-equipped writer, and an advocate for the musical consumer.

While wearing each of these hats simultaneously, one must also make sense of the world he covers; each review or article should reflect the reality of the year and place in which it is written.

Daily newspaper critics, like all working journalists, cover the news as it happens. This means the critic will attend concerts in the evenings, on weekends, and whenever they take place. He will be on call to conduct interviews when, and often where, the subject agrees to talk. He will also be expected to attend press conferences when they promise to offer breaking (as opposed to already leaked) news.

One prepares for the profession by studying music, listening to it for years, having broad musical interests and, ideally, if not always, being a member of one of the musical professions. As one grows in the job, he will acquire the skills of musicological research and interpersonal networking which will add to his effectiveness.

Have Varied Musical Experiences

Being a music critic is easy. Just get a job, then hold onto it.

You get a job by being qualified. Which means, if you are interested in classical music, you have experience in hearing, and writing about, opera, symphony, piano recitals, choral and vocal music, and the repertory of chamber music and instrumental literature.

There is no substitute for having known Beethoven's "Pathétique" Sonata (and Opus 7, or Opus 110) since the age of 13, or having heard "Aïda" (or "Bohème" or "Boris") regularly over a period of years. Or having hands-on experience of the chamber music repertory. This is knowledge which makes individuals civilized, and being civilized is an asset to a critic.

In addition, the music journalist should understand, by having observed, the workings of the music business and the day-to-day operations of symphonic organizations, professional presenters and academic institutions. What he does not already know or understand when he comes on the job, the conscientious critic should endeavor to learn or master. This means asking questions, keeping files, reading other periodicals systematically, and in general keeping abreast.

Ideally, the critic himself will have studied conducting, piano, voice, one or more instruments, composition, music theory and the history of the art. Such studies give you the background to observe knowledgeably the field you now cover.

Avoid Clichés

Your reviews should be descriptive, colorful, cogent and uncluttered by technical terms. An intelligent, music-oriented adult should be able to read and enjoy them without resorting to a dictionary.

Writing is easy: make a point and move on; keep it short; vary your vocabulary. Don't fall into ruts. Stay away from other people's clichés, and try to avoid inventing your own.

The verb "to be" is the bane of the critical profession; avoid it—nothing is as deadly as using the verb "was" time after time in describing an event. Use active verbs, find colorful alternatives, vary your sentence length. Short, declarative sentences are tonic, but they must be true.

Comparisons are the soul of reviews: "Krips' tempos emerged slower than Jorda's, but less articulate." "Rubenstein's approach to the ballade became muscular and gutsy, Brailowsky's more analytical."

The job of writing about music for a general audience demands an ability to describe performances and report events, a background of sufficient listening experiences to enable one to make refined and illuminating comparisons, an instinct for recognizing quality, and an ear and eye for detail. A sense of humor, always present, and judiciously applied, is a bonus for the ordinary critic, a necessity for the serious practitioner.

A critic must be incorruptible. His devotion to fair reporting must override all other considerations. There will be certain artists he cannot judge fairly because of friendship, bias, past association or present lust. He should decline to review those artists. And if he is true to himself and his standards, he will eventually command the respect of his readers.

A prize-winning critic, Daniel Cariaga began his musical life as an accompanist to singers and violinists, a pianist for dancers, and a pit conductor. He was for eight years the music and dance critic of the *Press-Telegram* in Long Beach, California. In 1972, he joined the music staff of the *Los Angeles Times*; over the years, he has interviewed for the *Times* numerous major figures in the field. He also serves as Southern California correspondent for *OPERA NEWS*. Since 1970, he and his wife, mezzo-soprano Marvellee Cariaga, have given more than 400 recitals in North America, and at sea.

T he arts and entertainment side of the features department at a newspaper is usually a little world unto itself. The larger the newspaper, the more focused and specialized the jobs become. The theater critic has one of those most specialized of jobs. It's not a place where a general assignment reporter can come in and take over. It requires an understanding and love of the theater. Magazines with theater critics present the same situation—the critics have to know theater and know it well. Once you start with that foundation you can begin to take Dan Sullivan's advice on how to break into the field and also how to discover if this is what you really want to do with your life.

How to Become a Theater Critic

Dan Sullivan

So you want to be a theater critic. Very well. Arise. You are now a theater critic. There is no accrediting committee. There is no qualifying examination. You are a theater critic if you can convince people that you are one.

This will involve getting your stuff printed. (We will get to the idealistic part of this essay in a minute.) You will probably not be able to get the editor of your local daily to print it because he has no evidence that you know the first thing about writing for a newspaper. Your PhD dissertation on "Doctor Faustus" will be of no help here. He wants to see clips of stories you have written.

If you don't have any clips, forget about working for a daily paper for the moment. Find the editor of a humbler publication—a community college paper, a weekly, a shopping mall handout. Tell him that you'd like to review plays for him and that you'll do it for nothing.

Get 50 reviews published and paste them into a scrapbook. Now you have clips. Go to see the first editor. Maybe he'll give you a stringing job. If not, tell him that you'll call him again in three months, and continue at your present post. But ask the editor for some sort of payment.

Well, how do you like it so far? Is it as much fun as you thought it would be, getting in to see all those shows for nothing? If the routine is getting burdensome after only 50 shows, then you don't want to be a theater critic. I have been attending shows for a living for more than 25 years and I still think it's fun. Some nights it's even fun to write about them.

It's work, as well. If only we could just say Yes or No to a show, and then go home! Unfortunately, we have to find reasons for our yeses and noes. This takes thought. Thought takes effort. Virgil Thomson, whose music criticism you should look up in the library, used to say that a review isn't an exam that a critic gives, but one that he takes.

And one that he takes in public. Let the critic attribute one of Lady Bracknell's lines to Miss Prism, and there will be a letter to the editor about it in the Sunday paper. (If you don't know who Lady Bracknell is, maybe you should think about reviewing TV.) As a critic you will also hear from people who were offended by something you wrote. Perhaps you'll hear from the leading lady's brother, a linebacker for the Minnesota Vikings.

The Bottom Line Is Truth

Should it bother you that your review upset somebody? Yes, a little. Critics who enjoy wounding artists are creeps. So examine your conscience. Did you accuse the actress in question of being a bad person? No. Did you say she was a bad actress? No. You said that she gave a bad performance last night, and here is why it was bad. In other words, you dealt with the work. In other words, you did your job.

What is the job? Theater people will argue that you and they are in the same business. You're both working towards "better theater" in the community. True. But they are in the business of putting on plays, while you are in the business of writing articles for a newspaper. Two different processes.

Your job isn't to promote theater. It is to say what happened at the theater last night. The reporter in you doesn't even care if the show was good or bad—either way, he's got a story to get out. Happily, the reporter in you is balanced by a theater lover who cares a lot whether the show was good or bad. But not to the extent that he will lie on its behalf. The critic's bottom line is the truth.

Whose truth? Why, the critic's truth. It won't be everyone's truth. Some nights it won't be anyone's truth but the critic's. But he is stuck with it. And if he sticks with it, and doesn't waffle, he and his readers will work out an understanding. I've had couples tell me that I'm an infallible guide to theater in Los Angeles: If I hate something, they'll love it. Fine, we're communicating.

But if I start to hedge, the line goes dead. Say your "noes" with respect, then—but say them. Not only does it keep you honest, it keeps the theater community honest. As Claudia Cassidy of the *Chicago Tribune* used to say: "The critic who puts up with the second-rate, will soon find himself presented with the third-rate."

Do Your Homework

Be careful to make your yeses and noes specific. Specifics are arrived at by asking oneself a series of questions. Was it useful to have Lady Bracknell played by a man? Was it a good idea to set the tea party scene by a Hollywood swimming pool? Why did you like Gwendolyn but not Cecily? The more times the critic has seen the play, the more informed his answers will be.

But he must never stop doing his homework. This poses a problem for the critic who also serves as his paper's theater editor. Too much time will go to office chores—making out schedules, arranging photo calls, proofreading copy, explaining to one's publisher that we can't cover his niece's high school show without covering them all— and not enough to preparing himself for the evening's exam. Yet ultimately that's what he's graded on.

Another pressure is that of the deadline. Whether your deadline is midnight or noon, you'll always wish that you had ten more minutes. Sometimes you'll hear yourself grunting at the typewriter as you try to nail down the particulars of a performance. At other times—when the show is either wonderful or wonderfully horrible— you'll write with ease. You will write in good moods and in bad moods, in sickness and in health, always trying to keep your eye on the show, not on your own private twitches, which will manifest themselves without help. Virgil Thomson again: "Keep your opinions in your back pocket. They'll come through anyway."

Criticism *is* personal, though. I'm sometimes asked if I ever do any "real writing." Reviewing is real writing. Compared with the fiction writer, the critic may be "hugging the shore," to use John Updike's phrase. But he does get into the boat and push off. His subject isn't just the play. It is himself at the play, and things happen to him there. Watching *Death of a Salesman* with Dustin Hoffman, I was so moved that I almost stopped taking notes. If you can relate to that, you'll probably make a very good critic.

> Dan Sullivan has been a theater critic at the *Los Angeles Times* for 20 years. Before that he was a theater critic at the *New York Times*, and reviewed theater and music for the *Minneapolis Star Tribune*. He is writing a biography of the playwright William Inge to be published by William Morrow, Inc.

I f you think you might want to be a film critic, it will be painful to read Stephen Hunter's piece on becoming a critic. He does a head count and finds that there simply are not that many film critics in this country. Should that discourage you? Yes, if you are not 100 percent certain this is what you want to be. But if you're 100 percent certain, then you will have no choice but to fight for one of those 650 slots. Once you have made that decision, you will find Hunter's advice very useful.

Becoming a Film Critic

Stephen Hunter

If they don't ask directly, they ask with their eyes or in the halting, shy, worshipful way they address you. And who can blame them? For years I myself wondered, and would have given anything for a succinct and practical answer.

The question is: How do you become a movie critic?

And yet now that I've been one for eight years, I still haven't got an answer, or at least a satisfactory one. I can tell them how *I* became a movie critic, which had to do with internal politics, a shift in management theory, some success that validated me outside the newspaper itself; but that's not it, not it at all. What they want to know, really, is how *they* can become movie critics.

Of course there is no typical way; a lot of it is the sheer physics of the right-place/right-time, which cannot be managed without inordinate amounts of luck; but a lot of it is desire, wanting it so bad you want no other thing.

I tell them this is foolish, although it's a sin I committed daily from the time I was 12 until the time I was 33 when someone who owned a big newspaper finally said, "Okay, you're a movie critic." I tell them there are reasonable jobs to want that can be gotten in journalism. Do you want to be in a Washington bureau and cover the fastest track of all, national politics? It can happen. Most dailies have bureaus; most bureaus have rotating staffs. This means openings come and go and enterprising reporters can get to Washington, sometime, if that's what they want. They can get overseas, if they work hard enough. They can cover whatsoever it is that tickles their brains or imaginations; they can have interesting, fruitful, passionate lives. They can count.

But can they be movie critics?

Probably not. There are about 1,300 dailies in this country; probably less than half of them have full-time movie guys, the rest filling out the page around the movie ads with wire service copy. So there are probably fewer than 650 of us. We do not want to give up these jobs, for reasons that are obvious — they are the best jobs in America, and only a fool would give up soft hours, a sniff of glory, and the subversive pleasure of turning down interviews with beautiful women. Women who in real life wouldn't spit upon you.

So this is how you get the job: Any way you can, that's all. Does a degree in theory from film school help, or an M.A. in Criticism from one of the well-known master's mills? How should I know? I have neither. So the interesting question isn't how you get the job, it's how you keep it. You work like hell, is one way, the best way. In my town, one man, if he hustles and doesn't treat himself too preciously, can pretty much cover the market and throw himself against the 250-odd feature and art films that hit the screens every year. Of course distinctions must be made. When I first got the job, in a blast of crazed missionary zeal, I saw and wrote everything. I do mean *everything*, and that was one of the big years of the teen death-o-rama movies, where men in hockey masks shish-kebabbed entire graduating classes and cheerleading squads. The first year I saw more than 300 movies; I must have seen a thousand people die, in revolting detail, learning secrets that only surgeons should know.

Finally, I said enough is enough. I was losing the capacity to discriminate and was dreaming about slicing up a few producers. I decided to skip a few of the more odious atrocities, such as *Dr. Butcher, M.D.* Nobody noticed, and that was years ago. If you won't tell them, I won't.

Recipes Ruin Writing

Still, seeing the movie is only the smallest part of it. The most important part of it is writing the review. It's really the only thing you do.

I have no recipe for writing a piece, and if I did, I'd advise you to tune me out. Recipes ruin writing for the same reason they help cooking: they make it turn out the same each time.

I can tell you that the spine of a piece of newspaper criticism must be a discrimination delivered as an argument, and that it must adhere more to the topic at hand than the mood in mind. People sense when critics become more interested in themselves than their movies and, rightly, they turn away.

The review begins with a judgment, sometimes rushed to, sometimes not discovered until the last paragraph. But a judgment there must be.

I make that judgment based on certain things: First, my own emotional reaction. I don't try to ignore my feelings and become some remorselessly mechanical creature, Robocritic. I try to put my politics and prejudices aside, and become a blank slate, and let the movie strictly happen. It doesn't work, of course; but the effort is important, because if you cease to make the effort you soon become a set of inevitable political twitches, tiresome and grating no matter how correct. Back to feelings: I try to cultivate and refine them, to ask myself why I feel what I do. But no movie exists in a vacuum; I try to put it in some larger context, relate it somehow to its genre and then to the culture that spawned it.

And, yes, of course, each movie is comprised of six elements, and each movie emphasizes one more than the other. It may be a movie of performance, where the actors pull you into the story by the neck; it may be a movie of effects, thrilling you with dark and troubling visions no man has ever seen before; it may be a movie of its auteur's voice, where you sense the director's artistic sensibility in every frame, like it or not; it may be a movie of photography, where the cinematographer is the principal creator, evoking an exquisitely lit patina of muted fuchsias and glistening magentas, so vivid the look is the movie; it may be a movie of pace, so seamlessly edited it whistles you along; or it may be a movie of ideas, written by someone who knows exactly what he means. You've got to know which of these is important enough to mark in 600 words; and which can be ignored.

Then, having worked that out, I labor to find a voice to express it. Perhaps this is the hardest trick of all: In some sense, the film critic is the newspaper's gigolo. He—among few others—is permitted, indeed encouraged, the indulgence of a personality. He is paid to charm, to beguile, to infuriate, to be the Robin Goodfellow of the dim gray pages of the grown-up newspaper.

So how do you "do" it? The answer is, you don't. It's not a thing of doing, it's a thing of being. You are it, or you're not. It helps if you've seen a million and a half movies, but you'll always bump into somebody who remembers the name of the seventh gunfighter in *The Magnificent Seven* when you can't; it helps if you've read a lot of film criticism, and mastered what we now think of as "the voice": ironic, sarcastic, allusive, articulate, vivid, passionate. It helps if you have some talent, and this sort of thing comes naturally to you, the words seem to bleed from your fingers. But if you don't, perhaps you can make up for it by working very hard, rewriting until you bleed, beating yourself in some way into a publishable critic. Some critics don't write well at all; but they know movies back and forth and their judgments are considered and provocative.

I think, really, it comes down to neither talent nor luck, but to a belief in the medium. No matter how many dozens of movies you've seen that month, or how many that day, you try to cling to an essential, childish part of you that was, many years ago, first enchanted by the power of the movies. You try to recall that icy, delicious shiver that overcame you alone in the safe dark when that white and piercing beam of light fired out of the darkness and smeared itself across the screen.

You've got to remember the part of you that always said, when the lights went down, "Hey, neat. A movie!" If you can't, you ought to get a real job.

Stephen Hunter is film critic of *The* (Baltimore) *Sun*, where he has also been a feature writer, the book review editor and a copy reader. A graduate of the Medill School of Journalism at Northwestern University, he is also the author of five novels, most recently *The Day Before Midnight*.

Y ou are not going to make a living from writing book reviews, but of all the ways of breaking into print this may be the easiest. And Elliot Krieger of the Providence *Journal-Bulletin* points out many of the non-monetary benefits. But can it really be an entrée into the writing field as Krieger contends? Well, read the piece by Maralyn Polak later in this chapter. The magazine editor at the *Philadelphia Inquirer* read her book reviews, contacted her, and for more than a decade and a half she has been writing a weekly interview for that same magazine.

Writing Freelance Book Reviews

Elliot Krieger

Don't stop to figure out how much money you can make by writing book reviews. You'd find the answer too discouraging.

Most newspapers pay from $25 to $50 for a book review. That's not too bad a pay rate if it takes you, say, two hours to write the review. But you also have to read the book, and sometimes that's the hard part. A $50 paycheck for reading and reviewing a 500-page novel doesn't work out to a particularly profitable use of your time.

But who's in this for the money, anyway? There are lots of other reasons why you might want to write book reviews.

The book review is the best way for a freelance writer to influence taste and opinion and to address the literary and intellectual community. Editors, publishers, agents and writers all read reviews — especially of their own books — avidly.

Also, the book review is the best way for a beginning freelance writer to get some clips. Most likely the book pages use more freelance writers than any other section of the newspaper. Newspapers with book sections are always hungry for reviews and on the lookout for new reviewers.

Writing book reviews keeps you sharp and fresh. You're really forced to think about what you're reading, to engage your mind in active debate against or discussion with the author and with a huge potential readership. And there's always the reviewer's special pleasure in being among the first to read a new book.

Getting Review Assignments

I was the books editor at the Providence *Journal-Bulletin* for four years. During that time I published reviews by more than 200 freelance writers. Many had never written for a newspaper before. I always welcomed hearing from freelance writers who wanted to review for us and I kept an active list, which I consulted regularly, of potential reviewers.

The best way to get on an editor's list of potential reviewers is to write to him or her. Phone calls and visits tend to be annoying interruptions in an editor's day, but a good query letter stating your interests and credentials is a perfectly sensible way to get the editor's attention.

You have a much better chance of getting a book review assignment if you're quite specific in your letter to the review editor. A would-be reviewer who says, "I read just about everything" is of no help at all to the book review editor. What kind of fiction do you read—mysteries? horror? highbrow? European? What's special about your background and education that might lead the reviewer to assign you a particular book? Did you live in Australia as a child? It's true that the editor may only rarely assign books on Australia for review, but it's also likely that there are relatively few people with that interest or expertise on his list.

Let's face it: everyone wants to review top quality fiction. And a surprisingly large number of people want to review poetry. (Everyone who reads poetry wants to review it, I suspect.) If you want to break into reviewing, you'll probably find poetry and literary fiction to be crowded fields; you'll also probably find that most newspapers have a columnist who regularly reviews the major genres: mysteries, science fiction, children's books.

But there are areas in which the review editor is always looking for reviewers. It's hard to get good reviewers on contemporary affairs. And it's especially hard to get people to review mainstream bestsellers. If these are your interests, you're a step ahead of the game.

On the other hand, it's inadvisable to request a particular book for review in your initial query letter. For the most part, by the time you've heard of a book, the review editor has already decided who, if anyone, is to review it.

You may want to review that new novel by John Updike or Anne Tyler. But I've got news for you—so does everyone else, and a review editor is unlikely to assign a plum to a reviewer he's never worked with. Yet if you ask to review a particularly obscure book, you'll probably raise the editor's suspicions about your motives. When I started in the job I was burned several times by people who asked for particular books to review; it turned out they were reviewing books by their friends or colleagues—a nice favor to the friend, but bad journalism and a sure way to scotch your reviewing career.

It's a great idea to enclose a résumé in your letter of inquiry to the review editor. Also enclose clips of your past stories, especially reviews if possible. If you've never published a review, don't let that stand in your way. I'd suggest writing a review of a recently published book and enclosing that with your inquiry letter — not in hopes of having that review published (although who knows?) but at least to show the editor the quality of your writing.

Writing the Review

Ah, the quality of your writing — there's the rub. A book review, like all newspaper writing, should be clear, concise and accurate. It should have an enticing lead paragraph. When scanning a review I would often apply this test: If the author could have written the lead paragraph without reading the book, it's not a good review.

The review should give the reader a sense of the flavor and style of the book, but it should not rely excessively on quotation. It should let the reader know what the book is about, but it should not devolve into plot summary or synopsis. It should place the book within a context, but the references — to other similar books, to other books by the same author, to other works in the same field — should not be obscure or pedantic.

That's admittedly a tall order, and not all reviews measure up on all scores. But clarity is the most important. If you can at least describe the book comprehensibly you have a shot at getting your review published.

Where to Get Started

Once you've drafted your query letter and written a sample review, what do you do? Send it to book review editors, of course. But to whom? Your best bet for starters is the major metropolitan newspaper in your area. It's true that the largest newspapers — the *New York Times*, the *Los Angeles Times*, the *Washington Post* — make no regional distinctions when assigning books for review. But most newspapers do prefer to assign reviews to writers living within their circulation area.

Many smaller papers do not run book reviews, or else they run only wire service reviews. Still, I think an enterprising reviewer might be able to break into print through one of these smaller papers — even if it means buying the books yourself and convincing an editor to institute a new feature. You'd be surprised how eager editors are for good copy and for reliable writers.

You can get a list of book review editors at daily newspapers from *Literary Market Place*, an annual reference available at larger libraries.

All this said, the fact remains that reviewing books is unlikely to become a lucrative sideline—which is a roundabout way of saying no one ever got rich from writing book reviews. The standard fee at the midsize metropolitan dailies (circulation from 200,000 to 500,000) is about $25 to $50 for a 750-word review. At larger dailies, perhaps you could get $100. Only the largest dailies, with circulations higher than 1 million, regularly pay more—and they're much more particular about assigning reviews.

Still, a good reviewer can expect to get regular assignments, and perhaps a boost in pay once your reliability is established. You can also expect to get—and should certainly request—more pay for reviewing a longer book. To be crude about it, an approximate rate of 10 cents a page ($75 for a 750-page book, for example) seems a fair minimum.

Remember that when you're assigned a review, the editor is usually buying only onetime rights (check to be sure); if so, you can try to sell that review to newspapers in other circulation areas. Many reviewers send copies of their reviews on spec to a large number of newspapers. If only one or two pick the review up, the reviewer has still come out ahead.

In addition, your first published review can be a calling card that will get you in the door elsewhere. You can begin to build a file that can get you more and better assignments—perhaps review assignments at larger newspapers, or feature assignments at a newspaper or magazine.

The best way to keep on top of events in the book review field and to get in touch with others who write and edit book reviews is through the national Book Critics Circle. The group publishes an annual membership directory that lists reviewers seeking assignments and editors seeking reviewers. For membership information, write to Dave Wood, *Minneapolis Star Tribune*, 425 Portland Ave., Minneapolis 55488.

Elliot Krieger was the books editor at the Providence *Journal-Bulletin* in Rhode Island for five years. He is now the editor of the newspaper's *Sunday Journal Magazine*.

S ince fashion writing in magazines and newspapers is often secondary to the photographs, it is an unusual field of expertise. Indeed, Ellen Kampinsky of *The Dallas Morning News* notes that, at times, fashion writing is simply reduced to cutlines running next to photographs. Sure, there are longer stories; however, often the fashion "writer" is a hands-on person who keeps in touch with the fashion community, searches and gathers the right clothes for the photo shoot, and may even have to dress the models for a well-styled photograph. Of course, at larger publications, fashion stylists are hired to pull the clothes and dress the models, but in entry positions the fashion writer often does it all. The freelance writer who wants to break into fashion writing may want to become a hands-on expert as well as learn all the other traditional writing and reporting skills.

Fashion Writing

Ellen Kampinsky

You could put the philosophy of fashion writing in a fortune cookie. Good fashion writing is good writing. Period.

But it's not that simple. For one thing, no one is really writing stories about clothes anymore. Page through the autumn issue of any major fashion magazine and you'll see what I mean.

In one 386-page issue of *Elle*, you'll find about 250 pages of advertising. Of the 130 or so pages of editorial copy left, there are five pages of stories profiling designers, two pages of writing about short hair, three pages extolling the merits of bathing, and two pages of reviews of fashion books. Everything else related to fashion is photos. And captions.

Captions are the essence of fashion writing.

They are condensed emotion, tiny poems, half-haiku. They deliver the message with a whiplash of wordplay. "These boots are made for stalking," notes *Elle*. "All's fringe on the western front."

The good caption is elegant in its inevitability. It does not repeat what's in the picture but adds an extra dimension to it. It produces in the reader a silent "ah" of satisfaction. Only *those* words could go with *that* photo.

Thus the first prerequisites of the would-be fashion writer are a good ear for language and the gift of synthesis. In fact, they are good requirements for any writer. After all, Dorothy Parker got her start writing captions for *Vogue*: "Brevity is the soul of lingerie."

Of course, there is more to fashion writing than captions. But even in newspapers, which traditionally place greater emphasis on words, the craft is turning into something of a headline service. In my own paper's weekly "Fashion! Dallas" section, stories on fashion trends have been getting shorter and shorter. A lead piece on the latest in sweaters might once have been a thousand words. Now it's down to as few as 200.

What's replaced the long-winded descriptions of garments is the brief, to-the-point overview. And lists. Five things you need to know about suede. Six top picks for your fall wardrobe. Be quick about it, and be clever.

Clever, yes. Clichéd, no. Unfortunately, fashion writing has been even more stereotyped than sports reporting. Generations of writers and editors have distorted the style of the late, great editor Diana Vreeland, who made *pronouncements*. One movie parodied her with the character of a fashion editor who ordered minions and readers to "think pink."

Vreeland gained legend status a half-century ago with her "Why Don't You" column in *Harper's Bazaar*: "Why don't you wash your blond child's hair in dead champagne, as they do in France." (Humorist S.J. Perelman countered that he'd let his blond child go to hell in her own way.).

At their worst, fashion writers overuse the imperative and hyperventilate all over the page. Throw away your animal prints! These are skirts to die for!

What arrogance. Nowhere else in journalism do we order readers about as if they were servants. The fashion writer's job is to inform, not badger.

A Letter to Mother

Finding the proper voice in which to tell a fashion story isn't always easy. My newspaper's current fashion writer joined us after working at a retail store. When she wrote her first piece for us, we bounced it back like a bad check. It read too much like an advertisement, something on the order of, "You'll love this season's new swimsuits."

Frustrated, the writer called her friend and predecessor in the job. The friend's advice was good: Write the story as if you were writing to your mother. People talking to their mothers usually don't use the second person, they don't throw around a lot of French words, and they don't sound like commercials. They use simple, descriptive language.

Besides being able to write, the fashion writer must be able to see. He or she must be able to vacuum up and process everything that comes into view, to recognize style not just on the runway but in the streets, not just in the cut of a dress but in the precise placement of a plastic hairclip or the lacing of a sneaker.

The good fashion writer is like a character in one of Nabokov's stories, "a giant eyeball rolling in the world's socket." Everything is useful. Billboards and MTV and Janson's *History of World Art*. The dedicated fashion writer will go into debt subscribing to foreign magazines.

Beyond Just Clothes

The fashion writer should love fashion, but not be obsessed with it. It is important to have a perspective, to realize there is much more to life than just clothes. Good things don't just come in $5,000 packages with a designer's tag on them. It helps to have a sense of humor.

Where do we find such fashion writers, those with perfect pitch and unerring eye? Sometimes, but not necessarily, at journalism schools. At my paper we've hired former ad copywriters, as well as ex-cop reporters and former city editors.

Such latitude is possible because fashion journalism extends beyond the coverage of clothing. In fact, while the amount of copy written about clothes is dwindling, fashion coverage is expanding into areas that traditional journalism explores.

First, and always, there is the news. In fashion, the news is made in Milan, Paris and New York. Twice a year, designers show their new collections six months ahead of when they will appear in the stores. When it's spring in Italy, it's autumn on the runways.

Covering the collections is a rite of passage for any fashion writer. It requires the stamina of a marathoner and the strength of a pack mule. The shows attract thousands of apparel buyers and manufacturers and wholesalers and media from around the world. They descend on the city and gather in front of a tent or showroom for hours in a life-threatening crush. Then they wait inside the tent for another hour or two for the show to begin.

There is a blast of music and a swirl of color as scores of designs parade before eyes heavy with jet lag. Afterward the audience waits in another mass to emerge from the tent. They do this six or eight times a day. It is all very glamorous. In retrospect.

Seeing the Trends Firsthand

Writers working for major newspapers file daily stories from the shows. While it is important to get this news to the general public, it is only half the reason to go to Europe or New York. The real value is that the writer gets to see firsthand what the trends are, both in the tents and on the streets. Months later, when the clothes begin arriving in Des Moines or Dallas and it's time to run stories about what's new and available, the writer will be able to make intelligent, informed decisions.

Not all the news is made at the collections. Fashion is a big industry. Most media cover the news of sales and mergers and deals and acquisitions on their business pages. But the good fashion writer must know what's going on in the trade, even if it serves only as background. The best fashion writers will cover the business angle as well as the designs.

The other main area of fashion coverage is features. One of the most heartening developments in recent years has been the willingness of fashion publications to tackle consumer issues.

Readers benefit from stories that tell them what anti-aging creams will and won't do (mostly won't), explorations of why clothes cost so much, and comparisons of designer dresses and half-price knock-offs.

To cover news and features and investigative stories properly demands that fashion writing be held to the same standards as the rest of journalism. This means fairness and balance, good research and proper sourcing.

After all the hymns to creativity and integrity have been sung, the main thing to remember is, it's only fashion. And fashion should be fun. Once it stops being fun for the writer, it stops being fun for the reader. And when that happens, it's time to quit.

Ellen Kampinsky is assistant managing editor of *The Dallas Morning News*. She oversees all of the newspaper's feature sections. In 1978 she started the *News'* weekly "Fashion!Dallas" section, which has been called the most widely copied newspaper section in the country. It is the nation's longest-running free-standing newspaper fashion section.

Lighten Up! Get Some Humor Into Your Writing

Leonard Witt

I don't think you can teach someone how to write humorously. It comes naturally. I know the best of the humorists are funny in person as well as on paper. I have heard Art Buchwald, Dave Barry, Russell Baker, and Calvin Trillin speak in person, and they make audiences laugh.

Now this does not mean you can't put levity into your writing. You certainly can, but if it doesn't come naturally, you will not be able to do it on a regular basis as the humor columnists do.

The nonfiction writer will see the humorous situation and go for that. That doesn't mean he will make fun of people, but he can write lines such as the one Sam Hodges of *The Orlando Sentinel* did about a bird watching expert: " 'You'll see birders in action!' promised . . . a Chattanooga nurse anesthetist, who is surprisingly lively for someone who puts people to sleep for a living."

Or let's take another example from *The Orlando Sentinel*, where writers have been given latitude to have some fun. In this story about ugly Muscovy ducks, Michael McLeod begins his piece like this:

Maybe the Muscovy duck was on a peaceful reconnaissance mission. Or maybe it had a kamikaze attack in mind from the beginning.

But something made the Muscovy swoop out of the sky and zero in on the wavering little object in the water below.

What seemed like a perfectly legitimate target to the Muscovy duck was actually the sun-dappled, bobbing head of a little girl playing in the small neighborhood lake, unaware that 15 pounds of poultry was bearing down on her from four o'clock high.

Having a duck land on your head can be something of a shock. At touchdown, the little girl screamed, floundered and windmilled towards land.

The Muscovy flapped towards shore behind her, where ground

forces awaited it. Someone who had just seen a duck try to use her granddaughter as an aircraft carrier mounted a simple but effective counterattack: She grabbed the duck and tried to wring its neck.

Then the grandmother, a quiet, respectable, mid-50ish woman, did something ungrandmotherly. In the sober officialese of the police report, she "picked said duck up by the neck and swung said duck into a nearby tree."

Said duck somehow survived and wisely retreated into the pond. The grandmother jumped into the water and splashed after it, but the duck eluded her.

Call it a tie. Call it an air assault repelled by an amphibious counterattack. Call it just another webbed footnote in the history of the Muscovy Duck War.

Lines like those above won't make your reader fall off the chair in laughter, but they certainly put levity into the story and set a light, fun tone.

If the story line is appropriate, work for the humorous quote, the humorous observation or the humorous twist. Editors at magazines and at newspaper feature sections around the country are telling their writers to lighten up. Newspapers, especially, are too serious.

T he story I like best about Denise Grady isn't in her essay. Several years ago, she and I were graduate students at the University of New Hampshire studying nonfiction writing. She had read in passing that Time, Inc., was planning a new magazine called *Discover*. In the article the potential editor was named. Denise wrote to him and said if the magazine was ever started she would love a job. Months later it was indeed started. The editor called her and she was hired as an original staff member and worked there during the magazine's early years. I like that story because it shows a little moxie coupled with talent can go a long way to gaining success. Now on to morbidity and mortality.

Hooked on Morbidity and Mortality

Denise Grady

Listen to this, I tell my husband. We have just had dinner, and he is trying to read the newspaper or do some work, and I see him cringe when he looks up and notes what I am reading—the *Morbidity and Mortality Weekly Report* from the Center's for Disease Control in Atlanta—but I cannot seem to help myself. This week, a fourteen-month-old baby in Missouri has a fever and diarrhea, and the lab tests turn up a weird tropical bacterium that's hardly ever found in the U.S. (except once in a while in people who eat raw oysters). But the baby hasn't been anywhere, except to day care and her babysitter. (And who would give a baby raw oysters? What baby would eat them?)

Eventually, the state health department finds out that the babysitter keeps piranhas in an aquarium, and the aquarium is also full of the same kind of bacteria that infected the baby. And, well, yes, the babysitter admits, it is possible that she might have given the baby a bath immediately after dumping the aquarium water into the bathtub. The baby is treated and cured, the babysitter is told to clean her bathtub with bleach every time she empties the fishtank there, and, in the meantime, the health department tests 18 aquariums from around the state, and finds the nasty bacteria in 22 percent of them.

My husband finds all this pretty disgusting. I am enthralled. How exactly did the health department find its way to the fishtank? Didn't the bacteria make the piranhas sick? How did the investigators get the sitter to admit that she "might have" bathed the kid right after cleaning out the tank? (I imagine her sweating it out under a spotlight, during interrogation by a bunch of nerdy-looking guys in white coats.) God, I love this stuff, I say to my husband. He replies (good-naturedly, I think) that I have a sick mind.

I don't know if you need my particular kind of sick mind to write about medicine and science, but it certainly doesn't hurt. I'm hooked on *Morbidity and Mortality*. It covers everything from the flu to cholera, toxic shock, AIDS, syphilis, salmonella, dengue, rabies, and people falling into holes on the job. I read the case histories in medical journals, hoping to guess the diagnoses (I'm usually wrong), and the first stories I generally turn to in newspapers and magazines are the ones about health. I still remember the details of a *New Yorker* article by Berton Roueche, which I must have read at least 15 years ago, about a man who turned orange from eating too many carrots. I get huffy sometimes and try to convince myself that I am a Writer, as opposed to a medicine- or health- or science-writer, but the fact is that nine-tenths of what I write concerns medicine.

I find medicine endlessly interesting. I have always been curious about biology and physiology, but what really sustains me is that medicine is the one branch of science that touches everyone's life: At one time or another, we are all patients. Medicine has people, and real stories with beginnings and endings. It has mystery, drama, suspense, life, death, birth, heroes, villains, tragedy, triumph, right and wrong: all the corny stuff that everybody likes to read about, even if we're loath to admit it. Medicine stories even have the potential to do some good; how often in life are we afforded the privilege of helping someone else?

If I seem to be dwelling on how wonderful medical writing is, it's because I want to emphasize that to be any good at it, you've got to like it. Of course, that's true for all types of journalism, but it's surprising how often people will ask science writers how to take dry, boring material from journals and make it interesting to the general public. The best answer I can think of is, if you find it boring, don't write about it. Bored writers produce boring stories. Granted, some stories are more interesting than others, and we who write for a living don't always have the luxury of picking our subjects. I have written a few clunkers. So I don't mean to sound flippant. But I still think it's possible to find a different, interesting angle on most stories, even those that have already had a lot of play in the media.

For instance, it has been widely observed over the past few years that doctors are delivering far too many babies by Cesarean section, and that cesarean rates can and should be reduced. I have seen article after article about it. I have just finished writing a magazine piece that includes several interviews with women who want no part of the movement to protect them from unnecessary cesareans: They insisted on cesareans even though their doctors encouraged them to try giving birth naturally. I got the idea for that piece from my own experiences with childbirth, as well as those of many friends and acquaintances. In another article, I examined the public outcry over supposed health risks from the "tropical" palm and coconut oils used in so many processed foods — and found out some disturbing things about the domestic oils that will be used to replace the tropical ones.

Just today, I saw a newspaper story that begged for better reporting: Medical researchers have found that when people switch from regular to decaffeinated coffee, their blood cholesterol goes up, increasing their chances of having a heart attack. The scientists think the effect may be related to the different beans used for regular coffee vs. decaf. The news story left so many questions unanswered! Could chemical residues from the decaffeination process have been the culprit? Did the groups really drink the same amounts of coffee? Did they lighten and sweeten it the same way? The type of bean used for decaf is also used for instant coffee; do people who drink instant have higher cholesterol, too?

I cannot overstate the importance of trusting your instincts and your intellect in this type of writing. Ask the questions that come to your mind, no matter how weird they seem. Take nothing for granted. And don't repress or disregard your own opinions and impressions about your subject. People who read features are looking for more than just the facts: they'll respond to the writer's sensibilities. Whether they agree or disagree, love you or despise you, they're more likely to finish your story if it takes a stand.

Readers Want Information

One of the worst pitfalls in this field is getting jaded and failing to see a good story because you've written about the subject before. People will always be desperate for information about heart disease, cancer, obesity, arthritis, backaches; there's so much research going on in these fields that there's often something new to say, and you might even have a chance to do a little good. It doesn't matter what you've written before; most people haven't read it anyway, and those who have probably forgot about it. The few who remember it are probably so interested in the subject that they'll want to read about it again. And there will always be people who've suddenly developed a burning interest in your subject because it has suddenly come to bear directly on them or their families.

I once worked in the science section of a general interest magazine, with two reporters who knew so much medicine that I was actually scared of them. You couldn't propose a story that one of them hadn't already done. Frequently, they would scan the week's medical journals and scornfully toss them aside, saying there was nothing worth covering. But I soon came to realize that I could pick up the same journals and find two or three articles that I thought deserved a story; most of the time, a day or two later, the wire services and daily papers would cover the same subjects I had picked. I'm not trying to say I'm a genius. I just have a certain type of news judgment that comes from identifying very closely with my audience: We happen to be interested in the same things. I am the kind of person who reads the kind of stuff that I write.

A number of years ago I covered a conference about cancer at which a doctor described research showing that chemotherapy worked differently and caused different degrees of side effects, depending on what time of day it was given. This doctor figured that the variation had to do with the body's own circadian rhythms — daily fluctuations in hormone levels, metabolism, cell division and so on — and that these daily changes might alter the effectiveness of all sorts of drugs.

This was news to me. I found it fascinating. I love stories in which science confirms ideas that appeal to common sense and intuition and logic.

Two other reporters — both at least 15 years older and more experienced than I — tried to discourage me from doing the story. One of them was from the same city as the university where this doctor's research group worked. The other reporter's attitude was, basically, hey, kid, you don't know it, but this guy gets up every year at this meeting and says the same thing, we're sick of him already; it's an old story, don't give him any more publicity.

I think they were, in part at least, trying to help me avoid being taken in. They did make me feel naive. But I still liked the story. As it turned out, my editors at *Discover* loved it. None of us wanted to make that much of it; we ran it as an item of 40 lines or so, in a department called "In the News." The headline was "Fascinating Rhythms." *Reader's Digest* picked it up right away, and ran it in their "News from the World of Medicine" department. It may still be that the other reporters were right about this doctor talking up the same study over and over again, but I still think their news judgment was off: people wanted to read that story.

I cannot resist concluding this piece with a list of miscellaneous advice for people who want to write about medicine: Beware of plastic surgeons and diet doctors with their own public relations people. Remember that your readers are not planning to splice genes in their kitchens, so you can spare them the "methods" sections of technical papers, which even I find boring, although you should read them yourself to make sure nobody has tried to pull a fast one. (If, for some reason, you must include an explanation about teeny little enzymatic scissors snipping up bits of DNA, at least pull it out into a box so that it doesn't mess up your story.) Check your facts thoroughly on the telephone, but don't let your sources pressure you into letting them "review the manuscript for accuracy." Even if you believe in peer review, you're a reporter and they're scientists — not your peers. Don't waste your space (and you reader's time) by naming every last test tube washer on the research team, or every agency that chipped in for the research. Even though you want to keep your sources happy, your first obligation is to your readers, who don't care where the money came from. Avoid, if possible, the kind of piece that pits six experts on one side of an issue against six experts on the other side, without any resolution; articles that take a stand are more satisfying. Finally, in moments of righteous indignation, remember that even bad publicity is better than none at all: I once wrote what I thought was a scathing denunciation of a quack arthritis remedy, only to have readers call and ask me where they could buy it.

> Denise Grady spent five years as a staff writer at *Discover*. She has also been an editor at *The Sciences* magazine, the *New England Journal of Medicine* and other scientific publications. Her work has appeared in *American Health, Time, Reader's Digest, Self* and other magazines. She has won several awards for science writing.

E ach week Maralyn Lois Polak interviews a different celebrity for the *Philadelphia Inquirer*'s Sunday magazine. That's a wonderful assignment for a freelancer. So she must be an outgoing person who has a way with celebrities, right? Not quite. Read on, and remember that the way people write often has nothing to do with the way they act. In fact, writing allows those of us who are not perfect to polish and polish until we indeed sound as if we are.

The Celebrity Interview

Maralyn Lois Polak

I can't talk. That's why I write. I stutter, I stammer, I flush, I blush, I falter, I sweat. I'm desperately petrified of audiences. When I started doing interviews, I was shy — a real wallflower-type who couldn't even think of what to say to strangers at parties.

Paradoxically, I have come to specialize in interviewing mostly famous people, like Ralph Nader and Jimmy Stewart and Oprah Winfrey and Brooke Shields and the late Andy Warhol. That happened accidentally, when an editor of the *Philadelphia Inquirer*'s Sunday magazine invited me to write for him in 1974, after he noticed some zany book reviews of mine. I did not begin as an interview specialist, but developed an expertise as I progressed. More than 15 years later, one interview each week, 52 interviews a year, I'm still learning.

Interviewing looks easy, right? Two people talking? Hah! No matter how often I do it, writing interviews is always hard work for me. But the actual process is enjoyable. First I research the subject's background. I go to the library. I read newspaper clippings. I check the computer files. If they've written a book, I make sure I read it so I can look them straight in the eye. Then I think of my questions and list them on yellow legal paper. Then we're ready for the interview itself, which I record on tape.

We usually talk for about 90 minutes. Then the tape's transcribed — a horribly boring, tedious and time-consuming process. Why do I tape instead of taking notes? Accuracy and verité. I want every word, every gasp. Then I pore over the transcript and search for a theme I can explore in 1,500 words.

Interviewing celebrities has ameliorated my shyness somewhat. As long as I have my list of interview questions on a sheet of yellow legal paper, as long as I've done my research, I'm safe. That's my script. I walk in, and drop my notebook. I'm a klutz, my cord is tangled. They see I'm no threat. My clumsiness makes them feel superior. This puts them at ease. They open up. This usually works with even the most reluctant folks. They trust me. I transform my vices into virtues. And, usually, then, we have a *conversation*, not an inquisition. Try forgetting the intimacy is simulated.

Making Discoveries

I like doing interviews because I'm interested in psychology, human development and character formation — why people are the way they are, how they became that way. I like reading, thinking, reasoning, and making connections between ideas. I love making discoveries about a person. That's my personality — and my secret for keeping fresh despite doing the same thing, week after week, for so many years. Each person I interview represents a different puzzle to be solved to my satisfaction — and hopefully, to readers'.

Even if you're a student, an aspiring feature writer, or a new freelancer, it should be possible to break into celebrity interviewing. Remember, almost everyone you read about (or write about) is selling something, or has something to sell. That's when they're ripe to be approached for an interview. Don't assume that because you write for the college paper or a small-town daily, you won't ever get anyone famous to say yes to an interview.

Check your region's listings. Who's coming to town to give a speech? Anyone famous? Who's making a special appearance at a department store in a shopping mall? Any authors on autograph tours? Any actors doing a play? What music group's performing nearby? Who's promoting what on local radio or TV talk shows? Call the stations' managers or the concert hall promoters. Ask for the shows' publicists. Have them send you all the background information they have and get more phone numbers from them. Then call the star's agent or manager or public relations person and try to set up an appointment. It helps if you have an approved assignment from your publication, and can give a brief summary of what size and type of audience your article will reach. You might have to show them some clips of other pieces you've done. You have to start somewhere.

Framing Questions

If you're not sure what to ask your celebrity, you might begin collecting good general questions you notice in other articles. Often, long questions get short answers, and short questions get long answers. Be direct, and thorough. Some journalists ask the questions rephrased several different ways. What you ask may be less important than how alert you are, how acute you are, how quickly you respond to an opening, how mentally sharp you are in this tennis game of wits that *you* are conducting. It's your interview. You're in charge, no matter how famous your interviewee is.

Courtesy is always a must. Confidence and charm are also helpful. Think of it as a highly compressed "date." Make them like you.

Be calm. If you're a fan, leave your swoons at the door. You're working. Don't be intimidated. You're just two people talking at a table. If you're nervous, don't have a drink to relax—you'll probably ramble on and forget what points you're interested in exploring.

Begin the interview with a compliment or positive remark—but *be sincere*. Insincerity has a way of boomeranging back in your face.

If your subject launches into a filibuster, politely but firmly excuse yourself and interrupt, moving on to what else you wish to cover.

Memorable Interviews

Every interview is a challenge. In this business, you learn you can't really have heroes. Dick Cavett, for instance. He was sitting eating lox and bagel and cream cheese, with a snaggle of smoked salmon hanging from his incisor, and suddenly he starts saying, hey, kid, why don't you get your boss to buy a better tape recorder? He used humor as a weapon to deflect intimacy, and I liked him a lot better before we ever met.

My favorite interview subject is always the person I've just talked to. Memorable interview? John Cardinal Krol, a formidable Catholic leader in the city of Philadelphia, who explained that his badly scarred knuckles originated in a high school job he had at a butcher shop. "You can't get good soupbones any more," he lamented. I confided to him that as a teenager I wanted to be the first Jewish nun. "Come to us now," he urged, his eyes twinkling. "You're ripe."

Portrait painter Alice Neel, who compared herself to Gogol by echoing his "I am a collector of souls," was wonderful. She confessed, "My dear, all my men philandered. That just gave me more time to paint." Commenting on her unhappy Philadelphia suburban childhood, she recalled, "I was so bored I would sit on the front porch and will my blood to stop flowing."

I learned to expect interview moments that catch me by surprise, but enrich the story. Singer Kate Smith had a huge boil on her cheek, and during our chat, the scab fell to her plush carpet as we stood admiring her magnificent collection of Hummel figurines. And once a local TV weatherman dropped to his knees and begged, "Don't print this interview; marry me, instead."

Artist Andy Warhol was one of my most unusual interviews. I was on guard in case he had sent out an Andy Warhol look-alike to do the interview for him. I think the one I met was the real one. I asked him what he thought about sex. "I'd rather sweep up," he revealed.

Buckminster Fuller was a short fireplug of a man who rambled perilously. He listened to himself so hard he seemed deaf. I felt I was in the presence of God—possibly because he thought so, too.

Some interviewers, like the indomitable Italian journalist Oriana Fallaci, pride themselves on being aggressive adversaries who seek to intimidate their subjects into deep revelations. Fallaci may come on strong. But that's dangerous. My theory is if people get mad at you, they tend to throw you out, or leave, and then you don't get your interview. Save the tough, prickly, controversial questions for the end.

Be a *listener*. If I have to, I'll come on like an awed little girl. Fallaci uses being a woman differently. She wants the men she interviews to feel she is as powerful in her way as they are in theirs. They often rise to that challenge and reveal more of themselves than they might to a male interviewer. Can you imagine Henry Kissinger boasting to, say, David Letterman or Pat Sajak that he once wanted to ride off into the sunset as a cowboy?

I'd like to think that the interviews I do are unconventional. The structure is not standard alternating paragraphs of quotes and summary in chronological order. I do not go in for celebrity worship. I do not fawn or glorify or promote. I do not seek to regurgitate biographical details or reprint mundane facts. What finally concerns me is gesture, nuance, epiphany — the expression of personality, the essence of character. What intrigues me is the ineffable made real.

My technique seems to be the absence of technique. Alternating between richly detailed narrative and occasionally inspired banter, I seek to achieve a level of revelatory discourse rare in fiction, let alone journalism. My sly, droll questions can range from humorous prods to impertinent goads. Frequently, through my subjects, I meditate on the fleeting significance of fame.

Sometimes, though, I wouldn't mind a bit of celebrity reticence. From the lead of my Oprah Winfrey interview: "Little or nothing is sacred, secret or left to the imagination with TV talker Oprah Winfrey, who seems compelled to reveal, confess, admit, expose or share every last flaw, thought, fault, crack, fissure, fact, feeling, detail and speck of her personal and professional self . . ." The last line in the piece indicated I had finally become drenched and oversaturated by her confessional zeal. "Thank you, Oprah," I wrote. "Now, please, hush up."

Granted, interviewing can be like getting paid to be a voyeur. People actually tell me their secrets! Journalism aspires to extract and reveal these secret parts of people. And yet, I deeply hope there's a shrine hidden deep in the heart of each of us that no interviewer could penetrate or plunder or publicize — a shrine, however, where a poet might kneel in ecstasy.

Maralyn Lois Polak — poet, journalist, editor, teacher, lecturer, radio personality — has, since 1974, written a weekly celebrity interview column for the *Philadelphia Inquirer* magazine, where she is contributing editor. Her work has been nationally syndicated by Knight-Ridder and also appeared in such publications as *Mirabella*, Andy Warhol's *Interview* and *West*. Her book of author interviews is *The Writer as Celebrity* (Evans).

End Words
Afterthoughts: More Points to Remember

1. If you want to be a critic, you have to be a student of your discipline. You have to learn all you can because criticism, like any other kind of writing, is based on knowledge, and requires converting that knowledge into information for your readers.

2. Big newspapers and magazines have only a few full-time staff jobs for critics and columnists, and the chance of landing one is remote. On the other hand, freelancers who cultivate an expertise have many opportunities open to them, especially on a regional level. Even in small metropolitan areas there are regional magazines, alternative newspapers, shoppers and big dailies. All run a host of specialized columns, and finding the right people to write them is not easy. If you are good, you will get assignments.

3. Often specialists aren't writers, and writers aren't specialists. Freelancers who mesh writing talents with expertise in theater, finance, food, travel, fashion, home decorating, health, science, media, film, arts or literature have a real chance of placing stories regularly or even gaining contributing editorship recognition on the alternative or regional magazine's masthead.

4. Even a tiny publication will help you gain access to the stars and experts in your field of expertise. Whether you are a freelancer or staff writer, you'll get a chance to meet the celebrities passing through town. Once you start writing for a local publication, you will also better see local trends that will help you develop stories for national markets. In this business, success, no matter how small, breeds greater success.

5. The best way to make contact with editors of smaller publications is with a well-thought-out letter of introduction. Tell what specialty you can bring to the publication. Make the letter lively. Include a résumé and, if you have been published, include copies of your best stories. If you don't hear from the editor, follow up with a phone call. Then another letter. On the one hand, editors complain about nuisances; on the other, they like people who are aggressive. Aggressive reporters get good stories. Figure out a proper balance. If you get a rejection, then what? Don't quit. Get more writing experience, and then try again. For most of us, this is a business of small steps, each leading further up the career ladder.

6. Conflict of interest worries editors, so if you can't be a full-time writer, you are sometimes better off making your field of expertise an avocation rather than a vocation. In other words, a homemaker who knows a great deal about food and takes writing seriously may have a better chance of becoming a contributing freelance food critic than a chef employed by a particular restaurant.

7. In talking about television criticism, John Voorhees gives the following advice that can be translated into any form of criticism: If the critic is intelligent, perceptive, has curiosity, an active mind, and can write, it's likely his or her criticism will reflect those qualities and be interesting and thoughtful to read.

8. Once you begin to write for a publication, no matter what its size, be sure the editors send you all the press releases they receive in your specialty. And get yourself on mailing lists. If, for example, you aspire to be a TV critic, write to all the local channels and also to the networks. Ask to be put on their mailing lists. Much of it will be junk mail, but occasionally the nugget will be there to set you up for a story.

Exercises

1. Compare how the television critics write in *USA Today*, the *New York Times* (or *Los Angeles Times*), and a smaller regional paper. Compare them over a few days and keep notes on your observations. What is each paper's story selection like? Are they giving in-depth analysis or just a brief overview of what is going to be on tonight's

TV? Are they cheerleaders or truly critical? Do the critics concentrate on one show or many? Which fits your style best? After you have compared the television coverage, you might try other disciplines.

2. Now you be the critic. Find a recently released book and write a book review. Or go see a film and write a review. Or go to a play and review that. Try your hand at whatever specialty you favor. When you are finished, go to the library and look up reviews of the same piece of work you reviewed and compare. How did you do?

3. Following celebrity writer Maralyn Lois Polak's advice; try to track down all the celebrities who are coming to your area in the next couple of weeks. Check your region's listings. Who's coming to town to give a speech? Anyone famous? Who's making a special appearance at a department store in a shopping mall? Any authors on autograph tours? Any actors doing a play? What music group's performing nearby? Who's promoting what on local radio or TV talk shows? After you have made your list, think if there is any local or national market where you might convert your findings into a celebrity interview and story.

How the Pros Do It
Writing Sample Number 5

I first saw this story by Steve Sonsky while judging a major feature writing contest sponsored by the J.C. Penney Company and the University of Missouri. We awarded it a first prize in arts and entertainment writing. There were stories that required more resarch and more important stories, but none that fulfilled their own missions as well as Sonsky's piece did.

He wanted to show how five years of "Miami Vice" on television changed a city. He did so with solid research, but also with a pace and tone that never made the story sound academic or dull. He did his homework. This story is filled with facts, but he turned the right phrase when it was necessary.

Like most of the examples in this book, this story is not beyond the capabilities of most feature writers, yet after judging the contest I realized how poorly focused articles can be and how perfunctory the writing often is. Some writers are so interested in letting the experts speak that we never hear the writer's voice, or get a sense of his style or tone.

Sonsky's voice is here, but it never overpowers. You hear it when necessary as you feel the tone he sets. In one section he writes about "Miami Vice's" quick cuts and when he does, his own writing pace quickens also. I've marked several other places where his words fit the subject he is writing about. If you get a chance, look at some "Miami Vice" reruns and see if you can match Sonsky's tone and the tone of the show itself.

Bye, Pal!
Miami's Vice: It Was a Case of Art Imitating a Slice of Life and Life Imitating the Art

By Steve Sonsky
The *Miami Herald*, Florida

We take like one-tenth of one percent of the objective reality of Miami and that's what we render. What we capture is the spirit.
— "Miami Vice" executive producer Michael Mann, after the first season.

Whenever possible look for legitimate connections, as Sonsky does in this opening.

In the end, we find our best metaphor for "Miami Vice" in its very beginnings.

As the fresh images recede into the eternal loop of Rerunland, perhaps it is the question asked by a confused Crockett in the very first show that we need to be considering again.

Maybe you still remember the scene from that September 1984 Sunday premiere, 107 adventures ago—a bookend to tonight's denouement. It was the most vivid image in a pilot movie full of stylish visuals, the beginnings of a show that would go on to change the way television looked—and the way Miami looked at itself—forever.

Betrayed by his partner, abandoned by his wife, Crockett was on his way to the final shoot-out with drug lord Calderon when he suddenly pitched the original black Ferrari to the side of the road.

By making this description so vivid, the writer helps blur the line between reality and art.

A ghostly phone booth glowed in the dark. The skyline was hazy in the distance. The car had kicked up a silvery dust. An ephemeral pink and blue neon sign hung in space over the phone booth. A still life in celluloid.

Crockett was calling his wife Caroline. He needed to know, he told her, nearly pleading, needing an anchor . . .

"It was real—wasn't it?" he asked.

"Yes it was," she said.

It was real—wasn't it?

It was far more real than we perceived it to be at first, back before Michael Mann's .1 percent solution, his fictionalized essence-of-Miami, became the reality.

Wasn't it an extraordinary thing to watch? Art imitated a slice of life. Then life imitated the art. The slice became the whole loaf.

Five years of shows and he picks just the right line to set up his story.

It happened because NBC wanted a TV show that "looked contemporary," and Miami became the lucky beneficiary of innovation. For as it reinvented the look of television, "Miami Vice" reinvented the look of Miami, too, reinvented the way Miami was perceived by the world.

And we in Miami liked what we saw. And began to replicate it.

Richard Brams, Vice's co-executive producer who oversaw logistics in Miami, notes how in the early years they had to build sets for the indoor looks they wanted. Later, they were able to do more location-shooting as "Miami began trying to duplicate much of what we designed as discos, or entertainment places," Brams says. "We saw people designing their new establishments the way we had dressed our sets."

Interview material helps prove writer's premise that Miami imitated art.

It wasn't always that they had created the vision either, Brams points out.

"It was here," he says. "It was the real world of Miami imitating what was already here, but not in such volume. I mean, look at South Beach now. It's not that they copied us. They responded to those things that we spotted and (put on film).

"They rehabbed and went back to the original look, the integrity of what was there in the beginning."

We knew the city was dangerous. We didn't need Vice to tell us that. But we needed them to show us how we could be cool, and look exotic, as well.

Mann had his crew shoot in a style he'd begun to perfect with his cult film *Thief.* No earth tones. Water down the streets. Slick and shiny. Quick-cut editing. Electronic score.

Notice sentence tempo change when he talks of quick-cut editing.

(Tangerine Dream in *Thief.* Jan Hammer for Vice.) It was a compressed reality, too—from Arquitectonica's Pink House in Miami Shores, to the steel and glass towers of Brickell, to a post-modernist dreamhouse on Indian Creek Island, to SoBe. (Which in '84 was merely South Beach—

Sneaks in a Sonny Crockett line just at the right time.

where folks feared to tread. Nightclubs? Restaurants? You're dreamin', pal.)

The car-chase in-an-instant was an hour-commute in real life. Mann took the one-tenth kernel of Art Deco/postmodernist truth, and edited it to make it seem the whole burgh looked this way. Eventually, more of it did.

"Miami Vice" reinvented Miami in the eyes of the world—that was not surprising. TV does that. What was unusual was how Miami then bought into the vision—how a city reinvented itself in the stylized, glamorized image that a TV show had of it.

Humble Beginnings

Vice's beginnings were humble.

It was the vision first of Anthony Yerkovich, an Emmy-award winner for his writing on "Hill Street Blues." Yerkovich had been fascinated by a newspaper clipping reporting that one-third of all the unreported income in the United States either originated in, or was channeled through, South Florida. Guess why.

Even while working on Hill Street, he began to accumulate more information about "the drugs, the life-style, the immigration influx." He began to formulate his own variation of the Miami-as-Casablanca theme, Miami as the epicenter of the drug holocaust. "A sort of Barbary Coast of free enterprise gone berserk," he once called it.

He pitched the Miami idea as a two-hour series pilot to NBC President Brandon Tartikoff. Tartikoff had an idea of his own, scribbled on a piece of notepaper. "MTV Cops," he had written—a notion of how to give a new twist to an old network standard: Integrate what were essentially music videos into the context of a drama show. There would be a separate budget of $10,000 an episode to buy the rights to actual tunes—unprecedented for TV.

The ideas were merged.

A few months of writing and research later—traveling around Miami with undercover cops and dopers—a script by Yerkovich called "Gold Coast," later retitled "Miami Vice," was born.

It's hard to think back now to all the local hubbub preceding that initial show. In the wake of the *Scarface* fiasco, local xenophobes were again up in arms over a film project whose violence, they feared, would further reinforce Miami's image problems. The county suggested it wanted

Watch the research material make the story solid.

Esoteric facts; readers read to learn.

script-approval powers if it was to cooperate; at the very least, couldn't they take Vice out of the title? No and no, said Universal, and if the county didn't want to cooperate, the studio would simply do the show in L.A.

They cooperated.

As the show kicked off, much of the early criticism about story lines—beyond the ubiquitous complaints about muddled plotting and style over substance—was directed toward the drug-crime emphasis and crooked cops. Unrealistic! Overstated! cried the critics. Why is the show about drugs and police corruption every week?

> Listen to the writer's voice.

In this era where the phrase "national drug epidemic" is part of the lexicon, it's easy to forget that just five years ago, this sensibility had not yet matured. Vice was prophetic in yet another way: in Yerkovich's and Mann's recognition that drugs were so pervasive, and not just in Miami, but nationally. That it was where the bulk of vice resources were increasingly being targeted.

In the midst of the criticism, Mann was buoyed, he once recounted, by something several real-life Miami vice squadders had told him: "You guys," they said, "haven't scratched the surface of what's actually going on down here." By 1986, Miami Police Chief Clarence Dickson was saying that 10 percent of his force was corrupt.

> The author knows the show and he knows Miami. The artist speaks, then the reality expert speaks.

Ratings Struggle

In that first year, Vice was struggling in the ratings. The turning point was a *New York Times* piece on Jan. 3, 1985. "The most talked about dramatic series in the television industry since 'Hill Street Blues,' " the *Times* gushed. *Newsweek* followed, then a *Rolling Stone* cover, then this from *New York* magazine, with John Leonard carrying on about "Miami . . . A dream city . . . Seen through filters of psychedelic lollipop, dissolved in montage, piled under by superimpositions of the ghostly and the slick, angled at from stars and sewers—a surreal sandwiching of abstract art and broken mirrors and picture postcards . . . There is no murder; there is only art."

> Never forget how helpful a library can be.

The public's curiosity was piqued.

The show ended that first season ranked 47th but during summer reruns, it moved into the top 10—and stayed there through season two, which began with another media blitz: the covers of *People, Us, TV Guide, Rolling Stone* again, even *Time*.

Dumped in
chocolate
saves the writer
from explaining
just how un-
known the actors
were. Always
search for ways
to economize.

[Philip Michael] Thomas and especially [Don] Johnson, just a year earlier journeymen actors who graciously allowed themselves to be dumped in vats of chocolate for a local charity function, were now national icons. A relative snubbing by the Emmys—just four awards from 15 nominations (the only Emmys Vice would ever receive), for art direction, editing, cinematography and to Edward James Olmos for best supporting actor—hardly slowed the rush. Nor did, at first, a succession of indecipherable scripts.

There were parades. Department store chains featured Miami Vice fashion sections. Anyone wearing socks was uncool. Crockett-like stubble was all the rage.

Generalization
quickly backed
by facts. More
research. But it
never intrudes.

The stars' every move was chronicled in the tabloids—sordid tales of Johnson's romance with a teen model, of Thomas' several illegitimate children. Johnson and Thomas were invited to a state dinner at the White House. "A couple of cops from the most talked-about show on television stormed the White House Tuesday night, nearly upstaging a president and a prime minister," the *Washington Post* wrote.

The tragedy of "Miami Vice," from a creative sense, was that the height of its popularity was never in sync with its best work.

It was the ninth most popular show on TV its chaotic second year but in its superior year three, following Don Johnson's celebrated contract holdout, after NBC committed the strategical blunder of moving it to 9 P.M. to blunt "Dallas," it dropped to 16th. A new white Ferrari, and darker duds for the boys were no match for "Dallas' " stratagem of bringing Bobby Ewing back from the dead.

There were occasional sparks, but the script quality was never consistent and the public grew further disenchanted.

Uses description
to prove a point.

Attempts to develop Crockett and Tubbs as fuller characters seemed like afterthoughts—as did co-stars Saundra Santiago, Olivia Brown, and Michael Talbott, whose roles as Gina, Trudy and Switek grew more limited each year. Only Olmos' Lt. Castillo, a stark triumph of black-garbed minimalism in a sea of cinematic overstatement, was able to escape Johnson's shadow.

The writer has a
point of view,
and it is pulling
the reader
through the
story.

The series never got the credit it was due for some of the timely, politically inspired tales it spun. One example: The chilling show in October of '86 with convicted Watergater G. Gordon Liddy playing a retired right-wing renegade general illegally recruiting American mercenaries to fight alongside the Contras in Nicaragua; it aired a week before Eugene Hasenfus' plane was shot down.

But those occasional brilliant episodes were lost among the too-frequent missteps.

A parade of big-name guest stars didn't help. In season four, despite another flurry of publicity over Crockett's marriage to a character played by singer Sheena Easton, ratings continued to erode. Down to number 44 among network shows.

The cliffhanger fourth season ending—Crockett getting amnesia and thinking he was his drug dealer alter ego, Sonny Burnett—did nothing to stem the tide. Early this season, Mann announced that year five would be Vice's last.

Even Johnson's uncanny knack for staying on magazine covers—in the fall it was the romance with Barbra Streisand; in the spring it was the reconciliation with former wife Melanie Griffith—didn't help. Vice's average rank this year was 65th—NBC's lowest-rated full-order series.

After the big event "finale" airs tonight, NBC actually still has four more new episodes it's quietly looking to shoehorn somewhere in the schedule. So Vice, no matter its reception tonight, is assured of dying not with a bang— which would have been appropriate—but with a ratings whimper.

Vice Legacy

So in the end, what will we remember "Miami Vice" for?

In the television world, it's credited with irrevocably up- **More facts.** grading the quality of TV-filmmaking. It showed that TV viewers do appreciate superior imagery—as well as superior sound. Pop sound tracks, from "The Wonder Years," to "China Beach," to "Tour of Duty" to "Wiseguy" are now de rigeur.

It leaves behind a $20-million gap in the local economy—the estimated money it spent here each season.

But it also leaves behind a movie-making infrastructure, and a local corps of expert film professionals, that didn't exist when it first blew into town. Moreover, as Vice continues to be syndicated abroad—it's now shown in 136 countries, from Abu Dhabi to Zimbabwe—more foreign filmmakers are drawn here.

Which brings us to the final, big question about "Miami

Vice's" legacy: As its immediacy recedes, will it be remembered more for the Miami, or more for the Vice in it?

Above, the writer as critic delivered his point of view. Here, outside of his field of expertise, he lets the real experts speak.

Bob Dickinson, treasurer of the Greater Miami Convention and Visitors Bureau, is bullish on the aftershock. Tourism, as measured by resort tax collection, has been up every year since Vice began. The jury's already in, he argues. The cachet Vice has lent the town far overshadows any reinforcement it gave to our shoot-'em-up image.

But Mike Collins, vice president of marketing for the tourism bureau, disagrees. "The steady stream of stories involving drugs and violence have a kind of cumulative effect (after the) beauty of the scenery fades away," he theorizes.

Maybe the larger issue:

Was it real, Crockett asked?

Now that the show is gone, will the Miami panache fade, too, like an illusion? Will the new facades on the old buildings crumble? Will the SoBe clubs wither and die? With the cameras off, who will define us? Do we cease to be cool when TV stops watching?

Now, the next step in Miami's evolution: Now, we just have to dress ourselves.

Ending takes us full circle back to the beginning.

Goodbye, "Miami Vice." And thanks. Thanks for the memories. Thanks for lending the vision. In the end, it has been real. For in this town, you were more than just a TV show. You were life.

CHAPTER SIX

Selling Freelance Stories to Feature Sections

T he definition of a freelance writer used to be "a man with a type-writer and a working wife." Today we would amend that to say "a man or woman with a word processor and a working spouse or significant other." The point is, freelancing is not an easy way to make a living, and never has been. But it is not a bad way to bring in the occasional check to help pay the rent or subsidize a vacation. However, every so often you'll meet some very talented person like Neal Karlen who makes his living from freelance writing. And in these days of the larger magazine paying somewhat more respectable rates, it is possible to write important stories and be paid well for them. Plus there are the intangibles. I tried freelancing and never made a financial success of it. But I tried and will never have to go through life thinking I missed out on trying something I wanted to do. And more importantly, from every freelance article I tried, I learned. Each provided me with another story for my clip file, and I am convinced freelancing helped me move ahead of others who didn't take chances. Am I advocating taking chances? Sure, just take a look at what happened to Karlen.

How to Approach a Feature Editor

Neal Karlen

I can still recall the exact moment when I decided to try and make my living as a freelance writer. It was four years ago, and I was sitting in my office at the fancy-sounding national magazine where I held a fancy-sounding staff writing job.

Opening my mail one day, I came upon an interoffice envelope stamped CONFIDENTIAL. Inside was a letter from the corporate benefits department telling me how much money would be in my retirement fund if I stayed with the company until June 25, 2024 — my 65th birthday.

I was 26, and had never before considered my own retirement. Now, seeing in print the actual date that I would receive my gold watch and be pensioned off, I panicked. Looking into the future, I saw my life as a series of bureaucratic promotions. One day, I knew, the promotions would end and I would begin my countdown to June 25, 2024.

Two weeks later, I was seated in the office of the magazine's editor in chief. I had just told him that I was quitting in order to become a full-time freelancer. My disbelieving editor, staring at me across his ping pong table-sized desk, reacted as if I had just told him that I was running away to join the circus.

He'd always liked me, and now seemed genuinely concerned about my welfare. He got up, closed his office door, and asked if I was *sure* I wanted to do this. Was I positive I could make a living freelancing?

"Of course," I said with that special brand of cockiness reserved for 26-year-olds who don't know what the hell they're doing.

Still, I had been freelancing for pin money for a couple of years, and already possessed a handful of what I thought were pretty snazzy clips from *Rolling Stone*, *Esquire* and *New York*. I was positive that I had enough contacts and salable story ideas to pay the rent. At that point in my life, with neither dependents nor a mortgage, I wanted to fly free without a net. "Well," said my editor with a handshake and a kindly sigh, "good luck."

The Cold Reality

A few weeks later, I couldn't get out of bed. Hiding under the covers, I tried to make sense of what I'd just done to my life. In one corner of my apartment sat my silent computer. In the opposite corner sat my equally quiet telephone. I had about a month left of savings, no job and no assignments. Every single one of my story ideas had either been shot down or ignored by every single magazine editor I'd called.

My two options seemed starving to death, or crawling back on my knees to my old magazine in the hopes they'd let me start over in the mail room. Neither choice seemed too appealing. So, knowing the MasterCard secret police would soon be after me if I didn't get going, I forced myself to get up. I wandered to the phone, dialed, and affected what I thought to be a professional sounding voice.

"You know," I said to one more editor, "I've got a couple ideas I thought you might be interested in."

That call didn't end in an assignment, nor the next. Nor even the one after that. But then, a strange thing happened: the phone rang. Would I be interested, asked an editor, in flying to Hollywood in 12 hours in order to spend several days hanging out with and interviewing Cher? No, this would not be the assignment that would win me a Pulitzer. But it probably would be fun, and most definitely would help with that MasterCard bill.

"I might be interested," I said into the phone, trying to sound cool and coy. Hearing silence on the other end, I resorted to the truth. "Yes, yes, yes!" I said. "Please, please, please!"

Now, four years after I was saved from law school by Cher, I can actually say I'm making a living at this crazy business. I've occasionally thought of getting a job, but have always decided that for me, the neuroses that come from freelancing are much easier to live with than the neuroses that come from sitting in an office waiting for the gold watch. To get to that point, however, I had to learn a few things. The most important of which are:

Story Ideas: Where to Pitch Them and How to Get in the Door

Story ideas are the wampum, the currency of exchange, of the free-lance trade. When you are in front of your word processor, it is well and good to view yourself with the artful reverence of Marcel Proust. But when you are making the rounds of magazine and newspaper offices trying to get a feature assignment, it's best to see yourself as Willy Loman. Like Willy, you are a salesman working on commission, traveling on a smile, a shoeshine—and the salability of your story ideas.

Unfortunately, cooking up bright concepts for an article only gets one 20 percent of the way into print. What you need is a smart idea, pitched to an appropriate outlet. Nothing turns off editors faster than a story idea submitted by someone who doesn't really understand their publication. If you think *Rolling Stone* still prints 20,000-word counterculture screeds, or that *Playboy* buys pornographic fiction, or that *TV Guide* is written for saps, then it is time to go to the library, check out a year's worth of issues, and *study*.

If you're new to feature freelancing, the best and easiest place to break in is in your local publications. This is no time to be an elitist — a lengthy, well-written, bylined clip from a throwaway shopper is worth more in the long run to a freelancer than an anonymous blurb in the *Washington Post*.

No matter where you are, there are probably a few nearby outlets that are respectable, well read, and always open to fresh talent. In general, it's easier for a just-starting freelancer to place a feature story in a local newspaper than a magazine. True, papers don't usually pay as well as magazines. But they have an infinitely bigger newshole to fill, and are usually more open to letting someone without a lot of experience help fill up some column inches.

Newcomers can get the best of both worlds by investigating the Sunday magazine supplements of their local papers. They usually pay better than their daily editions, and are often open to giving neophytes a chance.

Mind you, it's not that the people running these magazines are necessarily kindhearted. Rather, their interest in fresh talent usually stems from the fact that most Sunday supplements are understaffed for the amount of copy that they have to produce. Further, their editors often have trouble getting stories out of their already overworked colleagues in the daily newsroom. And so, they need lots of freelancers, and lots of freelancers' ideas.

Ideas Are Everywhere

And where can you get suitable, colorful feature ideas that haven't already been covered to death? If no interesting and undiscovered local phenomena or characters pop into your head, a good place to head once again is the back issue section of your library. There, look through the recent life-style, trend and pop culture sections of *People*, *Newsweek*, and *Time*.

Did a small story run last year in one of these publications on people in Los Angeles who are hiring psychiatrists for dogs? Perhaps by now there's such a practitioner in your city. Was there an item about how more and more women are paying alimony to their ex-husbands in New York? Maybe it's happening where you live.

If you still come up dry, check the news blurbs for your state that run daily in *USA Today*. Editors at the local magazines often don't know what's going on in outlying areas—and the *USA Today* blurbs often provide a wealth of potential true crime and human interest stories.

Though it's a cliché, the best single way to come up with ideas is to keep your eyes open as you conduct your daily life. Last year, for example, I was assigned to do a profile of Patty Hearst by a well-known women's magazine. Hearst's press agent, the most powerful and notoriously unpleasant woman in the business, insisted that I come into her office to be checked out. When I reported to the press agent's headquarters, I was verbally insulted, then forced to listen to her conduct her nefarious business over the phone for an hour, then insulted some more. No, she finally said, Patty Hearst was not interested in the magazine I was representing.

So I didn't get that story. However, ten minutes into the agent's first torrent of invective, I realized I did have *another* story, a *better* story—namely, a first-person account of what it's like to sit in front of this powerful person as she does what she does for a living. *Spy* magazine gave me full rein to tell the tale, and it remains one of my best received stories ever. The moral? Stay awake.

So say by now you've come up with a feature idea or two. The next step is getting the idea to someone who can assign you the story. Here, the key element is making personal contact. Do you know anybody who is an acquaintance or colleague of an editor at the newspaper or magazine? Call that person and ask if he or she minds if you name-drop when you write the editor, à la "Dear Editor X, My friend, Joe Smith, suggested I write you concerning a couple of story ideas that I thought would be appropriate for your publication."

Even if you don't have a name to drop, send a brief letter introducing yourself to the articles editor, along with a handful of clips. Don't send in a formal query letter yet—just ask if they might be interested in hearing your ideas. If they write back and say no, you've saved yourself the trouble of writing a query. If they say yes, you're halfway home. If you don't hear from them—a likely scenario—you now have an excuse to call the editor two weeks later. In any case, you've made personal contact, and the editor is much less likely to let your correspondence mildew in the slush pile.

The Query Letter

If you don't have clips, then you'll nearly always have to send along a formal query with your letter of introduction. Even if you do have clips, publications usually require writers trying to get into their pages for the first time to send along a written description of the story that they would like to do.

Every freelancer I know hates writing query letters. After a while, when you know enough people at enough magazines, you'll be able to pitch stories over the phone. But whether you're pitching verbally or on paper, the main thing to remember is to make the query short and to the point. Don't get cute, fancy or carried away with descriptions of your lead. Simply describe what the story is, how you plan to get it, and how many words you think it deserves. If you're writing, never let your query run more than a page, and whenever possible, make it shorter.

Beyond that, there is no formal standard or template for writing queries. I have spent several days crafting thoughtful, well-written queries, and had them ignored for months. I've also scribbled down seat-of-the-pants ideas in an editor's office, and had an assignment in 15 minutes. Just use your own voice, and *get to the point*.

Also, don't flood an editor with ten story proposals at once. Instead, try to get the editor interested in one or two solid ideas. If those bomb, try a couple more in a couple of weeks. Then try a few more a little later. If you query smartly, something will eventually hit.

Also, don't be afraid to tackle the national magazines. True, the chances are infinitesimal that a newcomer will be assigned a long feature by one of the major publications. But that doesn't mean you're shut out. Many of the biggest magazines run short feature, service or regional pieces written by freelancers. Though these pieces are difficult to get at first and don't pay much, don't sneeze at the opportunity.

For instance, the first thing I wrote for *Rolling Stone* was a 300-word bylined blurb on a convention of Mr. Ed fans. Within less than a year, I was writing cover stories and major features for the magazine. At *New York* magazine, my first assignment was to write 200 words on the funeral of a local radio celebrity. Not long after that, they gave me a 4,000-word feature.

Whatever you do, whether you're trying to break into a national or local market, persist. Politely!

After the Assignment

Okay, you've landed a story. You've agreed on an acceptable fee, have a realistic due date, an approximate word length for your assignment, and are in a general agreement with your editor on what this article is *probably* going to end up being about. You've done the necessary reporting, and have begun writing. What should you keep in mind as you near that dreaded deadline?

First off, you should remember that editors are looking for writers who are going to make their lives easier. They may work with a prima donna if he or she is sufficiently well established, but what they want from a newcomer is reliability.

That means not being late. Not turning in a story that is three times longer than it's supposed to be. Not changing the complete focus of an article without at least discussing it with the editor. Not telling the editor that if he moves one comma, you're taking your name off the story.

Of course, unforeseeable problems arise. If, for any reason, you know you can't get your story in on time, call your editor as soon as possible. If he or she was counting on that story for a particular issue, the editor will need to fill that space—and will be happy to have the news now, rather than two days before the article was supposed to go to press.

Recently, for example, I succeeded in pitching a full feature profile to *GQ* on Bill Musselman, the controversial basketball coach of the Minnesota Timberwolves, an NBA expansion team. Musselman was a fascinating character, but the demands of putting together a new team forced him to cancel several interview sessions.

I was in trouble. The article was scheduled for the issue that would coincide with the start of the basketball season, and my deadline was nearing. Musselman kept canceling, and I kept fretting, trying to figure out how I was going to write a colorful profile with so little information.

Finally, a week before the story was due, I called my editor. I had only done one feature for *GQ* before, and was sure this would now be my last. My editor listened to my song-and-dance, paused, and said, "Well, if you don't have it, you don't have it." She gave me another month, and then a warning: "It better be good."

Temporarily off the hook, I began breathing again. That afternoon I set about doing whatever I had to do to pin down the wily coach. And yes, in the end, *GQ* gave me another assignment.

All of these caveats might make freelance feature writing seem like a pretty horrific business. Unresponsive editors, nonpaying payroll departments, killed stories, impossible deadlines, disbelieving fact-checkers—at times, I must admit, I've thought about throwing in the towel.

Then, I remember how much fun it is to be your own boss, have your words and ideas in print, and observe people and places that you'd never experience if you were stuck working in the corporate widget factory. It's a wonderful way to see the world or your town, and then get paid to let other people see it through your eyes.

To make a full-time living, I often end up having four or five stories in different stages of production going on at once. What I do to make sure that I don't get burned out, blasé or cynical—which is my definition of a hack—is to make sure that I absolutely love one of those articles. Love, not for the money, nor for the prestige of the magazine it will appear in, but because the story itself fascinates me.

For example, one of my favorite profiles appeared in *Manhattan, inc.* about an old-time New York politico named Jerry Finkelstein. A back-room fixer, he was a character right out of Damon Runyon who had never agreed to talk for publication before. "The reason I'm trusted," he told me is "because I keep my mouth shut around wiseguys."

It took me three months' worth of tri-weekly, off-the-record breakfast meetings before I could convince him to talk. It took me another three months to get him to start telling me the juicy details of where the bodies were buried.

The reason I kept at it wasn't because of the money. If I calculated how many hours I spent with Finkelstein, compared to my fee, I would undoubtedly find out that I would have been better off financially working at Burger King. But the story was one I couldn't resist—and one I couldn't have done had I been stuck in some office somewhere watching my retirement fund grow.

Someday, of course, I'll probably want that pension fund, not to mention dental insurance. When that happens, I'll go back. In the meantime, I just keep thinking of the question my editor in chief asked me that day four years ago when I told him I was quitting my staff job to freelance.

"Are you sure you want to do this?" he asked.

"Yes," I still answer.

Neal Karlen is a contributing editor to *Rolling Stone,* and a former associate editor on *Newsweek's* national affairs staff. His work has also appeared in *GQ, Esquire, Spy, New York, Mirabella* and several other national publications.

He's collaborating with Henny Youngman on *Take My Life, Please,* the comedian's autobiography which is to be published by William Morrow and Co.

A few people like Maralyn Polak of the *Philadelphia Inquirer* magazine have long-term freelancing relationships with a newspaper — in her case, providing interviews to the paper's magazine each week for 15 years. In the future, as newspapers continue to look to cut costs, they will probably take more freelance material simply because freelancers don't need to be paid higher full-time wages and benefits. The best markets are with the larger papers. Aside from their Sunday magazine sections (those that are still around) the papers' daily feature section, sometimes called the Style or Life-style sections, are probably the next most fertile place for freelancers.

In the piece that follows, Mary Hadar, assistant managing editor of the *Washington Post*'s Style section, tells how one great newspaper works with freelancers. Although each paper makes different arrangements and has different needs, much of her advice, especially when she talks about accuracy, is universal.

What a Newspaper Feature Editor Wants From Freelancers

Mary Hadar

An editor views an unknown freelancer with mistrust and suspicion. No matter how compelling the story idea, no matter how gracefully phrased the query letter, at the back of the editor's mind linger the questions: Does this person have the reporting basics? Will she be objective? Will he get me sued?

Thus the uppermost value for a successful freelancer is accuracy. Double-check your facts, your spellings, your titles, your quotes. Take no shortcuts. Fail in other areas, but if you fail at this one, you won't be invited back.

Next on the checklist is authority. A newspaper has probably asked you, rather than a staffer, to write this story because you have a special knowledge — of the subject matter, or the players, or simply of the geographic location.

Your story should be imbued with this knowledge. Let the reader see you know what you're talking about. A special knowledge of a subject makes you more valuable to the newspaper.

The *Washington Post* Style section, for instance, has a large, carefully selected stable of writers on staff whom we will send to cover stories of major importance. But we maintain a continuing relationship with a New York freelancer, Judd Tully, who covers all the major art auctions. This is particularly useful to us during the big sales each spring and fall at Christie's and Sotheby's, but it also comes in handy for the odd, newsworthy auction during the rest of the year.

Judd has made himself an expert in this field and has established reliable contacts with the auction houses and many of the key bidders. We occasionally call on him for takeouts explaining why the market is acting the way it is and how this affects the public at large. He, in turn, pays special attention to any Washington angles in the events he's covering.

The relationship makes sense for the *Washington Post* for two reasons: a) Judd knows more about the subject than our reporters and b) it costs us less to pay Judd for these stories than it does to send a reporter to New York and put him or her up at a hotel.

Geographic Needs

A major feature story in another part of the country would most likely be assigned to one of Style's regular reporters. But if time were of the essence, we would be more likely to call on a freelancer who lived in that area.

Similarly, if the story we were looking for were on the short side — say, 25 inches — we might consider it more cost-effective to farm it out. Enterprising freelancers have sold us stories on regional writers' conferences, World Series fever, local productions that were bound for Washington. A freelancer in Paris, Peter Mikelbank, supported himself quite nicely in 1989 by writing a host of entertaining pieces about the French bicentennial celebrations. We kept buying them because he utilized that rarest of feature commodities: humor. He wrote about guillotine chic ("Parisian fashion to die for") as well as the invention of the brassiere ("arguably France's most uplifting cultural achievement of the last century.").

All things being equal, we would like our freelancers to show some flair in their writing. Most of our staff writers have distinctive voices that make their pieces identifiable even without their bylines. But a little voice goes a long way, so don't fall into the trap of over-writing. Much can be told by simple details, judiciously selected. Particularly with emotional stories, you're better off letting the accumulation of facts evoke the emotion.

Finally, there is one month when the *Washington Post*, and most other newspapers, are most receptive to freelance ideas. That month is August. Nothing's happening and half the staff's on vacation. The knowledgeable freelancer will stockpile those August ideas and shop them around when the days become sultry. The remaining ideas should be saved, of course, for that most dreaded of weeks: the one that falls between Christmas and New Year's.

Mary Hadar has been assistant managing editor in charge of the *Washington Post*'s Style section since August, 1983. During this time she has won three consecutive Penney-Missouri awards for producing the best feature section in the country. Hadar joined the *Washington Post* in 1977 as a copyeditor on the Style section. In 1979, she became night editor of Style. Prior to coming to the *Washington Post*, Hadar was foreign editor of the *Jerusalem Post*. She has also worked at *The* (Baltimore) *Sun*.

What a Magazine Editor Wants From Freelancers

Leonard Witt

As an editor of a regional magazine with no full-time writers on the staff, I am totally dependent on freelance writers. My situation is typical: Magazines everywhere need freelancers, and editors are always searching for better stories. Even in metro areas as large as Minneapolis and St. Paul, there are never enough great stories to go around. We have two city magazines, two alternative newspapers, and business publications all vying for the same freelancers' time. And the best of the freelancers are also writing for national publications.

The best way for a freelancer to break into the market is to be good or at least to be smart. Being good means having excellent writing and reporting skills. Being smart means realizing your talents might not yet be developed enough to write full-length features, but recognizing ways to break into print.

In our magazine, *Minnesota Monthly*, we run a section called "Monitor." Just about every magazine has some type of up-front feature. Often they are quick paced, relatively light reading to add balance to the longer features. Most often they provide one piece of information. In an upcoming magazine we will run a piece on a Prairie School-designed home that is opening soon to the public in Minneapolis. A visit to the house, a look at the press releases, short interviews with the principals involved, and presto—a quick 250-word, brightly written story is done. It will not pay a lot, but it shouldn't take long to write either. In *Philadelphia Magazine*, another regional, a writer turned a quick piece on homeless people going to see the art films at the public library. Both stories are quick and done in a style that just about anyone can imitate. As a freelancer you just have to capture the style and start selling. We need you.

Also in our book is a section called "Vitae," that reads a bit like a long résumé. The subject is always an interesting person, someone not necessarily worthy of a longer feature story. The story itself is broken into Who, What, Where, How and Why sections. It's another place a writer doesn't have to be an expert stylist or have years of writing to make a sale on. In the back of the book is a section called "Just the Facts," not much more than an interesting listing of facts that varies from month to month on subjects ranging from pontoon boats on Minnesota lakes to the making of the Pillsbury Doughboy. Any novice in the Twin Cities interested in breaking into our market should be studying those features and writing for them. The front of the book material and those two features alone account for almost 100 stories a year, many of which could be done by freelancers. Look at other magazines; most offer those same type of opportunities to smart but not necessarily great writers.

If you have a specialty in food, entertainment, books, health, education, media, restaurant or theater reviewing, we need you, as do all magazines. But we only need you if you have proven yourself to be a dedicated reporter and writer. You have to know your specialty and have to know how to present it to a lay audience. Throughout this book writers tell you to start at small publications and work your way up. As an editor I tell freelancers who call me to send clips of the work they have done. If their style fits what I am looking for I will call them immediately. It doesn't matter to me what publications they have written for. All that is important is the example of their writing in front of me. If it is great, I will be on the phone to them in a minute setting up a lunch or office meeting. Later, if a writer backs up those clips with a great story, as freelancer Jim Thornton did for us recently, I might just start negotiating to put him or her on a retainer as a contributing writer. We need great writers.

For the main features, I stay awake nights worrying that the material coming in might not be good enough. We always want it to be better.

How do you become good enough? You study the markets, find out what the editors want. Study the best stories (don't try to emulate all the stories, just the best. Frankly, every magazine has its dogs that are run out of necessity rather than choice.) Once you see what genre of stories the magazine uses and have studied its style, ask yourself if you want to write these kinds of stories and if the style fits your expertise. If so, begin the process of contacting editors. Sending a query letter like the one at the end of this chapter is the best method, and if the editor doesn't know you, supply examples of your past stories.

To excel in freelance magazine work you will need to be a good reporter, a good researcher, a good interviewer, a writer with a voice, a writer who uses description, a writer who is organized. In other words, you have to be very, very good, and you have to be willing to work very hard. And if you are going to write for magazines, you also have to be dedicated. You must care about the things you are writing about. You will probably not make a financial killing, but those people who write for my magazine do make a difference in the community. They do get read and they do have a wonderful showcase for their work.

Remember, to get published in magazines it takes smarts, hard work, skills and talent. Any one of those will get you published somewhere. Putting them all together will get you published everywhere you send in stories.

L ook in most newspapers and you will see a ton of syndicated material. If the paper is a large one such as the *New York Times* or *Los Angeles Times*, instead of buying syndicated material, it will be selling it to papers around the country. Although individual newspapers don't pay much money, a syndicated piece can, if it is good enough, be sold to many newspapers. Since the syndicate acts as a middleman, it takes a healthy split of the profits. As Dan O'Toole points out, newspaper syndicates are a tough market, most lucrative for authors who are already selling to magazines and then recycling their material through a syndicate. But as you will see from his examples, syndicates will buy if you provide the right story.

Feature Writing for Newspaper Syndicates

Dan O'Toole

Newspaper syndicates represent a small, highly specialized market for the freelance writer. They're not a market for the novice. In fact, the market is so tight that even established freelancers will have trouble placing their work with a syndicate. Most syndicates that offer one-shots to newspapers (a "one-shot" is a feature that is sold once rather than on a continuing basis) have only two or three slots available to freelancers on any given week. The financial arrangement is usually a fifty-fifty split of sales. Thus, smart freelancers use syndicates as a tool for squeezing extra dollars out of an already published story.

A syndicate one-shot editor is looking for stories that sell themselves, stories that are intriguing and not easily duplicated by a newspaper's staff. Previous publication is a plus, because phrases such as "in this article from *New York* magazine" or "written for the *Los Angeles Times*" are great selling tools. Stories can range from three-to-five part series, two-part articles, to single articles.

Most series offered by syndicates are five-part excerpts from newly published books. A syndicate editor will only accept a series from a freelancer if the topic is one that is an irresistible read for a newspaper editor. One memorable syndicated series written by a freelancer for the *Los Angeles Times* syndicate was "The National Enquirer Capers," in which a former stringer for the tabloid recounted several bizarre adventures he experienced while gathering information for inquiring minds. Among them were a narrow escape from the clutches of the Secret Service during a raid on Ronald Reagan's trash, the infiltration of a nuclear power plant, and hijinks on Capitol Hill when an attempt to catch a Congressman in the act of taking a bribe backfired and resulted in a keystone cops-style chase all over Washington.

Another successful series looked at the big buck buys and leases that occur in the world of celebrity real estate. It revealed that Barbra Streisand paid nearly $6 million for a barn and that Roseanne Barr pays $20,000 a month to rent a Beverly Hills house.

Single Articles

Syndicatable single articles come in many shapes and sizes. Most common is the life-style or trend article. A few that have done well in the market include an article on how tabloid TV — Geraldo Rivera and Oprah Winfrey, for example, exploits crime victims by making them public spectacles, an article about 40-year-old Yuppies having their first babies in an effort to delay the aging process, and an article about some of the bizarre methods churches are using to lure un-churched Yuppies into their flocks.

The celebrity profile always sells, especially if that person is or will soon be in the news. Recent celebrity articles that did well were an article in which Joanne Woodward told how she and Paul Newman have sustained their 31-year marriage despite their intense professional rivalry, one in which TV actor Fred Dryer revealed his unique formula for success, and a third in which Chris Evert unveiled her plans for a post-tennis business career.

Perhaps the easiest story to sell to a syndicate is the "geewhiz" story. "Strange But True From Science," "Game Show Horror Stories," "Exploring the Unexplained World" and "The World's Weirdest Clubs" are some recent best-selling titles.

Opinion articles are a special case in syndication. They absolutely must be previously published, preferably in a major newspaper. And the writer must be a recognized expert on the subject being written about. No newspaper editor is going to publish an article about the Middle East by Joe Sixpack.

Travel, business and humor articles can also do well in syndication. But again, they must be really unique to be salable.

Syndicating a Column

A freelancer's chances of landing a column with a syndicate are slim indeed. Most syndicates develop one or two new properties a year, and generally they are by writers with established reputations in the field they are writing about — Henry Kissinger and Jeane Kirkpatrick on politics, Lee Iacocca on business, Jim Murray on sports, Edith Lank on real estate, etc.

Syndicate editors normally receive 50 or more submissions a week, many more than they can comfortably deal with. To increase your chances of a sale, you should write a cover letter telling the editor why your submission will sell itself to newspaper editors.

As with any other freelance submission, always include a self-addressed, stamped envelope; if you don't, your rejected submission could end up in the round file. Always put your name and phone number in one of the upper corners on every page of your piece. In syndication, if your piece is going to be accepted, you're going to get a phone call, not a letter. And most important of all, when you're selling that syndicated article to a magazine, make sure you retain second rights. If you don't, the magazine may make its own deal and successfully market your article to a syndicate before you have a chance to do it yourself.

Dan O'Toole is the special series editor for the *Los Angeles Times* Syndicate. He purchases articles and book excerpts for newspaper syndication.

Several writers in this book (and I'm among them) advocate taking chances with your writing when you are starting out. If you are a feature writer, your only power is going to come from writing better than the people around you. You want to find a voice. You want to develop a style of your own. You want to distinguish yourself from the writing masses. One place to accomplish some of these goals is the alternative press. Of course, what follows is not mainstream advice, but then Sandra Shea has spent most of her life outside of mainstream publications.

Don't Forget the Alternative Papers

Sandra J. Shea

"Alternative" is a concept that died in the '80s. The idea of anything existing and thriving outside the mainstream was obsolete the minute the mainstream collapsed its boundaries to include almost everything in the universe. Rock songs, drugs and Russia are all former alternatives. Now they only serve to prove the notion it's a small world after all.

While most publishers and editors will tell you "alternative" is an outdated word to use in relation to their newspapers, in fact, the alternative press is about the only alternative-anything left. I can't, for example, think of an instance of Knight-Ridder or Gannett wanting to make one part of their chains.

The secret to the alternatives? As George Bush would say, it's the vision thing. Most of the surviving, successful alternative papers are still being published by their founders. Take a ride in the way-back machine with these guys, and you find them in their early days to be bright, passionate and driven. Driven not only by a mission, but by a feeling of being outside of things and by a commitment to maintain that position. (Outside, after all, is where art happens, although I doubt anyone thinks much about art where newspapers are concerned.) Suffice it to say, people with strong personal visions know they are rarely ever going to feel like a jolly brother or sister in the happy family of man.

Anyway, they published their newspapers. Weirdoes found a natural home there. Some of them were brilliant. Some could write. Everybody had, if not fun, at least an interesting time. Because ideas lived. People discussed them, sometimes in very loud voices. People cared.

It was the modern-day equivalent of putting on a musical.

Come back to the 1990s: the founders are a little older. But they are still there, either in body or spirit or both. Weirdoes still are attracted to the papers. Fortunately, some of them can write. Screaming discussions can still be had. People still care about ideas. That's the most remarkable thing—very talented people still put in long, underpaid hours toiling at these places with shoestring budgets trying to meet impossible demands. The demands, while impossible, are completely seductive: make it different. Push yourself to do it better so it *stands out*. So it's not like every newspaper on the stands. All of this, of course, is not only heaven for a staff full of driven, talented people with their own vision, it can make for a very good newspaper.

Let Your Voice Be Heard

It is youth's duty to misbehave. It is not their duty to dissipate their energies over a series of boring town meetings thinking they are learning about being writers. They will learn about the inverted pyramid. But they can do that anytime. As writers, their job is to find *their* voices and let them be heard.

Alternatives let them do that. Because if alternatives are doing their job, they are always looking for opportunities to beat the dailies at stories by doing them first or doing them better.

How do we think about doing them better or first?

One of the luxuries we have is time: A weekly schedule leaves a lot of room for time to report, to write, to shape a story. Time is the most oft-cited distinction between weeklies and dailies, but there's more.

Only Connect

Another luxury of alternatives is their ability to identify completely with their audience. It's partly a function of the readership of the alternative press, wherein you have a bunch of people fairly narrowly defined by age, interests and other demographics. You don't have that luxury on dailies, who by their nature must appeal to a wide range of people, from fifth graders to 95 year olds. So alternatives provide room to carve out a clear voice and address people directly.

The ability to identify with the readership is also partly a function of being an editor who considers herself a reader first, an editor second. If it doesn't connect with me, it won't connect with the reader.

How do things connect with me? There are a few things I look for:

Out of an average of 10 to 15 queries that come in over a given week, the majority may be okay stories, fine in their own right, judged by their own merits. Most conform to typical standards in query-writing. But the best ones make me think: this person has something to say.

For example, let's take a typical query:

Recent legislation suggests that Massachusetts car insurance rates will continue to rise. I'd like to do a story to find out why, and maybe talk to some residents around the state to gauge their reaction.

My response: go ahead. But do it for some other paper.

Here's another one:

Few bad tastes rival the unsavory one you get licking the envelope that contains your car insurance payment. Another $269.12, gone for good. Probably more than a thousand bucks in premiums for the year. Even if you drive in Boston, chances are you won't get your car smashed, stolen, or burned enough this year to get back as much money as you put in. Mostly, the cash seems to disappear into some mega-corporation's bank account.

What's going on here? I'd like to find out.

This is a much more compelling query, because here's someone who has something to say, suggesting a story that will connect with the reader.

Connecting With the Reader: A Different Spin

The eternal search for a different spin eventually uncovers that manna for alternatives (and good publications everywhere): people with skewed views of the world. It's supreme manna when a sense of humor is attached.

According to my unofficial survey, at least 50 percent of those who have entered college have left wanting to be a writer. Of that number, 27.8 percent want to be a humor writer. Which is usually a good thing. When people claim they want to be humor writers (or their cousins, satire writers) they often have something to say. They probably won't necessarily end up as humor writers, but if they keep writing, chances are they will be strong stylists.

Not that alternatives go out searching for humor writers to nurture, although they should. But they do look for wise asses, who tend to make good writers.

Connecting With the Reader: The First Person

Another popular misconception in journalism is objectivity.

I happen to abhor the first person. (Perhaps a better way to say that is "The use of the first person should be avoided.") It's easy to get people to quit writing in first person when they shouldn't. But one of the hardest things is getting people to use it when they should. I'm referring specifically to writers who have had drilled into them that they must eschew their own feelings and write an objective piece without realizing that sometimes, the third person is just a device to hide behind. For example, I once spent many weeks and countless hours getting one young and gifted writer who usually scrupulously avoided the first person to write a personal account of his stand on animal rights.

I thought he'd do a good piece not only because he grew up on a farm, but because it was the last story on earth he wanted to write. His resistance suggested he had a lot of confused feelings on the issue, but he clearly had thought a lot about it, and therefore had something to say. He ended up writing a powerful, moving piece.

I advise this with extreme caution, though. In fact, here's a rule of thumb: If you really really want to write about a painful, powerful or evocative event in your life, don't. It will only be very good if you are scared to write about it and have to be forced.

Take Risks

A few years ago, we produced a special section on AIDS, from the standpoint of how the disease was affecting human relationships and the way people negotiated them. Sober, well-reported pieces ranged from AIDS' effect on gay and straight relationships to the relationships between hookers and clients and between the porn industry and their customers. But the most memorable piece in the package was a short up-front humor piece called "A Girl's Guide to Condoms," probably the first piece to focus on this symbol of the most significant yet mundane change in the intimate relations between men and women for decades. Because it was a story related to AIDS that also happened to be funny, it was risky. But it worked.

For a profile of a candy factory, another writer played with the voice of the piece to the extent that it slowly deteriorated from that of an adult to that of a kid. By the end, she was writing in the voice of an 11-year-old. It could have bombed or been stupid, but in this case, the risk was also worth it, (if I do say so myself).

Newspapers and magazines have been around for a long time, and their traditions — from the inverted pyramid to the five Ws — are firmly established. Alternatives are relative kids on the scene, so they are more fluid. What they offer is freedom, and the opportunity to take risks — even to misbehave. In creative terms, that means elevating the ordinary by finding a new way to look at it. Which ultimately makes for good newspapers. And good writers.

Sandra Shea wrote this as features editor of *The Boston Phoenix*. She has spent much of her working life associated with alternative newspapers — in addition to *The Phoenix*: in Connecticut (the *New Haven Advocate*), in New Hampshire (the *New Hampshire Times*), and in California (*The San Francisco Bay Guardian*). She is now features editor at the *Philadelphia Daily News*.

End Words
Afterthoughts: More Points to Remember

1. Neal Karlen mentions that when you're trying to sell a story, dropping names of people who know the editor never hurts, and the truth is it may not. But don't think that just knowing someone will sell a story. It won't. It might cause the editor to spend more time looking at your query, but only good ideas, well presented, will sell. In the long run in this business, it isn't who you know, or even who you are, but rather how good the stories are that you produce.

2. Neatness does count. Magazine and newspaper editors get tons of unsolicited query letters. Ones that arrive neatly typed and well organized get points over those that come haphazardly stuffed in an envelope. A dot matrix printer is okay, if the ribbon is in good order. Don't send letters with crossed out typos and poor quality photocopies of previous stories. Take the extra time and money to get them done properly at a place with decent photocopying machines. In other words, make yourself look professional.

3. Here is what one magazine editor likes to see arrive on his desk: A query letter on good quality letterhead stationery with name and address. If the writer is new, an introductory letter, copies of

previously printed stories, and a short, well-thought-out query letter. Be sure to put in your phone number. It is amazing how often, when an idea is truly compelling, the editor will get right on the phone and make contact.

4. On the other hand, as a freelancer you must learn to be patient. Rarely do things work at the speed you would like them to work. You send in a query, and it often will sit on an editor's desk for days or even weeks. There is a good chance it will get rejected. You'll have to send it off to another editor. Again another wait. If it does get accepted, the finished story might sit again. Often editors will be so busy putting out the present magazine that they have put aside future stories. Finally it is read, then it might be sent back for revision. More time passes. If it is a monthly, it could be several months before you see your story in print. But that is the writing life. The first letter to an agent suggesting the idea for this book was sent out three years before the book finally got into print.

5. If things take this long, should you send out multiple queries to various editors? Books on freelancing are divided on the subject, but it is often impractical for writers to keep sitting on story ideas. Unless you know that editors are fussy about multiple queries, (e.g. editors for directly competing publications) I would send them out to more than one place. It is best to tell the editor you are doing this. But at least one writer in this book admitted privately that he sends out the same query to several publications at a time and never has been caught. The reason: Rarely does more than one editor accept an idea.

6. What happens if you get a query or, God forbid, a finished story rejected? Cry. Okay, don't cry. Bust up some furniture instead. Do what you must to work out the pain and frustration of rejection. Then resubmit it somewhere else or rewrite it. Don't give up on it immediately. One story that recently was rejected by *Minnesota Monthly* later showed up in a law journal and then in a city paper. The writer could have just trashed it. He didn't.

7. What happens if an idea or story eventually gets nowhere? Move on to another story. If you let rejections paralyze you, you belong in another business. All writers have had plenty of rejections and probably a few poorly written stories in their pasts. Those who have succeeded learned by their mistakes, but did not dwell on them.

8. Since we are on the subject of time, it is very important for freelancers to be aware of deadlines and publishing schedules. Something written for a newspaper feature section can be written and in print in a day. Monthly magazines, on the other hand, often demand that stories be finished months before publication. Even if they want to get something timely in the magazine, it will probably have to be submitted at least a month before publication. So if, for example, you are going to cover a onetime event in July, most monthly magazines will not want it. After all, it would have to be a fairly super event for anyone to want to read about in October. On the other hand, you might be able to sell an annual event for the next year. Yes, you have to plan that far ahead.

9. Once you have established yourself as a freelancer and have developed a specialty and style, let editors know that you are available to accept their assignments. Your specialty or specialties can be anything: the outdoors, theater, architecture, home design, crime, sports, politics, general interest. Every editor wants to build up a stable of dependable writers with a good track record and is always looking for new talent.

10. Keep alert to editorial changes at all publications. They happen with great frequency. Contact the new editor with a letter. Congratulate him or her, then introduce yourself. Present your specialties, even if they don't fit in with the magazine's past. Include past story clips. Each new editor brings a new mind-set to the magazine or feature section. Your ideas might be exactly what the editor wants.

11. Have some moxie. Study a magazine or newspaper feature section. See what you think is missing. Can you fill the niche? For example, if you are a food writer and see a magazine that could use food coverage but doesn't have it now, make a pitch. You have nothing to lose except some time.

Exercises

1. Find as many local publications in your hometown as possible. Even in moderate-sized towns you will find shoppers, daily newspapers, suburban newspapers, statewide papers, outdoor tabloids, religious publications, parenting tabs, women's papers, gay

issue papers and advocacy papers for just about every organization. Write a little synopsis about each, describing its apparent audience, its quality of writing, and its tone. Most will not be very well written, but if you find one that catches your attention and matches your interests, go to it immediately. This could be your best chance of breaking into the market.

2. Find a city or regional magazine in your area. Analyze it from cover to cover. Study the masthead. Does it have any staff writers? Now look at the short pieces that are not staff written. Make a list of ten ideas. Pick the one you think is the best of the ten. Do a little research about it. Now type up a query letter directed to one of the editors on the masthead. You have now taken your first official step as a freelance writer.

3. Now it is time to write. Write. And write. Keep a journal. Write interesting letters to friends. Write every day. Every day. And keep querying editors. Write articles even if you are not sure there is a market. This goes against all advice, but if you are new to this profession you will need to polish your skills, and the only way to polish them is to write. Eventually, it will pay off.

Further Reading

1. *Writer's Market* edited by Glenda Neff (Writer's Digest Books). A comprehensive listing of freelance markets, payments and guidelines for writers. A must for every freelancer looking for the best markets for his or her stories. Updated annually.

2. *Basic Magazine Writing* by Barbara Kevles (Writer's Digest Books, 1987). An excellent look at all phases of writing and selling magazine articles. Much of the information, like querying editors, is transferable to freelancing for newspaper feature sections.

3. *The Complete Guide to Writing Nonfiction* by The American Society of Journalists and Authors (Harper & Row, 1988). More than a hundred professional freelancers share tips on all aspects of nonfiction writing, from researching to selling.

How the Pros Do It

Writing Sample Number 6

Unless you have personal contacts, you will have to rely on query letters like professional freelancer Steve Kaplan does when he approaches a new market. In fact, he says, each time he has broken a national market he has done so with a query letter.

In looking for potential places for his stories he uses sources such as *Writer's Market*, but he also says, "I use my eyes. I go to magazine stores." For example, when looking through *Family Circle* magazine he noticed a feature called "Women Who Make a Difference." He filed that away in his mind, knowing someday he would find a woman who made a difference, and indeed he did in Sue Watlov Phillips, who helped transform shelters for homeless people.

As he always does for editors who don't know him, he did plenty of research before putting together the query. Then he wrote it, in this case with a very specific market in mind. And he sold the editor and eventually the story. When I read the query I thought it might be a little long, but it did exactly what a query should do—it set up a sale. Here is an excerpt from his query letter.

A Query Letter That Found a Story a Home

By Steven Kaplan

Stephanie Abarbanel, Editor
Women Who Make A Difference
Family Circle
110 Fifth Avenue
New York, NY 10011

Kaplan matched his idea to a specific editor and a specific department of the magazine. No shotgun approach here.

Dear Ms. Abarbanel:

Sue Watlov Phillips has just returned to her tiny and very cluttered office in a Northeast Minneapolis church after a grueling four-day trip to Washington, D.C., and three state capitals. Phillips is much in demand by legislators these days, because she is one of the few people in the U.S. who actually has a workable solution to the problem of homelessness.

Makes Phillips come alive by putting her in motion. Immediately knows why Phillips is important.

The pilot program she devised has been so successful in

THE COMPLETE BOOK OF FEATURE WRITING

Gives specifics to back up that she is doing something important.

Started out as a lowly volunteer. The editor hears Phillips talk.

Certainly sounds like an amazing feat.

Giving a title allows the editor to visualize the whole package.

In essence this is an outline of the story. Editor can quickly see how it will unfold.

If you have the freelance credits, let them be known. If not, try to give other sensible reasons why you are qualified to do the article.

The editor considered and eventually bought and ran the story.

re-integrating the homeless back into society that it has been adopted for use by the entire state of Minnesota and is now being copied by 28 other states across the nation . . . a possibility she didn't even dream of when she first volunteered at her neighborhood shelter, back in 1983.

. . . She volunteered to serve coffee and doughnuts at the shelter and was horrified at what she saw . . . "People, entire families were forced to sleep on cots on our church floor," she recalls. "It was shocking and appalling to me. I decided that I had to try and do something about it."

What Phillips did about it was to listen . . . They told her that temporary shelters kept them out of the cold, but what they really needed was a home they could call their own for long enough to get their lives back together again.

Out of those beginnings, Phillips devised the Elam Baptist Transitional housing program which has since become a model for the nation. Elam's success rate is nothing short of astounding: almost 90 percent of the homeless people who go through the program end up with a steady job and living in their own homes. . . .

We would like to do a story about Sue Phillips, perhaps entitled *The Volunteer who Found 10,000 Homes.* Phillips is a living example of how one concerned volunteer with a good idea can literally improve the lives of millions . . .

The story would tell how Sue discovered the homeless problem; how her new idea grew from paying attention to her "clients" rather than the shelter professionals; the difficulties in getting her church, and then government, to provide assistance to attempt a new concept; and finally the national triumph of her ideas.

We are a journalist team, writer and photographer, who are contributing editors of, and frequent contributors to *Mpls./St. Paul* magazine. We have published in many national magazines including *Horizon, Family Circle, The Robb Report,* the *Los Angeles Times Sunday Magazine, The World and I, Writer's Digest, Atlas, Prime Times, Changing Times, MD, Vista* and many others.

Many thanks for any consideration you give this article suggestion.

Sincerely,

Steven Kaplan   Larry Marcus

CHAPTER SEVEN

Getting to The Top

N o new writer will totally enjoy Jon Franklin's advice on becoming great. You see, he offers no overnight formula. But he does offer a long-term plan, a plan good only for those willing to stick to it as he did. And for him it paid off with two Pulitzer prizes. He shares more of his secrets for writing dramatic nonfiction in his book *Writing for Story* (A Mentor Book, New American Library, 1986).

How Feature Writers Become Great

Jon Franklin

Like many of my students today, I came to journalism as an orphan child of fiction. I had literary ambitions and, given that, would far rather have written short stories. That, after all, had been the training ground for the Great Ones, for Hemingway and Steinbeck and all the rest.

But they lived in a kinder world. I was of the first luckless generation to enter my apprenticeship after the extinction of the magazine giants and the concurrent demise of the short story as a commercial form. The door had slammed shut in my face; there was no way I could feed a family writing short stories.

Hemingway's edict was clear, though: If you were going to be a writer, you had to write. The ante, then as now, was to put a million words through your typewriter.

Worse, those million words had to be *published*. History was very specific on that point. Exposing your writing to editors and audiences and suffering the consequences was critical. If you got applause, you learned something; if you got raspberries and rotten tomatoes, which was more likely, you still learned something. You never learned much of anything when writing for yourself, which was why writing for yourself was to real writing what masturbation was to sex.

It was also necessary to get paid for what you wrote, a truth that in my case had to do with family responsibilities, but which also had larger implications. For, as W. Somerset Maugham had so acidly reasoned it through, writers were supposed to be smart, weren't they? And it was definitely not smart to starve. Therefore, the phrase "starving writer" was a contradiction in terms.

Given these realities I looked around and saw only one opportunity: journalism.

What? Covering muggings and traffic accidents, quoting politicians, sitting through town council meetings? Me? To a young man of my literary pretensions, this was not a very satisfactory answer.

Still, it seemed better than, say, selling insurance.

And besides, I told myself, I'd only be doing it for a while. I'd be slumming, but they'd see real quick what a fine young writer I was—too good for the newsroom, clearly. So they'd move me over to the feature desk. I'd make my reputation writing features. Then, when the time came, I'd take some time off and write the Great American Novel.

Facing Newsroom Realities

The ambience of the newsroom, of course, was anathema to all this.

The city room culture, then as now, was dominated by the Jack Webb school of journalism. Just the facts, ma'am. Who, what, when, where and why . . . always assuming there's time for a why.

Keep it under 14 inches. Can I quote that? Is that "Philip" with one "l" or two? *Whadda you mean you don't know? What kinda reporter are you?* Copy over!

Hey, Franklin! The cops have a floater at the inner harbor. Run down and find out what's going on! Take a photographer with you!

It was a brutal experience, the truth is, for one whose heart so warmly beat to the rhythms of Joyce, say, or Remarque. I responded in the only logical fashion, which was by trying to write it better than the normal stuff you see wrapped around the tire ads.

The gods aren't totally cruel, though. There always seems to be an editor around who does care, someone who will play mentor for a young writer. I had one . . . or maybe, come to think of it, he had me. In any event, one day early in my career he pulled me aside.

"Franklin," he said, "you tried to make this a great piece. Well, it's not.

"It could have been, maybe, but who knows? All I know is that it's not—and that there's only one way of making sure that you won't write a great piece, and you found it."

I stared at him, waiting. Well? Well?

"The only way to insure that you won't write a great piece," he said, articulating very precisely as though I was a seven-year-old, "is to set out to write a great piece."

I stared at him, bewildered. Now, what kind of thing to say was *that*? What did he mean?

Did he mean I was being too self-conscious? Should I spend more time being conscious of the self-consciousness of my copy? I could have grabbed him by the necktie!

What was I supposed to do? Tell me what to do!

He looked at me sort of sadly, for a long time.

"Nah," he finally said. "Nah. Forget it."

So what was one to make of that? Was it some kind of code? Was he supposed to understand?

Was he supposed to understand *any* of what was going on?

And what does one do, the young artist, when some fool of an editor strips off the whole first paragraph of his story, thus deleting a half-day's work and agony . . . and then sends the rest of the piece through mostly unchanged?

And how does the young artist react, in the secret, sensitive artistic center of his mind, when some Hun of an assistant city desk man laughs at him for the way he uses commas?

Well, one slinks away and licks the wound in private.

What the hell is so funny about my commas?

And what was wrong with the lead?

And then, in simple self-defense, one sets art aside for a day or two and learns everything there is to know about commas. That way, the next time that idiot makes a snide remark about your commas you'll make mincemeat of him!

Life is cruel, though, because no word is ever said again about commas. There are instead other slings, arrows and humiliations.

Hey, Franklin! Where'd you get this sentence? Outta a textbook in some college library?

And so again the young writer slinks off, setting aside his literary ambitions for yet another little while, to spend the time instead brushing up on the niceties of sentence construction.

Hey Franklin! You got three paragraphs here. Gawd, they're beautifully written! Love the syntax! Get off on them verbs! Oh wow, lookit them metaphors! Only thing is . . . you don't say anything . . . yuk, yuk, yuk!

Oops.

By this time the writer is getting very good at, if nothing else, slinking away from the city desk. He plops down in his chair and glowers at the computer tube for a while. In his mind he dismembers that editor, starting with his fingernails. And then finally, and with resignation, he calls the story up, deletes the offending three paragraphs, and starts over.

It is a deadly combat, an endless circle, a Sisyphian task. You try, you rail, you try again, you fail, you try again, you succeed. Then, having succeeded, you reach farther . . . too far, oh Lord, too far . . . and you fail.

You lose track of small things, like the passage of years.

You forget why you came here in the first place, and what you were going to do. The place where once you were an artist is now nothing but a hollow ache. You ignore it.

In your struggle with the desk editors you arm yourself with knowledge and skill. You learn ever finer points of syntax, of sentence construction, of paragraph sequencing, of story structure. You learn to use character, and the specific but limited uses of the quote.

More and more, the problem becomes clear. There is a world out there, and in that world inexplicable things happen. You are supposed to understand these things, and represent them in a simple way in your copy. When the reader reads your copy, some more or less accurate picture of reality should appear in his mind.

Transitions, for instance . . . you once thought transitions were merely ways to get from point A in your copy to point B. But no. They are much more. They are the fault lines in the psychological world, the seams of reality. They can be sewn, and unsewn. James and Faulkner showed us the techniques; even a humble newswriter can adapt them and use them.

The newswriter can defy everyday logic by flitting from one scene to another, or from one group of people to another, or even from one era to another. For example, in one paragraph I have kids walking down an alley, and then in the next paragraph I have a man in an adjacent house traversing the world.

Using these logic-defying stream-of-consciousness transitions in modern newswriting is a simple idea, a simple thing to say. You can argue with it, if you like. Discount it. Whatever. But the writer, this one anyway, spent two years analyzing the possibility. *Two years.*

They passed quickly, so absorbed was I. At the end, I was using stream-of-consciousness transitions. The editors loved them. Well, anyway . . . they loved them until I made the mistake of pointing out what I was doing.

(That's another rule you learn. Never, ever, tell your editor what you did. Stories are like sausages. Nobody wants to know what goes into them.)

But two years pass.

Time Keeps Moving

More years passed in wrestling with the subtle idea of *clarity*. What is clarity, exactly? Can clarity be truth? In an unclear world? Or is it a construct? How can you clearly describe something that's intrinsically unclear and, if you do, are you adequately re-creating reality . . . or are you writing fiction?

Then there were more years devoted now to the study of structure. Note, if you will, that the nut paragraph of an analysis story corresponds to the proposition or contention in an argument or the complication of the short story. And be aware, if you would write well, that good analysis stories also have summary bolt paragraphs at the bottom, the same way arguments have conclusions and short stories have endings.

And words, interestingly, are the inadequate measures of story length. Words are evocative and, being evocative, draw forth other words and images that are not to be seen on the printed page but exist there, nonetheless.

"Elephant," say, draws on the whole encyclopedia of ideas and images, from the parable of the blind men and the elephants to childhood stories about Dumbo. "Elephant" is an evocative word with roots deep in the reader's mind, and the writer who uses it draws on those roots.

The word "neurotransmitter," on the other hand, is not evocative (unless you're a neurochemist). It can't be used without being explained, and the explanation is no good if it doesn't put down roots of its own so that, later in the story, it can be treated as evocative.

Words can be classified that way, for their evocative potential. They also have various degrees of emotionality. There are hot words and cool words, and all temperatures in between. And such meanings, of course, are often not in dictionaries. They come to the reader through his culture, and they change by the day. A writer must know these things, think of them consciously, keep track of what "elephant" means today and what it might mean tomorrow.

And there are levels of meaning, too, far above words. In fact, words turn out not to be the basic transmitter of message, after all. The unit of writing is the active phrase, which is to say a phrase or phrases constructed around a verb. "The sprawling oak tree" has no meaning unless it falls, or casts shade, or is used to hang a criminal; if it falls in the forest, and there is no writer to hear, it indeed makes no sound.

And patterns . . . there are patterns, and patterns of patterns, and patterns of patterns of patterns. We report on events, but patterns of events are even more interesting, and patterns of patterns can electrify. What are the stereotypes about your story, and why are they stereotypes? What does that tell you about your story? What are the accepted patterns by which your characters explain the world around them? How do those patterns render the characters' worlds predictable? What does their choice of patterns have to say to us, and our readers?

And when you really look at patterns . . .

This goes on, and on, and on. Writing is technique, techniques for seeing, techniques for remembering, techniques for analyzing, techniques for clarifying, techniques for writing itself. If you are a writer, these things are your life. You become totally absorbed in them, art forgotten, greatness no longer a viable concept.

And it is then that the Zen of it works its magic and you hear, out of left field . . . you hear someone yammering . . . some critic, perhaps, or some professor, saying, hey, look at feature writing! Look at what the new generation of writers are getting printed in, of all things, newspapers! Lookit, lookit, lookit the new art form! Look at these writers! Some of them are great!

Art form?

Great?

Oh.

Let the Audience Worry About Greatness

And here I was, Jon Franklin, feature writer, writing this piece to address the question of greatness. And what did I do? I drifted off, into that other world, the writer's world.

Sorry.

Yes, I'd wanted to be a great writer. I wanted, in the yearning, egocentric secrecy of my heart, to be Shakespeare. It was only later that I learned that Shakespeare wrote not for art, but money . . . not to be cheered, but to be fed, 'cause the baby needed new shoes.

Greatness is a different matter — and one of very minor interest. You see, greatness, and the quest for it, has but one purpose. Setting out to write a great piece is the only surefire, 100 percent way to make sure you don't write a great piece.

"Greatness" is simply not a writer's word. It's an audience word, a word that an editor, a critic or a reader chooses to use, or to withhold. It has to do with power achieved, and perhaps with batting average — with how often the writer writes something that moves or changes the audience.

A writer who is preoccupied with greatness is by definition still a beginner. He is still a member of the audience, wanting to crawl up on stage, wanting applause, wanting, wanting, wanting . . .

He is still too conscious of the payoff, and not conscious enough of the performance. He is thinking about what HE wants, and not about what the audience wants. He is self-indulgent. He is lacking both humility and confidence. Therefore he will produce nothing great.

The young writer's mind is full of such excess baggage — a humiliating condition, brought to the fore usually by editorial criticism. For the greatest and least forgivable sin of the editors is that, usually, they turn out to be right.

Students come to me, now, as I once came to editors, bearing copy. They have their literary pretensions, their sweaty little egotistical desires, just as I had. They try to conceal the fact that they're not really committed, that they're slumming. But in this they are totally transparent. The fact oozes from their pores, and from their copy.

What they want is for me to look beyond their copy, and to tell them of the greatness in their artistic souls.

That's not my job, of course; their artistic souls are *their* problem, not mine. My eternal job, as editor and coach, is to discuss with them the inadequacies of their skill as reflected in their copy. This is hard on both of us — and, to them, humiliating.

I remember so well, as I tell them all the things they least want to hear, things about commas and getting names right and the clarity of simple sentences.

And of all the things they don't want to hear, what they don't want to hear most of all is that art, whether journalistic or otherwise, takes time.

Why, at this rate they'll be old and wrinkled before they're really great!

Well, yes. But they will get old and wrinkled anyway, barring the even less acceptable alternative. The trick is to make an investment toward that day. And if you want to invest in yourself as a writer, the first thing you need to learn is patience.

Greatness in writing, like greatness in most else, arises from the acute consciousness of detail. Truth emerges not from art but strong verbs and well-placed commas. You can't change the world if you can't define the semicolon. Syntax matters. Grammar matters. Reporting matters.

Art submits to these things and grows out of them, not vice versa. So does the writer, who becomes a writer only by virtue of such submission.

The discipline that makes art what it is grows from the ability to observe both details and patterns of details. Seeing, for instance, is the core of the writer's art — and "seeing" has to do with consciousness. The writer who doesn't bother to notice how many "l's" there are in Philip Jones is a poor seer as well as a poor reporter. A good writer, in the end, must be an excellent reporter.

And it doesn't matter, in the end, whether the writing itself is classified as fiction or nonfiction.

Jon Franklin is chairman of the journalism department at Oregon State University at Corvallis, Oregon. He was previously a writer for *The* (Baltimore) *Evening Sun*. In 1979 he won a Pulitzer Prize for feature writing and in 1985 he won a Pulitzer for explanatory journalism. He is an author of the book, *Writing for Story*.

F eature editor Ken Doctor provides plenty of tips for getting training, but the one bit of advice that deserves to be repeated is that the onus for growth will be upon you. Writing and journalism courses, mentors and wonderful working conditions may or may not help, but only you will make the difference. Only you can map out your life. There will be plenty of obstacles, surely some detours, but ultimately success will be in your hands.

Ten Surefire Ways to Train Yourself for the Next Millennium!

Ken Doctor

If you are wondering where your first (or next) job is going to come from, and what training you'll need to get it, you're not alone.

Print journalism absorbed more changes in the 1980s than it did in any other decade of the century. Wall Street tightened its oversight of major newspaper and magazine companies, making clear the bottom line was the only line of type that counted. *USA Today* started out as a joke in most newsrooms and by the end of the decade had forever changed the way newspapers thought about design and information and the use of color, forcing such a gray eminence as the *New York Times* to invest almost a quarter-billion dollars in a state-of-the-art color plant.

Specialized magazines of unbelievable specificity flourished in the marketplace. Where once a single health magazine occupied the newsstands, now more than a dozen compete for readers. There have been more titles and lots more circulation—magazines have doubled their circulation in the past 40 years, while newspapers have struggled to maintain what they had as the first baby boomers were entering the world.

Those newspaper readers, who are just now being introduced to the possibilities of audiotex and videotex, have voted with their ink-stained hands, tossing back the daily newspaper to the doorstep of the local newspaper company. As 1990 dawned, fewer than one of two Americans bought a daily newspaper. The journalism press has turned near apoplectic about the future of the industry and what could be done to save it.

Newspaper companies have responded by making the readership crisis the center of each and every conference. Take-it-or-leave-it journalism is out; give-'em-what-they-want-to-read is in. Sunday magazines are out; quick-read graphics are in. Reporters are out; clerks are in. At a recent meeting of New Directions in News, one top editor of a major newspaper group suggested that reporters could soon be replaced by community residents who just call in their "news" to computers, who (excuse me, which) could do the requisite sorting and dispatch it to readers.

It's an industry without a compass, one that can too easily leave a would-be features writer directionless. But, out of chaos comes opportunity. Yes, the 1990s will mean more information-gathering clerk jobs. Readers are hungry for more information about what's going on and about what to do. And newspapers are learning they don't need highly paid writers to do these "lists." Though they'll hire more clerks, newspapers in the 1990s will also have greater needs for people with what psychologists call higher-order cognitive skills — the writer's gift of explaining, analyzing and interpreting the vastly changing world to readers. As the two-tier system develops, prepare yourself for the top one.

Here, we'll skip the long, turgid story about problems of daily journalism and get right to the sidebar: how smart training can help you profit from the current depression.

1. I Meant to Get a Mentor

We think of ourselves as being the object of training. We dream of finding the ideal mentor, but fail to remember that we're in the driver's seat. Work hard to train *yourself* because the odds are long you won't find anyone else who can set and keep your own life and career on course.

You're a writer, right. Write it down. Today. Who are you? What are you best at? What do you want and need to learn? How can you do it?

What kind of training have you had; what kind do you need?

Make the list and update it at least once a year. Make it your birthday present. Need help with the list? See point 9 below.

2. Get Training: Formal Journalism Education

As you are allowed, pick and choose those classes that play to your strengths and weaknesses. Stress the skills classes: interviewing, writing, reporting, computer skills. Volunteer for role playing assignments. Talk to the professor out of class, seeking training and interning opportunity tips. Work on the campus newspaper. Immerse yourself.

If you're beyond journalism school, take the opportunity to refresh your mind with several good books on feature writing. A weekend spent with one of the following paperbacks may stimulate new thought:

Writing to Learn and *On Writing Well*, by William Zinsser;

Mastering the Message, by Lauren Kessler and Duncan McDonald;

Writing for Story, by Jon Franklin

Working journalists should also check out such in-service training opportunities as offered by the Poynter Institute for Media Studies in St. Petersburg, Florida, and the American Press Institute.

3. Get Training: The World Outside Journalism

Remember, journalism should only be an approach to the world, not a world unto itself. Get what you need out of journalism school and get into whatever other studies interest you. Don't think you have to stick to a straight liberal arts regimen. Consider film studies if you love movies, etymology if Greek and Latin roots could enrich your language, public health if you're interested in fitness writing, gerontology if you want to be ahead of one of the greatest demographic trends of the century, Middle Eastern cooking if you are hungry, Russian literature if you want to pull your writing away from newsese. Take a course in story telling, and apply these ancient techniques of oral history to what you do as a writer.

Don't forget your computer skills. The necessity of word-processing skills are self-evident, but don't forget on-line data research skills. In the coming age, when only the best and timeliest information will do, those who only use the *Reader's Guide to Periodical Literature*, in book form, will be unemployed.

Pick up these classes at four-year schools, community colleges, community education classes, or cooking stores — employers of the

21st century won't be checking where you went to school, but what you know.

4. Put Yourself in Training: On the Streets

Stop by the best magazine stand in town; the best bookstore. See what the readers are reading. Read something beyond your own local newspaper.

Forget writing for awhile. Volunteer to work with southeast Asian refugees, help out in a literacy program for the homeless, do communications for a local political campaign. Do the traveling you've always wanted to do. See the world differently, and then see what you'd like to write and what you now know to write about.

5. The Age of Generalists Is Dead, Generally Speaking

Have #2 pencil, will travel, is no longer what hiring editors want to hear. Unless you want to work a 60-hour week covering everything from bake sales to sewer board hearings for the local weekly, you'll have to specialize. What are your passions? Write them down and figure out what kind of writing you can do about them that will sell to current or potential bosses.

6. Focus on the Work, Not the Money

If you can afford this luxury, buy it. You may be able to obtain salaried work, or you may have to take it article by article. Journalism, unlike surgery or space science, allows you to work on speculation.

Remember, future employers will not hire you—for an article or for life—off your résumé. Journalism is a business of clips: the proof is in the paper. Find the situations that will yield the best clips.

After you've assessed your own abilities, write down a list of publications you believe may realistically accept your work. Inventory dailies, weeklies, monthlies, in-house organs published by corporations and hospitals, business-oriented publications, alumni magazines. When you've got your list, you're ready to go to point 7.

7. Time Is Time

Whether you are going to test life as a freelancer or want to develop your versatility as a writer, try the shingling exercise. "Shingling" is what Dick Neuberger, onetime-prolific freelancer and onetime U.S. Senator from Oregon, called his ability to spin the same subject into an endless variety of stories for different publications and different readers. Neuberger's facility was such that he even wrote articles in the Senate's cloak room, in odd moments between appointments.

For example, Neuberger covered the Depression-era opening of the Grand Coulee Dam, selling a primary piece to *Reader's Digest* and then following up with reports targeted to other readerships, recycling the same material, but adjusting the spin.

You should be able to shingle any story — assess the subject interest, find the people interest, the alumni magazine interest, the how-to interest, and the photo story interest. Build your writing house successfully without having to start fresh with each building material.

Shingling forces you to do what any good journalist should also do — develop a sixth sense of what the readers want to know. In a world rapidly devolving into niches and developing the technology to reach those niches, tailoring writing to specific groups becomes a basic of the trade. It also forces the recognition that there are an infinite variety of ways to tell any story.

8. Look Inside the Glass Cages

If you are looking for a job, look beyond the size of the building or the circulation of the publication. Work with people you can learn from. Pick editors who know more than you do and communicate with more than barks. Pick colleagues who want to be better jounalists than they are. Start a writers' group, if just in a tavern one night after work. Play the Outer Limits game: What could this story have been if it were to be written again. (It will be, some time, somewhere.) Learn from your mistakes, and your successes.

9. Double Your Fun

Pick assignments that will stretch you. As journalists, we have the unique ability to think up an idea and knock on anybody's door to ask questions. If you're interested in doing work overseas, find assignments that will allow you to interview those involved in foreign exchange work, international business, cross-cultural training. Get the training and education you want in the work you get paid to do. Not sure you want to be a feature writer? Interview a career counselor and get tested for free.

10. More Rigor, Less Mortis

Follow your plan. It's easy to be seduced by the comfort of any work situation. But if it's not training you to become the writer you want to be, make plans to move on.

> Ken Doctor is Associate Editor/Features for the *St. Paul Pioneer Press Dispatch.* He previously worked as managing editor for the monthly *Oregon Magazine* and editor and publisher of the weekly *Willamette Valley Observer.*

End Words
Afterthoughts: More Points to Remember

1. Almost no one becomes an overnight success. In the beginning your work will have problems. You will need to write and write and write and study the craft of writing and read and read and read. Self-doubt will nibble at your heels with each step, but success might just come for those who continue to grow and refuse to give up.

2. In pursuit of success you will have to master the fundamentals. But don't let not knowing the rules prevent you from getting started. Write first and learn the rules as you write. As important as grammatically correct writing is, almost one hundred years of research have found there is no correlation between knowing all the grammar rules and writing well.

3. Many newsrooms today are more like writing mills than places to learn. If you decided to go to a newsroom, be careful that production does not rule over quality.

4. Eventually everyone in nonfiction writing will be forced to use word processing. In putting this book together, almost 80 percent of the contributors sent in their work on disks. All of the first-line editing was done on a personal computer. It's a must that journalists be fluent with some form of word processing.

5. Feature sections at newspapers will most assuredly change in the years ahead. In fact, they could even disappear, and the trend

seems to be more toward a continuing emphasis on shorter stories. That could translate into an even smaller outlet for truly fine feature writing, which will mean that only the best writers will succeed. Of course, it could just happen that editors will wise up and realize that readers are not rebelling as much against length as they are against poor writing. Ultimately, it is up to you to show them what good writing is all about.

Exercises

1. If a journey of a thousand miles (or the journey to greatness) begins with the first step, then make sure the first step in your journey is studying William Strunk and E.B. White's *The Elements of Style* (Macmillan, 1959). Master its contents and you will know most of the important rules of usage, grammar and style. With fewer than 80 pages, it is a classic that every writer should read often.

2. Write a self-appraisal of who you are and what you want from your writing life. Then write the course of action or training you will need to attain your goals. Look at it again in a year to see how you are doing, and the next steps you will take.

Further Reading

1. *Writing for Story* by Jon Franklin (Mentor Book, 1986). Two-time Pulitzer Prize winner Jon Franklin gives a systematic plan to writing feature stories. Stresses nonfiction novel approach to writing stories.

2. *On Writing Well* by William Zinsser (Harper & Row, 1985). Another must for any writer's library. It's a book that will guide the beginner and remind the professional how to keep his or her writing fundamentally sound.

How the Pros Do It
Writing Sample Number 7

Of all the examples in this book, this one is the hardest to take apart and examine. Earlier examples, like Mr. Lucky and the blind boy, were well written, but rather easy to analyze. Mr. Lucky was really not so lucky and that was the theme of the story. In the blind boy story, the mother's relationship and her demand that his blindness would not stop him from living a normal life dominated the story.

In this story by Madeleine Blais, the relationship between mother and daughter and between Frank, who we rarely see, is much more subtle. In Chapter 2, Blais talks about the need to see and write about "grayness, nuance, something other than that sharp division that characterizes most news in which people have either won the lottery or they lost it bad."

This is a story about nuance. The lead is almost quiet to a fault, and some might see it as a fault. It doesn't exactly grab you by the collar and drag you into the story. Nonetheless, it sets the tone for the rest of the story. A beautiful story. In the story Hannah says, "A poem is as much what you don't say and what you imply as what you do say."

The same could be said about great prose writing. In the Mr. Lucky story the writer never once says Mr. Lucky is unlucky. It's implied. In this story, we never see a lot of Frank, but in the end his relationship with Vivian makes this story.

Blais spent weeks with Vivian and Hannah, but she centered the story around one day—the birthday. Often in feature writing, it takes time to find that right moment. If Blais had tried to write about all the time she spent with Hannah and Vivian it would not be much of a story. More often than not compressing the time makes unwieldy stories come together. It is much easier to see a beginning, a middle and an end. And in this story, the ending is brilliant.

The Poet and the Birthday Girl

By Madeleine Blais
From the *Miami Herald's Tropic* magazine

Victoria Hospital, private room: That's where Vivian Kahn was born on April 16, 1943. She does not hesitate to remind people of this fine beginning, especially when her birthday is approaching. Every year there is a big celebration. One time Vivian Kahn went to a Tony Orlando concert: "He kissed me once.

"He kissed me twice. And he called me one of God's special children. Which I am."

Her mother Hannah:

"When you learn your child has Down's syndrome, one of the first thoughts is: How will I get through the first

Christmas? The first major holiday. And then you think, how will I get through the first Mother's Day? The first day of first grade, when all the other children are enrolling in regular classes.

And then you think, how will you tell her about the womanly processes?

"But you can. And you do."

"How was work today, Viv?"

"Fine."

"What did you do?"

"Well, we said our address and when our birthday is and our social security number."

Vivian's speech is exceptionally clear for a Down's victim, and her vocabulary reflects her mother's love of language. "Marty said that on my birthday he's going to play music. He said he had something cooking up his sleeve, and we're really going to town. Ronni said she's going to give me a present." It is dinnertime and Vivian looks up quickly from her plate, anticipating her mother's disapproval. "I told Ronni a card would be plenty." Vivian swallows hard and repeats herself, "Plenty, Hannah, plenty."

Hannah: "One thing with retarded kids. They're not jealous. They are noncompetitive, nonmanipulative. One gets something, they're all happy. Call it pure soul or pure light or whatever you want to call it."

Vivian Kahn goes to "work" every day at the Association for the Development of the Exceptional, on North Miami Avenue. She is small, 4 feet 7 inches tall, and dresses young for her age: Hannah says that size 14 Polly Flinders fit best. She joins 50 other retarded adults who are taught how to count, how to take a bus, how to answer the phone. Her mother drives Vivian in the morning, and she is given a ride home to their apartment in the afternoon. Her mother, who has had a job selling furniture at Whitecraft Industries' showroom for 41 years, arrives home a couple of hours after Vivian, at 5:30. A few minutes before her mother's blue car pulls into the parking lot, Vivian goes to the window and looks for her, so she can wave a greeting at the woman with silver hair. Hannah has a remarkably energetic stride for a woman of 72; it is the always-hurried movement common in mothers of young children. When she is alone, Vivian can take care of herself. She can watch

> Notice all the information about the two women in this paragraph. Readers want information.

television or type a letter or answer the phone as long as "I don't give no information to wrong numbers. Frank taught me that. He taught me not to climb and not to touch the stove too."

Frank Kahn was Vivian's father and the stepfather, though he disliked the term, of Hannah's two sons from a previous marriage. Hannah Kahn was 19 when Melvin was born, 21 when Danny came. "No one could have been more scared with a baby than I was. I remember the doctor told me, as long as you've got a healthy baby, they'll probably turn out all right no matter what you do." Hannah Kahn's first marriage is a phase of her life about which she is uncommunicative, yet it has perhaps figured in some of her writing. For in addition to the steady prosaic life amid the rattan, selling the *étagères* and convertible couches, Hannah Kahn is a poet of some note, once considered a leading candidate for the title of poet laureate for the state of Florida. *Ex-Wife* is an early poem about which she says today: Too obvious, everything about it. The sentiments, the rhymes:

Wonder if my shadow / ever interferes, / do they know their laughter / as an echo of my tears.

Wonder if her love / is stronger than was mine? / I who only asked for bread— / She whose bread was wine.

Sometimes when the shadow / is intensified, / I can hear him breathing / softly at my side,

I can feel his fingers / reach across the night / and rest upon my eyelids / shutting out the light—

I have heard him tapping / on my window pane / and when I rose to answer / found out that it was rain.

Wonder when their beings / merge within a flame / does he ever call her / by my name?

Always try to get as much written research material as possible. It often works into the story.

Dinner over, Vivian helps clear the dishes. She inquires after dessert. "When God gave you to my house, Vivian, there must have been a contract requiring dessert with every dinner." Dessert is an apple. After dinner, Vivian says, "I'm cold, I'm chilled."

"What should you do when you're chilled?"

"Put something on."

Vivian was Frank's first child. Hannah had wanted a girl, and when Vivian was born Frank told Hannah, "It's a girl. You got what you wanted." Hannah recently came

The writer in the background watches, listens and later uses the material.

across the hospital bill: 10 days, $100.

Vivian has fetched her sweater. "Hannah," she says, very businesslike, "take your pills."

"See," says Hannah, reaching for her pills. "She watches over me."

She touches her daughter's soft pretty hair. "I was born with nervous hands," she once wrote. "What they loved they had to touch." — Nuances like this one make this story.

They found out that Vivan had Down's syndrome when she was 8 months old, just after Christmas: "We went to the doctor for a routine checkup. She was dressed in white shoes, a blue organdy dress. For the first time her hair was long enough for a narrow ribbon bow." — Remember Hannah is recalling an event 40 years ago. But she does so, so vividly it could have been yesterday. Writer has built a trust with subjects.

Frank and Hannah Kahn were left alone with Vivian in the examining room. The child's chart was on a table, open. The doctor had written, "Did you tell her that Vivian is a Mongoloid child?"

Hannah:

"In those days nothing was known about retardation. No one knew anything about an extra chromosome. Lightning strikes. I felt that I was the only person in Miami who had given birth to such a person. I can still remember the words of the doctor: "They Are Unfinished Children. During Pregnancy Because Of Some Endocrine Or Other Deficiency In The Mother That We Do Not Know, The Unborn Child Is Not Completed. She Can Never Go Beyond The Mental Age Of 5 Or 6 And It's Best For You And Your Other Children That She Be Placed In An Institution When She's 13 Months Old. There Is No Doubt About Our Diagnosis. See This, These Special Epicanthal Folds In The Eyes. (But her eyes are impish. . . .) Their Little Fingers, Short Curved Like A Fish. Their Hands Are Short And Stubby. (Her fingers which we had counted and re-counted. She's double-jointed. . . .) These Children Usually Are."

At home that night Hannah performed the usual tasks in a trance. She prepared the dinner, talked to the boys, cleared the table. Frank took Vivian into her room, changed her, gave her a bottle and put her to sleep. Hannah thought: I should have known. Should I have known? The pregnancy was so easy, too easy. I told the doctor the baby wasn't kicking as much as the others had. He said, "We'll take care of everything, Mrs. Kahn." At the hospital the nurses remarked on what a good baby Vivian was, how well she slept.

Frank came into the living room, dressed for the card party they had planned on going to. Hannah Kahn was incredulous. "Get dressed," Frank said softly. "Everything goes on." Hannah remembers only one detail from the evening. "I drank cup after cup of coffee. It tasted like blood."

"Frank established the rhythm. Frank set the pace. Without him I don't know how I would have survived. . . .

"We never actually sat down and told the boys something was wrong with Vivian. We said she was slow in some ways but advanced in others, like her dancing. Both boys were always good with Vivian. I remember Melvin used to go to the beach with the debating team, and every now and then he'd ask me if Vivian could come along. I told him, Melvin, the other boys aren't going to want Vivian to come along and he said oh, they do. Vivian walks around and she attracts the girls and helps us make friends. Danny told me that whenever he took Viv to the playground, he never thought she was slow. He simply assumed all the other children were very advanced.

"In whatever way Danny and Melvin might have been hurt by it, they certainly got to be more considerate people through their association with Vivian. By far she has enriched me. Without Vivian I would've had such an ordinary, take-for-granted life."

"Child," the mother once wrote, "give me your hand that I may walk in the light of your faith in me."

Blais often uses Hannah's writing to emphasize emotional high points in the story. Blais writes sparsely about Frank, but his presence is always felt.

From a letter Hannah Kahn wrote to a friend shortly after her husband's death in 1975:

"Vivian's relationship with her father was unique; everyone who knew them grieved doubly when he died, wondering how Vivian would adjust. She's been wonderful. . . . He taught her well.

"I don't have to tell you how grief comes in waves. Vivian sometimes sets the table for three instead of two.

"About six months ago he re-wallpapered our kitchen. The icebox goes in a niche. . . . He already wasn't feeling well—moving the icebox was difficult. I told him no one would know if he didn't paper behind the icebox. He looked at me, smiled and said, 'I would know.'

"Tomorrow I have to go to the lawyer's office and sign a new will. . . . Vivian's future is my greatest concern."
From *Betrayal*:

> *I walk among the headstones in my sleep —*
> *I read the names, the dates. I place two stones*
> *Upon your grave. I ask you to forgive*
> *That in some strange, distorted way I live.*

From *Metastasis*:

> *The cells divide*
> *and multiply*
> *My body is their battleground*
> *I am the field they occupy.*

Hannah Kahn had a mastectomy seven years ago. During a recent visit to the doctor "something showed up on the scan." Hannah now rehearses the reality of the future: "Someday our life together, as it is now, will end. Vivian's not going to be by the window and I'm not going to get out of the car." She is looking into Haven School, the possibility of placing Vivian there five days a week to accustom her to separation. "It has always been my unspoken dream that something would happen to her before something happened to me so Vivian would be forever sheltered."

"Hannah," says her daughter, "now please don't forget your pills."

Vivian Kahn has never been to her father's grave. She thinks he is buried in the clouds. On his birthday she always waves to him in the sky ("That's where Frank is, he's in heaven") and sings "Happy Birthday" including the second verse, *We love you, we do.* "Frank didn't want Vivian to see him sick in the hospital. Instead they spoke to each other over the phone. He never wanted Vivian to go to the cemetery. He didn't think she could handle the thought of the underground thing.

"At the time of Frank's death I was very worried about the effect it would have on Vivian. I didn't understand that for a child like Vivian who has two parents, when one dies, her life didn't change very much. She was in the same house, the same bed. There was no break," says Hannah, "in the rhythm."

This pill quote, placed here, seals the reader's understanding of the bond between Hannah and Vivian.

When it came time to tell Vivian about the womanly processes, this is what Hannah Kahn did:

"Frank would die if he knew this. He was a very modest man. I never sat down and told her. I took her in the bathroom with me and showed her and tried to behave as naturally as possible because I have discovered with Vivian if you're casual, she's casual. With Vivian, I don't know how much she needs to know. At Vivian's job, at A.D.E., they keep stressing Who-man Growth and Development, as Vivian pronounces it. I don't know what they're telling her. I don't know what she understands. I'll never forget the day Vivian was watching 'All In The Family,' and Vivian is yelling 'push, push' and I ran into the living room to see what was happening and Gloria was having a baby and my daughter's coaching her.

"At A.D.E. they say, this is reality. This is actuality. The children should know about these things. I look at Viv, and I see a child, in many ways, a child of 8 or 9, and I keep thinking: Who would want their 8- or 9-year-old child thinking about getting married?"

Only once did Vivian ever cross Hannah. That was when Richard gave Vivian an engagement ring, a diamond. Hannah told Vivian to return it. Vivian put it in her pocketbook.

Vivian often chooses to wear the clothing that Richard has told her turns him on. "What does that mean, Viv? Turning someone on?" "Actshully, Hannah, it means I light up his life."

Vivian has a notion her mother would like her to cool it with Richard: "I think she's wants me to be just friends."

Would she like to be more than friends?

"Be honest now. I would love to, but I don't know if my mother's going to let me."

Why Richard?

"Because he thinks I'm beautiful and so on and so on."

What's sex?

"I would suggest sex is good, you know why? I'm not embarrassed in saying it. Now making love is when you're kissing on the lips. My mother won't let me kiss on the lips. Sex means when you get VD."

Babies?

"I do have my dolls, Princess from Hungary and Granny from Russia. They are not real babies, they're dolls. But the only thing is how is my mother going to put up with it, it's a big job, supposing he starts doing something in his diapers."

Where do babies come from?

"Babies," she says, "can come from anywhere. The mother's stomach, a hospital, could come from God."

Vivian Kahn begins the celebration of her birthday on January 1st, with references to surprises and cake. On the first day of April she announces, "It's my month." This year was the first year in a long time that Hannah Kahn allowed Vivian to be her true age: 40. For years Vivian's age was frozen at 16. Hannah: "It was easier that way."

The festivities lasted two days. On Friday, April 15 Vivian received flowers at A.D.E. and everybody gave Vivian a kiss. There was a wondrous cake from a Cuban bakery. Vivian got to sit in the middle of the cafeteria next to a person of her choosing. She chose Richard. As the birthday girl, she was given the first piece of cake, but she made certain that Richard received the next piece. "Here Richard, this is the second piece." Marty, a man in his 50s who has spent his life in institutions and who has a gift for playing the piano without being able to read music, told Vivian "You ain't seen nothing yet." Then he sat down at the piano and played Vivian's favorite song, "You Light Up My Life." She got up and sang, So many nights I sit by the window waiting for someone to sing me a song. Vivian has told her counselor at A.D.E. she would like to be Debby Boone, or a secretary. Ronni gave Vivian more than a card, she gave her a bracelet and kept saying, "Happy Birthday. Many more 'til next year." Vivian clapped her hands and touched her bracelet: "I've never had it so good. The cake and this and the flowers." Marty was asked by popular acclaim to play "those Marine songs" which he did, and at the end of the hour, he got up, received a smattering of applause, and looking at his scruffy shoes when he spoke, which is his custom, he said, "I told you, you ain't seen nothing yet." On the next day Hannah and Vivian attended the annual luncheon of Women in Communications at the Omni, and Vivian stood before the hundreds of women in attendance to receive some birthday applause. A private party followed, at the Kahn's residence.

Hannah Kahn's *Eve's Daughter* was published in 1962. Her latest collection, *Time, Wait* will be published soon by the University Presses of Florida. By far *Ride a Wild Horse* is her most successful poem. Published first under the title *Into the Sun* in *The Saturday Review*, it has been in more than 20 textbooks and anthologies:

> *Ride a wild horse*
> *with purple wings*
> *striped yellow and black*
> *except his head*
> *Which must be red.*
>
> *Ride a wild horse*
> *against the sky—*
> *hold tight to his wings*
> *Before you die*
> *whatever else you leave undone—*
> *once ride a wild horse*
> *into the sun.*

Vivian has written two poems:

> *The Pink Carnation*
> *The Pink Carnation is wearing a white sports coat*
> *all dressed up for a date.*
>
> *The Ocean View*
> *I looked across the Atlantic ocean*
> *I see Europe*
> *the ocean waves are dancing just like diamonds.*

When Hannah Kahn is asked the difference between prose and poetry, she answers with a quote from one of her poems:

> *I wanted to write about the old men*
> *Who look at the dinner menu for a long time,*
> *And then ordered doughnuts and coffee.*

"I wanted to say, as quickly as I could, these men were poor and could not afford to order what they wanted. A prose writer might have said the same thing, but in a more complete way. A poem is as much what you don't say and what you imply as what you do say. A poem gives the reader the chance to add to or complete the thought.

"A poem can be about anything. It contains a certain moment you can almost take a picture of. It should capture a feeling or an essence or a scene. Something that stands out, that is not blurred into the momentum."

A certain moment:

After the guests had departed, Hannah and Vivian Kahn sat down to a light supper of gefilte fish and salad and chocolate mousse cake. ("I like my life," says Hannah, "but sometimes I don't like the facts of my life.") After dinner Vivian sat by the phone to collect more calls. More than once, she admired the flowers from her nieces and nephew. Vivian examined her gifts: The doll from Mexico, the Lollipop bloomers from Aunt Sylvia, the handkerchiefs. She wanted to play her new record, *Elvira*, sung by the Oak Ridge Boys, but she decided she better wait by the phone. Whenever it rang, and it rang a lot, it was for her: Danny and Phyllis in Spokane, Leslie in Washington, D.C., Estelle's son in California. Vivian decided that on the next day she would like to wear one of her new dresses. She thought it would be nice if her mother took her for a ride past Victoria Hospital.

Notice the use of the "certain moment" above and then here. You can almost take a picture of it.

At 8 o'clock Hannah said, "Viv, I think it's time. I think this is the time you were born."

"Oh, you think so Hannah?"

"Think so? I know it. It's 8:20, Viv."

Great writing is not a 9 to 5 job. If Blais hadn't been there at 8 P.M., there would be no great story.

Vivian rocked back and forth on the sofa. Her chin was buried in her neck, concealing the wide happy smile. The short stubby fingers clapped in delight. "Victoria Hospital. Private room."

"That's right. Nothing but the best for my daughter."

"Hannah, do you think we could go out on the terrace and say hello to Frank?"

The older woman stood, and crossed the room, her stride erect and swift, as usual. She opened the sliding glass door and made a sweeping motion with her hand, ushering her daughter onto the balcony. "That's because I am the birthday girl, right," said Vivian. The two women stood side by side. They held each other's hands. They looked up. The night was cloudy and still. Vivian took her hand and raised high the short bent fingers. She waved at the sky. In a soft shy voice she said, "Frank, it's my birthday today. Right now I will be born, be born, sure, Frank. Thank you for carrying me home from the hospital." Then her hand still raised, her face uplifted, Vivian stood utterly still and listened as only she can listen. "He says he remembers me," she said, her head beginning to rock. "He's singing 'Happy Birthday.' "

Ending ties into the beginning.

Finding a Staff Job

I f you like what you've heard about feature writing, and you are ready to spend time out in the rain knocking on doors as Jimmy Breslin once defined the profession, then you are ready to make a decision. You can either take the freelance approach or you can go for a regular job. Either way, you won't find it easy. Most in the profession have had to work their way up, and working your way up is harder now than it has ever been in the past. Feature editor Richard Cheverton provides some of the good news and some of the not so good news about finding a job in feature writing. Once again, the emphasis is on newspapers, but the advice applies to many other avenues in publishing as well.

A Great Editor Tells Who He Would Hire (and includes some dirty little secrets)

Richard Cheverton

First, Some Bad News

It's tougher to get a job in newspaper journalism than ever before. That's because there are fewer newspapers — and those that have had the good fortune to survive the shakeout of the past few years are being run by hard-eyed managers who are far more interested in ever-increasing quarterly earnings than in adding to fixed expenses by hiring more people.

In general, newspapers are finding ways to do more with fewer people. My own newspaper, *The Orange County Register* in booming Southern California, is a good example. Circulation is increasing at about 6 percent a year, outstripping the county's 2 percent growth rate. The paper was numero uno in advertising lineage in the country last year, displacing the mighty *Los Angeles Times*. We'll probably repeat that feat this year.

You'd think we'd be in Fat City when it comes time to figure the budget.

Naaah. Last year, we added two bodies to the features department—one, a restaurant critic (a highly specialized position that almost no beginner would be eligible to fill, unless his name was Wolfgang Puck).

The other position argued for itself.

And here we get to our first dirty little secret:

If You Are a Beginning Writer, and if You Don't Absolutely, Positively Burn to Write, Become a Copyeditor

Yes, the second position we added was on the desk. Growing newspaper equals growing copy desk: it's a gimme.

The nasty fact is that there is, generally, an oversupply of writers. If you, as an editor, want to put a lot of ink on a lot of paper, there are dozens of willing wage-slaves available.

But copyeditors?

Look at the ads in *Editor & Publisher* classifieds: My guess is that on any given week, help-wanted ads for copyeditors (always written with a slight note of yearning and desperation) will outnumber ads for writers (and, in particular, beginning writers) by a factor of ten.

There's a reason for that. Copyediting is tough.

Copyeditors do the grunt-work: they stare into VDTs all day; they wrestle with the myriad ways that writers fracture the mother tongue; they contend with the composing room; they live with the knowledge that, like the warrior-king in the Golden Bough, tomorrow always brings more problems, more errors . . . that the copyeditor's job always involves paranoia and defeat.

But . . .

Copyeditors are valuable little jewels to be collected and protected and guarded by the astute editor-manager. You could send every writer in a newspaper home, and the paper would come out on the morrow: you'd simply turn on the wire machines. But guess who has to turn raw copy into the stuff that comes off on your fingers?

Copyeditors. Without them, the operation grinds to a halt.

It's no surprise that so many managing editors or executive editors have come up through the copy desk route. On the desk, you have an intimate view of the way the newspaper actually works. Or doesn't, which is even more important.

So, my advice to someone who yearns to be in newspapering (and who wants, one day, to run the show) is: consider copyediting.

The work is there; you can chuck the job if the editor so much as looks cross-eyed at you and know, with certainty, that you'll be snapped up overnight; you'll have your choice of garden-spots and, if you are sufficiently footloose, you can copyedit your way across the country and back again.

So, end of aside: at least think about becoming a copyeditor.

(This message brought to you by the Desperate Assistant Managing Editor's Society of America.)

But, of course, you yearn to write, don't you?

(And, unfortunately, your father doesn't own the local daily.)

It's time to face another unpleasant fact.

How can one put this delicately?—it's tougher than ever before to break in if you're a white male.

Which is the reverse of saying: Times have never been better for women and minorities in the newspaper business. Many newspapers have very aggressive affirmative action policies in their newsrooms. At *The Orange County Register*, for example, all editorial managers must find a qualified minority finalist for each job opening. We're aggressive in promoting women into management positions, which means that, as women climb the ladder, they tend to be replaced by either other women or by minorities.

The hard, cold, inescapable truth is that white males now have to be extra-talented—almost irresistible—to muscle their way to the front of the hiring line.

And, as we've observed, the line is getting longer as the newspaper business shrinks. And, guess what? As the business contracts, people tend to cling to their jobs longer and take fewer risks. Job-jumping is way down; as the baby boomers mature, they put down roots. The "churn" that's so essential to opening up jobs to relative newcomers (or even mid-career types) is slowing.

And, while Newspaper Guild units are losing power at many papers, being a member in good standing is the closest thing to tenure outside a university.

Bottom line: Getting a good newspaper job is like jumping into a pool of molasses: you can make it to the other end, but it's going to be slow.

Which brings us to dirty little secret number two:

Hiring is a Crap Shoot . . . and Nobody Really Knows How to Play the Game

I have lost count of the number of people I've hired in my seven years at *The Register*. I'd guess it's 30 or so, and that's an extraordinary number for most editors. (But *The Register* has undergone an extraordinary period of growth and reformation; essentially, the newspaper's staff was replaced, top to bottom.)

In making those hires—and, thank goodness, most have worked out really well—I've come to know that hiring is the ultimate gamble. You never, ever really know what a person is going to do when he or she moves into a new job.

It's similar to what you see in major league baseball. A big-ticket free agent goes to a new ball club and has a terrible year. A star pitcher can't find the plate; a slugger goes into a two-year deep freeze.

I've seen the same thing happen in the newspaper business— so often, in fact, that I've finally learned that:

No Hire Is Predictable . . . for Either Party to the Transaction

It goes, I suppose, to the hiring process itself: The applicant shows up, freshly scrubbed, on his best behavior, alert, adrenaline pumping, slightly disoriented.

There ensues a ritual as elaborate as the mating dance of the prairie chicken. There's much preening and cooing, with each party to the transaction trying to discover what the other person really wants to hear. It's a classic courtship.

But—as with courtship—you can never know what the person looks like in the morning until it's too late.

Actually making a hire is really one of the great existential leaps of faith. Some editors tie themselves in knots, agonizing over real and imagined differences between candidates. One set of editors, who shall remain nameless, interviewed a flotilla of job-seekers for the better part of a half-year, then finally hired a person who worked at the newspaper and who was one of the first applicants they interviewed.

Did these editors really know what they were doing? Not likely.

The result is that a lot of bigger newspaper outfits — the chains, in particular — resort to elaborate stratagems to winnow out the potential .300 hitters from the future million-dollar bench-warmers. Knight-Ridder, for example, has its infamous hiring test, the most daunting quiz this side of the SATs, full of worrisome little traps (do they still analyze a candidate's handwriting?) and questions for which there are no "right" answers (and if you believe that, let's talk Florida swampland).

Having sat in on a few sessions with corporate headshrinkers discussing the potential of either job-seekers or current employees up for promotion . . . well, all I can say is that I was (and am) appalled. It's far too easy for managers to abdicate to the self-confident men in funny-looking sports jackets (who dresses most of these psychologists, anyway?); it's easy and it's harmful.

The newspaper business used to be the last refuge for the terminally different; for the square pegs who refused to be jammed into round holes. For people who bore some resemblance to the newspaper's actual readers, in all of their idiosyncrasies.

Now, the news biz is full of the certifiably sane.

Guess what newspaper executives discuss with alarm these days?

Declining (some might say plummeting) circulation and penetration and readership (particularly among the young) numbers.

Do you think that maybe, just maybe, newspapers are too sane? Think these problems are interrelated?

The prospective writer needs to know that, in many cases, he or she will be scrutinized by unseen persons . . . a shrink, perhaps, or a zealous personnel department.

I'm damned if I know what to tell an aspiring writer confronted by this, beyond: fake 'em out, if you can. I know this is heresy coming from a manager, but I'm convinced that any newspaper is better off with a few talented misfits.

You might as well be the one.

An Aside: Let's Talk Clips

The classic double-bind: how's the beginner supposed to amass a great-looking portfolio of clips? How important are they, anyway?

This, in turn, suggests yet another double-bind: how can the beginner amass good clips without being written into the ground?

It's my opinion that, while entry-level jobs are fairly easy to come by (there are always small newspapers willing to pay minimum wage to college graduates with several internships at major newspapers on their résumés), many of these jobs are perilous to the emerging writer.

Too many smaller papers are run by big chains that, putting it gently, have no understanding of journalism. It is a great tragedy of the business and of the country that many, many smaller papers have fallen prey to conglomerateurs and takeover artists who could just as well be putting together empires of toxic chemical plants.

A beginning job at one of these rural or suburban sweatshops is worse than no job at all. The editors at these papers will not give the beginning writer the kind of instructive editing necessary to learn the craft—let alone the art—of good writing. In many cases, they will insist that the young writer learn bad writing habits.

And, above all, they will cause the young writer to value production—sheer verbal tonnage—over quality.

As an editor who has hired dozens of people, I have seen too many candidates whose files are thick, brimming over, with clips. And all of them are formulaic, predictable, mechanical.

Personally, I think it would be better for the young writer to spend a little less time writing (and career-building) in his or her formative (meaning: immediate, post-college) years.

If you have to go to work, pick the brightest, quirkiest, most individual small paper you can find (yes, they still exist); work long enough to save some bucks and then travel. You'll find a good market for travel stories (and travel writing can be an entrée to a bigger newspaper). You can string for wire services or even for larger newspapers. Sometimes there are local English-language papers that count on the passing stream of traveling journalists.

Or take the opportunity to get involved in a political campaign; there's no better way to prepare for being a political reporter. Or find a garret and write the Great American Novel.

In other words: if you're young, you're supposed to take risks. Take them.

How About Something That's Not Quite a Newspaper?

In my opinion, some of the best nurseries for creating talented writers are the so-called "alternative" newspapers.

In case you haven't noticed, some of them have gotten very big: the *Phoenix* (Arizona) *New Times* prints tabloid issues of well over 100 pages. Their classified ads must bring tears to the eyes of the ad guys at the *Phoenix Republic* (which, in its usual, clumsy way, once tried to put the *New Times* out of business by publishing its own weekly entertainment tabloid, which quickly flopped).

The owners of the *New Times* have bought or opened papers in Miami and Denver. In Boston, the *Phoenix* is equally hefty. There are healthy alternative papers in just about every metropolitan area and, in general, the level of writing in most is far more passionate, more committed, more interesting than in most big metro papers.

Oh, the metro editors look down their noses at the supposed lack of "objectivity" in the alternatives but, again, ask the question: Who's getting the younger readers?

In plain truth, your future as a writer may not be with a big metro paper—which may, in fact, be a dinosaur stumbling toward a future tar pit.

What the hell; with the costs of desktop publishing plummeting, you can just as well start your own newspaper. (As A.J. Liebling said: "Freedom of the press belongs to the man who owns one.")

The newspaper business—big, troubled metros aside—is wide open to those willing to innovate, take risks, dare to fail. The future of newspapers may not involve "paper" at all. A person with a FAX machine has, in effect, a kind of printing press; who knows what impact these technologies will have on the business of communication?

But You Want to Work for a "Real" Newspaper . . .

Haven't talked you out of it?

Well, yes, there is the incomparable rush of going down to the press room and watching thousands of newspapers streaming off the big Goss presses; it's then that you begin to sense the real power of newspapers. These objects will be held, read, consumed by real people.

So, a final few thoughts for those of you who (like this writer) simply cannot imagine life outside a newspaper's newsroom. First, another rule:

There Are No Rules in Hiring

Every manager has his or her own quirks. Some like to do all the talking; others challenge the applicant to fill the silence. Some ask off-the-wall questions ("What's the funniest thing that ever happened to you?"), others revert to the formulaic ("What are your strengths and weaknesses?").

Some rely on clips—heavily. Others see them as a minefield, full of rewriting by editors who have covered up an applicant's fondness for libel.

Some managers succumb to the Romance of the Other—the idea that an operation always needs a transfusion of "fresh blood"; others seek stability and continuity by promoting from within.

Your job as a job-seeker is to do your research: call around, get a handle on the person you'll be confronting. It's a small, incestuous business: somewhere there will be someone with a book on the person you're going to be dealing with. An aside:

You Can Never Know Too Much

In hiring, I've been impressed by how little most applicants know about *The Register* or Southern California; how little, in short, they've prepared themselves.

An applicant with so-so clips could bowl me over by telling me what my problems are, what my newspaper needs to do to succeed, what that person can do for me in filling a gap in coverage.

It's not hard to figure out: there are materials available on most communities that can give you a fast picture of its demographics and of the newspaper's success in reaching its market.

A few calls to people who know the business will tell the job-seeker chapters about the internal politics of a newspaper. Ex-employees are invaluable in this regard.

Anything that will give you an edge is fair game.

I'll never forget how impressed I was with one job applicant. As a rule, *The Register* (and many other newspapers) asks candidates to critique the paper; we send out a dozen issues or sections and usually work the critique into our interviewing process.

This applicant did the critique—on videotape. He flipped through the pages on camera, told us what he liked, what he would do differently, what he'd change.

You can be sure that he had the editor's undivided attention. And he got bonus points for inventiveness and chutzpah.

Anything that will give you an edge—use it. A final insight:

You're Not Being Hired For a Job, You're Being Admitted to a Club

Whether or not a manager admits it to himself, when all of the clips have been read, all of the reference calls made, all of the tests or interviews totaled up, it comes down to a guess about the person's character.

And the big question is: How will this character fit the other characters in this newsroom?

It's a matter of adding to the mix; the smart hiring editor thinks of each job opening in relation to the strengths and weaknesses in each of the other persons holding jobs in the newsroom.

At *The Register*, we use the expression "tread life" (as in tires) a lot when we're hiring. By that, we mean that we're looking at that person's potential to learn and grow, to add to the "mix."

Yes, we're looking for people with edges, interesting rough spots, the square pegs for our round holes. But, still, it's every manager's nightmare that he'll hire someone who is talented, brilliant, qualified in every way, and that the person will come into the small, hermetic realm of the newsroom and create instant discord and havoc.

I've made a couple of those hires. It's an unending hangover.

What does this mean to you as a job-seeker?

I would be stunned (and impressed) if a job-seeker asked me, at some point, "How will I fit into the mix of people in this department? What do you see me bringing to the mix of talent that you need?"

I'd pay a lot of attention to that sort of applicant.

I'd also pay a lot of attention to an applicant who was concerned with what my newspaper could teach—in the near-term and the long run. In other words, an applicant who had a sense of what the newspaper was trying to do and how he or she could fit into that.

I'd be impressed.

And I'd probably try my damnedest to hire that person.

INDEX

A

Accuracy
  in freelance writing, 219-220
  in medical writing, 195-196
  in television criticism, 172
Allen, Henry, 146-147
Allen, Martha Sawyer, 62
Almanac of Famous People, 86
Alternative newspapers
  jobs at, 268
  writing for, 227-231
America: History and Life, 88
Americana Magazine, 80
Anecdotes, use of in profile-writing, 127
Anxiety
  about leads, 102-103, 112
  coping techniques for, 13-14
Art and Craft of Feature Writing, The, 104, 113
Art of Writing Nonfiction, The, 107
Arts and entertainment writing, 167-181
Atlases, 86
Audience identification, 228-230

B

Baldwin, James, 16
Basic Magazine Writing, 234
Beginnings. *See* Leads
Best Newspaper Writing, 39
Blais, Madeleine, 31-36, 252-261
Blundell, William, 83, 104
Body language, during interviews,
    62-63, 73
Book Critics Circle, 185
Book Review Digest, 87
Book reviews, writing guidelines for,
    182-185
Books in Print, 87
Boston Globe, The, 12
Boston Phoenix, 268
Breaking news story, vs. feature stories,
    5-6
Bridge of San Luis Rey, The, 6
Brody, Jane, 7

Brown, J.D., 162

C

Canadian Business, 80
Capote, Truman, 5-6
Captions, in fashion writing, 186-187
Cariaga, Daniel, 172-175
Carton, Barbara, 12
Cassidy, Claudia, 177
Catalog journalism, 161
Cates, Jo, 84-89
Celebrity profiles
  importance of contacting, 37
  interviews with, 196-201
  syndication of, 225-226
Character development
  importance of, in feature stories, 34-36
  in profile writing, 150-151
Chatwin, Bruce, 163
Cheverton, Richard, 3, 262-271
Clarity, 241-243
  in book reviews, 184
Clark, Roy Peter, 25-31
Clichés, avoidance of, in music criticism,
    174-175
Clips, importance of, 223, 267-268
Cobb, Nathan, 144-145
Coffeeline, 88
Columns, syndication of, 226
Communities as feature story sources,
    33-34
Complete Guide to Writing Nonfiction, 234
Computer databases, 88, 111
Computer skills, 247-248
Concise Columbia Encyclopedia, 86
Conflict of interest, in feature writing, 202
Conversation, interviews as, 72-73
Copyediting, as entrée into job market,
    263-265
Courtesy, importance of, in interviews,
    198-199
Crane, Stephen, 12
Criticism,
  guidelines for, 201-202
Cross-cultural training, 249-250

Current Biography, 86

D

DataTimes, 88
Deadlines
  importance of, 151-152, 217-218, 233
  as inspiration, 138-140
  working off, 16
Description
  guidelines for using, 129-133
  importance of, in feature writing, 16
  profile-writing and, 127-128
  as tool for writing leads, 106-107
Details
  avoiding gratuitous, 151
  double-checking of, 74-75
  importance of, in feature writing, 11-12
  profile-writing and, 128-129
  reporting skills and, 52
  successful writing and, 244-245
Discover Magazine, 195
Distance, in story structure, 97-98
Doctor, Ken, 245-250
D'Orso, Mike, 76-84
Dress, importance of, in interviews, 66-67

E

Ebert, Roger, 6
Economics of freelancing, 212-213
Editor & Publisher, 263
Editors
  hiring tips from, 262-271
  magazine editors, 221-223
  relationships with freelancers, 14, 18,
    91, 219-221
  skills of, 19
  techniques for approaching, 211-219
Education, for freelance writers, 247-248
Ehlert, Bob, 65, 129-133
Electronic research sources, 85, 87-88
Elements of Style, The, 85
Empathy, with story subjects, 10-11
Encyclopedia of Associations, 82-84, 87, 112
Encyclopedias, as research tool, 86
Endings
  guidelines for writing, 108
  as organizational tool, 94
  techniques for writing, 17

F

Face-to-face interviews, 110
Fact-checking techniques, 112-113
Fallaci, Oriana, 93, 200
Fame and Obscurity, 125

Fashion writing guidelines, 186-190
Feature writing
  definition of, 3-7
  importance of, 15-16
  as predictor of change, 16
  types of, 4-5
Film criticism, 178-181
Financial aspects of freelance writing,
    185, 248
  syndication, 224-226
Finkel, David, 51-61
First draft, as feature-writing tool, 131-133
First-person writing
  in alternative papers, 230
  limits of, 152
  techniques for, 134-140
  See also Writer's voice
Florida Trend, 8
Focus, need for, in feature writing, 91-92
Fontaine, Andre, 107
Food writing, 165-167
Forster, E.M., 32
Forthcoming Books, 87
Fox, Wendy, 149
Franklin, Jon, 40, 237-245
Free-Lancer and Staff Writer, 39
Friends, as idea sources, 137-138
Fussell, Paul, 161, 165

G

Generalist writers, demand for, 18
Glavin, William A. Jr., 107
Goode's World Atlas, 86
Goodman, Ellen, 137
Government agencies, as information
    sources, 110-111
Grady, Denise, 191-196
Greene, Bob, 139-140
Guinness Book of World Records, 86

H

Hadar, Mary, 219-221
Hamburg, Jay, 21-24
Harasim, Paul H., 145-146
Hard news, importance of, 15, 19
Harrigan, Jane, 89-100, 111
Harrington, Walt, 140-143, 155-156
Hart, Jack, 124-129
Hertz, Sue, 100
Hiring process, guidelines about, 262-271
Hodges, Sam, 190
Hohler, Bob, 98
Honesty
  importance of, in interviewing, 64, 110

in lead writing, 104-105
in theater criticism, 176-177
Hourglass writing structures, 96
How I Wrote the Story, 21
Humorous articles
    in alternative papers, 229
    importance of, in feature writing,
        190-191, 221
    syndication of, 225-226
    in travel writing, 163
Hunter, Stephen, 144, 178-181

I

Idea file, importance of keeping, 37-38
Ideas
    selling of, 37, 213-214
    serendipitous search for, 111
    sources for, 25-31, 214-216
Imitation, use of, by feature writers, 150
In Cold Blood, 5-6, 97, 155
Interviewing techniques, 11-12
Interviews
    with celebrities, 196-201
    as conversation, 72-73
    examples of, 69-70
    importance of, 59-60
    impressions gained during, 70-71
    multiple interviews, 63, 109
    picking locale for, 113
    preparation for, 66-67
    questions avoided during, 73-74
    role of, in television criticism, 171-172
    selecting people for, 61, 67
    techniques for, 55-58, 61-75
    timing of, 67-68
Iron Horse, 80
Isolation of freelancing, 14

J

Judgmental writing, avoidance of, 181-182

K

Kampinsky, Ellen, 186-190
Kaplan, Steven, 235-236
Karlen, Neal, 211-219, 231
Kister, Ken, 84-89
Klinkenberg, Jeff, 29
Knight-Ridder Inc., 266
Krieger, Elliot, 182-185
Kuralt, Charles, 139

L

Lavin, Cheryl, 105
Leads

anxiety about, 102-103, 112
    guidelines for writing, 12-13, 17,
        100-108
    ignoring rules for, 103-104
    mystery in, 104-105, 112
    as organizational tool, 93-94
    quotes and questions as, 107-108
    using description in, 106-107
Letter of introduction, 202
LEXIS information system, 88
Library, as research source, 76-79
Listening skills, importance of, during
        interviews, 9, 63, 200
Literary journalism, as type of feature
        writing, 6
Literary Journalists, The, 76
Literary Market Place, 185
Locale
    descriptive techniques and, 130-131
    importance of in travel writing, 164-165
Local information sources, 111
Localization of stories, 37, 58-60
Los Angeles Times, 263

M

Magazine editors, expectations of
        freelancers, 221-223
Magazine Index, 87
Manhattan, inc., 218
Martin, Claire, 114-123
Mastering the Message, 247
McLeod, Michael, 190
McPhee, John, 29, 76, 83
Medical writing, 191-196
Merck Manual of Diagnosis and Therapy, The,
        86
Merton, Andy, 144-150
Mikelbank, Peter, 220-221
Miller, Kay, 61-75
Minnesota Monthly, 3-4, 222
Minority hiring practices, 264-265
Molnar, Jim, 157-165
Morbidity and Mortality Weekly Report, 192
Morris, Jan, 162
Multiple sales, 248-249
Murray, Donald, 12-13, 15-18, 30
Music criticism, 172-175

N

Narrative line, profile writing and, 126-127
National magazines, guidelines for
        approaching, 216-217
Neatness, importance of, 231

Networking for freelance writers, 215-216, 231

Neuberger, Dick, 249

New Journalism, The, 154

Newspaper Index, 78-79

Newspapers
club atmosphere in, 270-271
as idea sources, 26-27, 38-39, 136-137
realistic ambience of, 238-241

Newspaper syndicates, 224-226

New York Magazine, 216-217

New York Times, 169, 245

New York Times Index, 87, 112

NEXIS information system, 88

Nichols, Mike, 163

Nonfiction novel, feature writing as, 5-6

Notes
as impediment to good writing, 94
importance of, in interviewing, 71-72, 109-110

Nouns, in headlines, 112

Nutrition, food writing and, 167

O

Observation, in feature writing, 9-10
during interviews, 62-63
in reporting, 58-60

Ode, Kim, 133

Offbeat perspectives, as source of ideas, 29-30

On Writing Well, 247, 251

Opinion articles, syndication of, 225

Orange County Register, The, 3, 263-266

Ordinary people
as feature subjects, 31-36
as idea source, 37-38

Organization, 111
importance of, for feature writing, 89-100

O'Sullivan, Bob, 164

O'Toole, Dan, 224-226

Outlaw Biker, 80

Outlines, as organizational tool, 95-96

P

Parallel narrative story construction, 97

Parker, Dorothy, 187

Patinkin, Mark, 133-140

People Magazine, 80

Perelman, S.J., 187

Persistence, importance of, 232
during interviews, 73-74
in freelancing, 213

Personal experience, as story source, 28-29, 37, 135-136

Personality theory, profile-writing and, 125-126

Philadelphia Inquirer, 7

Philadelphia Magazine, 222

Phoenix New Times, 268

Phoenix Republic, 268

Phonefiche, 87

Physicians' Desk Reference, 86

Pieces of the Frame, 154

Playboy Magazine, 142-143

Plot, importance of, in feature stories, 32-33, 38
in travel writing, 163

Point of view. *See* Writer's voice

Polak, Maralyn Lois, 7, 196-201

Practice, importance of, in feature writing, 109

Pre-publication approval, by subjects, 74-75, 110

Print sources, for research, 85-87

Profile-writing
guidelines for, 124-129, 150-151
interviewing techniques for, 66

Public documents, as research tool, 110

Public information sources, 110-111

Pyle, Ernie, 139

Q

Query letters
guidelines for writing, 216-217
neatness in, 231
sample of, 235-236

Questions
as story lead, 107-108
use of, in medical writing, 198-199

Quindlen, Anna, 135-136

Quotes
limits of, 36
as story lead, 107-108

R

Rand McNally Commercial Atlas and Marketing Guide, 86

Rand McNally Road Atlas, 86

Random House Thesaurus, 85

Ravin, Neil, 104

Rawson, Joel, 12

Reader's Digest, 195, 249

Reader's Guide to Periodical Literature, 78, 87, 247

Reading
about writing, 17

as source of ideas, 30
Reed, Jack, 53
Reference library, for freelance writers,
    84-89
Regional magazines, as freelance market,
    222
Regional stories, 38, 220-221
Rejections, guidelines for handling,
    232-233
Reliability, importance of, in freelance
    writers, 217-218
Reporter, as part of story, 140-143
Reporting, importance of, in feature
    writing, 18
Reporting skills
    guidelines for developing, 51-61
    importance of, in feature writing, 8
Research
    associations as source for, 82-84
    basic reference tools for, 84-89
    defining area for, 111
    developing focus for, 77-78
    electronic sources for, 85, 87-88, 247-248
    for feature stories, 75-84
    importance of, 18, 59-60, 110
    for interviews, 67-68
    in medical writing, 194-195
    print sources for, 85-87
    reporting and, 53-55
    skills development for, 112-113
    for theater criticism, 177-178
Restaurants, limits of, as interview locale,
    65-66
Risk-taking, in alternative writing,
    230-231
Rolling Stone, 216-217
Roueche, Berton, 192
Ruehlmann, William, 100, 109

S

Scanlan, Christopher, 7-14
Scene-by-scene story construction, 97
Self-censorship, by interview subjects,
    63-64
Self-confidence, importance of, 13-14
Serendipity, in story research, 111
Shales, Tom, 169
Shea, Sandra J., 227-231
Sheraton, Mimi, 6, 165-167
Shingling, 248-249
Showing vs. telling concept, 36, 128-129
Sidebars, in medical writing, 195-196
Siegel, Ed, 147
Siskel, Gene, 6

Sonsky, Steve, 203-210
Spatial story writing structure, 96-97
Specialization
    in book reviewing, 183
    in freelance writing, 201-202
    importance of, 18, 219-220, 222-223, 248
    in magazines, 245
    as marketing tool, 25
    as selling tool, 233
Spy magazine, 215
Staff jobs, guidelines for finding, 262-271
Stalking the Feature Story, 100, 109, 114
Standard & Poor's Register of Corporations,
        Directors and Executives, 87
Status indicator concept, in profile writing,
    128-129
Steinbach, Alice, 40-50
Stockpiling feature stories, 35-36, 218
Style of writing
    development of, 152-153
    experimenting with, 17-18
    in medical writing, 193
    story structure and, 98-99
    variation of, in feature stories, 4-7
    See also Writer's voice
Subjectivity in feature writing, 131-133
    in food writing, 166
    in television criticism, 168-169
    in theater criticism, 176-177
    See also Writer's voice
Subjects
    reporter's relationship with, 141-143
    selection of, in feature writing, 90-92
Success in freelance writing, guidelines
    for, 237-245
Sullivan, Dan, 144, 175-178
Summary sentence, guidelines for, 92-93
"Sunrise with Seamonsters," 106-107

T

Talese, Gay, 107, 125-129
Tape recorders
    for interviews, 71-72, 109-110
    as organizational tool, 92-93
    transcription of, 72, 197
Telephone interviews, 64-65, 110
Television criticism, 167-172
Tevlin, Jon, 103
Theater criticism, 175-178
Theme, importance of, in feature writing,
    130-131
Theroux, Paul, 106-107, 162
Thesaurus, as research tool, 85

Thomas' Register of American Manufacturers, 87
Thomson, Virgil, 176
Thornton, James, 102, 223
Throat-clearing syndrome, 103
Time management, 248-249
  importance of, 35-36
  role of, in television criticism, 169-170
Times Atlas of the World, The, 86
Tourism, impact of, 164
Training
  cross-cultural, 249-250
  in fashion writing, 188-189
  importance of, 173-174, 246-248
  role of, in film criticism, 179
Travel writing
  freelance opportunities in, 158-159
  guidelines for, 157-165
  historical roots of, 160-162
  syndication of, 225-226
Trends
  in fashion writing, 189-190
  in feature writing, 245-250
  as idea sources, 214-216
  localization of, for stories, 39
  research as tool for spotting, 80-81
  in travel writing, 162
Trust, building of, in interviews, 11-12, 70-71, 109
Tully, Judd, 220
Twain, Mark, 160-161

U

USA Today, 169, 215, 245

V

Vanity Fair, 140-143
Verbs, in headlines, 112
Vignettes, profile-writing and, 127
Voorhees, John, 167-172
Vreeland, Diana, 187
Vu/Text, 88

W

Wallace, Mike, 142-143

Wall Street Journal Index, 87
Washington Post, 220
Washington Post National Weekly, 142-143
Webster's Biographical Dictionary, 86
Webster's Collegiate Thesaurus, 85
Webster's New World Dictionary, 85
Whitman, Alden, 126-129
Who's Who in America, 86
Wilder, Thornton, 6
Winerip, Michael, 100, 148
Witt, Leonard, 3-7, 100-108, 190-191, 221-223
Wolfe, Tom, 128-129
Wood, Dave, 185
Word processing, learning to use, 250
Working conditions, for feature writers, 7-14
World Almanac, The, 86
Writers at Work, 17
Writer's Market, 234
Writer's voice, 223
  in alternative papers, 228
  in fashion writing, 187-188
  guidelines for developing, 17-19, 144-150, 152
  importance of, 91-92, 226
  judicious use of, 221
Writing for Story, 40, 247, 251
Writing for Your Readers: Notes on the Writer's Craft from the Boston Globe, 20
Writing samples
  human condition stories, 40-50
  issue stories, 114-123
  nuanced writing, 252-261
  query letter, 235-236
  reporter's presence in, 155-156
  slice-of-life story, 21-24
  television criticism, 203-210
Writing skills
  importance of, in feature writing, 18
  Murray's guidelines for, 15-18
Writing structures
  as organizational tool, 94-95
  types of, 96-98
Writing to Learn, 247

PERMISSIONS

"A Day in the Life of a Feature Writer." Copyright 1990 by Christopher Scanlan. Used by permission of the author.

Excerpt from "The Death of a Smoker," by Christopher Scanlan. Reprinted with permission of the *St. Petersburg Times*.

"Mr. Lucky Ends Mr. Clean Career," by Jay Hamburg. Reprinted with permission of *The Orlando Sentinel*.

Donald M. Murray, "Memo to a New Feature Writer." Copyright 1990 by Donald M. Murray. Used by permission of the author.

Roy Peter Clark, "Finding Feature Story Ideas." Copyright 1990 by Roy Peter Clark. Printed with permission of the author.

Alice Steinbach, "A Boy of Unusual Vision." Reprinted from *The* (Baltimore) *Sun*. Copyright 1984, *The* (Baltimore) *Sun*.

Excerpt about hearses from *The Virginian-Pilot* and *The Ledger-Star*, Norfolk, Va. by Mike D'Orso. Reprinted with permission of *The Virginian-Pilot* and *The Ledger-Star*.

Excerpt from article regarding the killing of Joy Griffith written by David Finkel. Copyright 1985 by the *St. Petersburg Times*. Reprinted with permission of the *St. Petersburg Times*.

"Living in the Danger Zone" by Claire Martin is excerpted from a March 26, 1989, story in *The Denver Post*. Copyright 1989 by *The Denver Post*. Reprinted with permission of *The Denver Post*.

"A Class Struggle" by Walt Harrington is an excerpt from *The Washington Post*. Copyright 1986 by *The Washington Post*. Reprinted with permission of *The Washington Post*.

Andy Merton, "Finding a Writing Voice That's Yours Alone." Copyright 1990 by Andy Merton. Used by permission of the author.

"Eating My Words." Copyright 1990 by Mimi Sheraton. Used with permission of the author.

"The Celebrity Interview." Copyright 1990 by Maralyn Lois Polak. Used with permission of the author.

"Hooked on Morbidity and Mortality." Copyright 1991 by Denise Grady. Used with permission of the author.

Excerpt from story on muscovy duck by Michael McLeod from *The Orlando Sentinel*. Reprinted with permission of *The Orlando Sentinel*.

"It Was a Case of Art Imitating a Slice of Life and Life Imitating the Art" by Steve Sonsky first appeared in the *Miami Herald*. Copyright 1989 the *Miami Herald*. Reprinted with permission of the *Miami Herald*.

Neal Karlen, "How to Approach a Feature Editor," copyright 1990 by Neal Karlen. Used with permission of the author.

Sandra Shea, "Don't Forget the Alternative Papers," copyright 1990 by Sandra J. Shea. Printed with permission of the author.

Mary Hadar, "What Editors Want From Freelancers Who Write Features," copyright 1990 by Mary Hadar. Used with permission of the author.

Jon Franklin, "How Feature Writers Become Great." Copyright 1990 by Jon Franklin. Used with permission of the author.

"The Poet and the Birthday Girl" first appeared in the *Miami Herald's Tropic* magazine, May 8, 1983. Copyright 1983 by the *Miami Herald*. Reprinted with permission of the *Miami Herald*.